**Extending Explanation-Based Learning by
Generalizing the Structure of Explanations**

D1742101

Jude W. Shavlik
Department of Computer Sciences
University of Wisconsin–Madison

Extending Explanation-Based Learning by Generalizing the Structure of Explanations

Pitman, London

Morgan Kaufmann Publishers, Inc., San Mateo, California

PITMAN PUBLISHING
128 Long Acre, London WC2E 9AN

A Division of Longman Group UK Limited

© Jude W. Shavlik 1990

First published 1990

Available in the Western Hemisphere from
MORGAN KAUFMANN PUBLISHERS, INC.,
2929 Campus Drive, San Mateo, California 94403

ISSN 0268-7526

British Library Cataloguing in Publication Data

Shavlik, Jude W.
Extending explanation-based learning by generalizing the
structure of explanations.—(Research notes in artificial
intelligence: ISSN 0268-7526)
1. Problem solving. Applications of artificial
intelligence
I. Title   II. Series
006.3

ISBN 0-273-08817-3

Library of Congress Cataloging in Publication Data

Shavlik, Jude W.
Extending explanation-based learning by
generalizing the structure of explanations.

(Research notes in artificial intelligence,
ISSN 0268-7526)
Includes bibliographical references (p.
1. Artificial intelligence.   2. Explanation-based
learning.   3. Comprehension (Theory of knowledge)
I. Title.   II. Series: Research notes in artificial
intelligence (London, England)
Q335.S466   1990   006.3   89-26957
ISBN 1-55860-109-0

Reproduced and printed by photolithography
in Great Britain by Biddles Ltd, Guildford

Contents

Preface and Acknowledgements

Creating machines that learn is a challenging, exciting, and rewarding enterprise. Machine learning dates back to the beginnings of artificial intelligence, and after years of relative neglect, has vibrantly re-emerged during the 1980's. This book presents several fully-implemented computer systems that reflect my theories of how to extend an interesting subfield of machine learning called *explanation-based learning*. In this type of learning, a specific problem's solution is generalized into a form that can later be used to solve conceptually similar problems. The explanation of how the specific problem is solved guides the generalization process. The PHYSICS 101 system utilizes characteristics of mathematically-based problem solving to extend mathematical calculations in a psychologically plausible way, while the BAGGER system and its successor BAGGER2 implement a domain-independent approach to increasing the scope of explanation-based learning. This book describes all three of these systems, explains the details of their algorithms, and discusses several examples of learning by each. It also presents an empirical analysis of explanation-based learning.

I hope this book proves useful to people interested in learning more about machine learning, especially explanation-based learning. In addition, those whose interests primarily lie in other areas of cognitive science and artificial intelligence may find portions beneficial. The PHYSICS 101 may prove relevant to those concerned with the psychology of mathematical problem solving, models of the transition from novice to expert, or intelligent tutoring systems. The BAGGER systems focus more on explanation-based learning techniques, but may be of interest to those interested in speeding up planners and other expert problem solvers; researchers in automatic programming may also find the BAGGER systems relevant.

I developed the PHYSICS 101 and BAGGER systems at the University of Illinois and created the BAGGER2 system after moving to the University of Wisconsin. (While several people have suggested that the logical next step is to develop BAGGER-N, this is the end of that research line, at least for awhile.) This book grew out of my Ph.D. dissertation, written at the University of Illinois and deposited in December of 1987. It is a heavily reorganized, updated, and extended version of that document. Thanks are due Pitman's anonymous review for his or her list of suggested improvements. I am also grateful for the assistance of Professor Derek Sleeman, the editor of this series, and Pitman's publishing editor Peter Brown.

A description of PHYSICS 101 is currently in press for the journal *Artificial Intelligence* [Shavlik90b], and one on BAGGER2 is currently in press for the journal *Machine Learning* [Shavlik90a]. The anonymous reviewers for these articles provided many beneficial comments and suggestions, which have also been incorporated into this book. In addition, Professor Pat Langley's editorial guidance and research suggestions about BAGGER2 are gratefully acknowledged.

The nearly four years I spent in the artificial intelligence group of the University of Illinois' Coordinated Science Laboratory was both intellectually rewarding and personally enjoyable. Foremost credit is due Professor Gerald DeJong, whose gently guiding leadership, along with that of Professors David Waltz and Robert Stepp, created a stimulating intellectual environment. Jerry DeJong was an exceptional advisor. I am grateful for both his providing me the freedom to pursue my interests and his insightful comments that led me to follow fruitful research paths. Many of the best ideas in my dissertation resulted from thought-provoking discussions with him. He was, and continues to be, an excellent role model, teaching me what it means to be a creative researcher.

Along with Professor DeJong, Professors Gregg Collins, Kenneth Forbus, Dedre Gentner, Brian Ross, and Robert Stepp served on my final Ph.D. examination committee. Their insights on learning, from the perspectives of both computer science and psychology, have been educational. In addition to being thankful for their comments and suggestions regarding my pre- and post-doctoral research, I enjoyed my interactions with them in classes and seminars.

While at Illinois I learned much from discussions with the other members of the explanation-based learning group. Interactions with Scott Bennett, Steve Chien, Melinda Gervasio, Raymond Mooney, Paul O'Rorke, Shankar Rajamoney, Ashwin Ram, and Alberto Segre stimulated many interesting ideas. Special credit is due Ray Mooney, now at the University of Texas. Interactions with him at Illinois, joint research with him since then, and general discussions about teaching and research have all been quite enlightening and enjoyable.

Since arriving at Wisconsin, several students have contributed to my understanding of machine learning in general and explanation-based learning in particular, especially Eric Gutstein, Richard Maclin, and Geoffrey Towell. They have begun exploring several exciting new research directions in machine learning that I anticipate will soon be producing significant results. I am also grateful to the exceptional graduate students who have taken my machine learning class and partook in thought-provoking discussions about this interesting field. Kevin Cherkauer, Eric Gutstein, Vasant Honavar, Jeffrey Horvath, Richard Maclin, and Charles Squires read portions of this book. I wish to thank them all, with special thanks to Geoffrey Towell who closely read the complete manuscript. The changes they suggested and the corrections they made have substantially improved it.

Finally, I wish to thank Zoann Branstine for being more than a close friend. Her love and understanding are greatly appreciated.

The research performed since I graduated was supported by the University of Wisconsin Graduate School. The research performed at Illinois was partially supported by the Office of Naval Research under grant N00014-86-K-0309, by the National Science Foundation under grant NSF IST 85-11542, and by a University of Illinois Cognitive Science/Artificial Intelligence Fellowship. A forgivable loan from the General Electric Corporation is also gratefully acknowledged.

October 1989
Madison, Wisconsin   USA

To my parents - Elizabeth and Raymond

1 Introduction

1.1 The Need for Generalizing Explanation Structures

One of the most essential properties of any intelligent entity is the ability to learn. From the earliest days of artificial intelligence, making machines learn has been one of its most exciting, challenging, and important goals [Rosenblatt58, Samuel59, Selfridge59]. One common, but powerful, way of learning is by experiencing solutions to sample problems. These examples can then be generalized so that they apply to a much larger collection of problems. Computers programmed to learn from examples have been successfully applied to such real-world tasks as soybean disease diagnosis [Michalski80a], word pronunciation [Sejnowski87], and electronic circuit design [Mitchell85].

Many real-world concepts involve an indefinite number of components, and many real-world plans involve an unbounded number of operations. For example, physical laws such as momentum and energy conservation apply to arbitrary numbers of objects, constructing towers of blocks requires an arbitrary number of repeated stacking actions, and setting a table involves places for differing numbers of guests.[1] However, any specific example of such concepts will only contain a *fixed* number of actions or components. Systems that learn from examples must be able to detect and correctly generalize repeated portions of their training instances. In some cases, the number of repetitions itself should be the subject of generalization; in others it is inappropriate to alter the number of repetitions. Explanation-based learning (EBL) [DeJong86b, DeJong88, Ellman89, Mitchell86] provides a computational approach to this issue. In this type of machine learning, abstracting the solution to a specific problem produces a general solution applicable to conceptually similar problems. The generalization process is driven by the *explanation* of why the specific solution works. Knowledge about the domain lets a learner develop and then generalize this explanation. The explanation of repeated portions of a solution dictates when it is valid and proper to generalize the number of times they occur.

This book primarily addresses the important issue in EBL of *generalizing the structure of explanations* [Cheng86, Cohen88, Prieditis86, Shavlik85a, Shavlik87b, Shavlik90a, Shavlik90b, Shell89]. This involves generalizing such things as the number of entities involved in a concept or the number of times some action is performed. Previous research on

---

[1] These three concepts are among those acquired by the systems described in this book. Details of their acquisition are provided in the following chapters.

explanation-based learning has largely ignored the generalization of number.[2] Instead, it has focused on changing constants into variables and determining the general constraints on those variables without significantly altering the underlying graphical structure of the explanation. However, this precludes acquisition of concepts in which a general iterative or recursive process is implicitly represented by a fixed number of applications in the specific problem's explanation. A system that possesses the ability to generalize the structure of explanations can learn, from a specific example, concepts that involve a range of possible numbers of actions or components. This book presents several such systems.

The central thesis of this book is:

> Explanation structures that suffice for understanding a specific example are not always satisfactory for generalizing the example. The explanation *structure* must often be *augmented* if a useful generalization is to be produced.

Evidence for this claim and techniques for augmenting explanation structures are presented throughout.

While generalizing the structure of an explanation can involve more than generalizing the number of times a technique is employed — for example, the *order* in which techniques are applied or the actual techniques used can be generalized — this book largely focuses on the topic of *generalizing number*. Usually this involves generalizing a fixed number of applications of a technique into a possibly constrained but unbounded number of applications. The phrase *generalizing to N* also indicates this process.

Generalizing number, like more traditional generalization in explanation-based learning, results in the acquisition of a new inference rule. The difference is that the sort of rule that results from generalizing number describes the situation after an indefinite number of world changes or other inferences have been made. Each such rule subsumes a potentially infinite class of rules acquired by standard explanation-based generalization techniques. Thus, with such rules storage efficiency can be dramatically improved, expressive power is increased, and, as shown in Chapter 4, performance efficiency can also be higher.

To see the need for generalizing explanation structures, consider the LEAP system [Mitchell85], an early application of explanation-based learning. The system observes an example of using *NOR* gates to compute the Boolean *AND* of two *OR*'s, and it discovers that the technique generalizes to computing the Boolean *AND* of any two inverted Boolean functions. However, LEAP cannot generalize this technique to let it construct the *AND* of an arbitrary number of inverted Boolean functions using a multi-input *OR* gate. The system cannot do this even if its initial background knowledge includes the general version of DeMorgan's Law and the concept of multi-input *NOR* gates. Generalizing the number of functions requires alteration of the original example's explanation.

Ellman's [Ellman85] system also illustrates the need for generalizing number in explanation-based learning. From an example of a four-bit circular shift register, his system constructs a generalized design for an arbitrary four-bit permutation register, but again, it cannot produce a design for an N-bit circular shift register. As Ellman points out, such

---

[2] Section 1.3 provides an introduction to explanation-based learning for the unacquainted.

generalization, though desirable, cannot be done using the technique of changing constants to variables.

Repetition of an action is not a sufficient condition for generalization to N to be appropriate. For instance, generalizing to N is necessary if one observes a previously unknown method of moving an obstructed block, but not when one sees a toy wagon being built for the first time. The initial states of these two problems appear in Figure 1.1. Suppose a learning system observes an expert achieving the desired states, and consider what general concept should be acquired in each case. In the first example, the expert wishes to use a robot manipulator to move a block that has four other blocks stacked in a tower on top of it. The manipulator can pick up only one block at a time. The expert's solution is to move each of the four blocks in turn to some other location. After the underlying block has been cleared, it is moved. In the second example, the expert wishes to construct a movable rectangular platform, one that is stable while supporting any load whose center of mass is over the platform. Given the platform, two axles, and four wheels, the expert's solution is to first attach each of the axles to the platform, then to select each of the four wheels in turn and mount it on an axle protrusion.

This comparison illustrates an important problem in explanation-based learning. Generalizing the block unstacking example should produce a plan for unstacking *any* number of obstructing blocks, not just *four* as was observed. However, in the wagon-building example the number "four" should not be generalized. It makes no difference whether the system experiences a pile of five, six, or 100 wheels, because exactly four wheels are needed to fulfill the functional requirements of a stable wagon.

Standard explanation-based learning algorithms (e.g., [Fikes72, Hirsh87, Kedar-Cabelli87, Mooney86]) and similar algorithms for chunking [Anderson86, Laird86] cannot treat these cases differently. These methods, possibly after pruning the explanation to eliminate irrelevant parts, replace constants with constrained variables. They cannot significantly augment the explanation during generalization. Thus, the *building-a-wagon* type of concept will be correctly acquired but the *unstacking-to-move* concept will be undergeneralized. Their acquired concepts will have generalized the identity of the blocks so that the target block need not be occluded by the same four blocks as in the example. Thus, any four

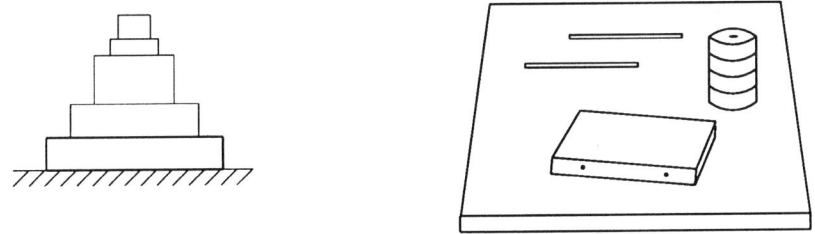

Figure 1.1   Initial States for Two Sample Problems

obstructing blocks can be unstacked, but there must be exactly four blocks.[3] Unstacking five or more blocks is beyond the scope of the acquired concept.

Note that EBL systems do not work ideally on the *building-a-wagon* kind of problem either — they just are lucky. They do nothing to augment explanation structures during generalization. It just happens that to acquire a plan to build a wagon, *not* generalizing the explanation structure is the appropriate thing to do.

Of course one could simply define the scope of EBL-type systems to exclude the *unstacking-to-move* concept and similar ones, but this would be a mistake for three reasons. First, the need for augmenting explanations is ubiquitous. Many real-world domains manifest it in one form or another. Second, if one simply defines the problem away, the resulting system could never guarantee that any of its concepts were as general as they should be. Even when such a system correctly constructed a concept like the *building-a-wagon* plan, it could not know that it had generalized properly. The system could not tell which concepts fell within its scope and which did not. Third, there is recent psychological evidence [Ahn87] that people can generalize number on the basis of one example.

One may argue that the fault for not properly generalizing lies with the module that constructs the explanations of specific examples. If this explainer used a vocabulary involving recursion, then it might not be necessary to alter the graphical structure of the explanation and a standard explanation-based generalizer would capture number-generalized concepts. However, such an approach places a much larger burden on the explanation module, as well as on the domain theory writer. Constructing explanations is a demanding, often intractable, task [Mitchell86]. Generalization is more focused and less computationally intensive; hence it makes sense to shift as much of the burden of learning onto this module as possible. If they are to scale to larger problems, EBL systems must not expect the explanation module to do more than narrowly explain the solution to the specific problem at hand. It is the generalization module's responsibility to determine how broadly applicable the solution is.

1.2 Overview of this Book

This book describes two basic approaches to generalizing explanation structures. Both approaches have been successfully tested by constructing complete implementations; detailed descriptions of these implementations are presented. Constructing programs serves several goals. First, it greatly aids in making ill-defined and incomplete theories concrete. Writing programs forces one to make the implicit explicit, address unanticipated interactions, deal with ambiguity, and be aware of computational complexity. With computers, one can not expect that ''the right thing will be (magically) done at the right time.'' Second, writing

---

[3] The SOAR system [Laird86] would seem to acquire a number of concepts that together are slightly more general. In addition to a new operator for moving four blocks, the system would acquire new operators for moving three blocks, two blocks, and one block, but not for five or more. Anderson's [Anderson86] knowledge-compilation process would acquire a similar set of rules.

programs can aid creativity. Just like scribbling on paper can help in the construction of mathematical proofs, "scribbling" on a computer can help in creating theories in artificial intelligence. Using a computer as a "knowledge medium" [Davis82] allows one to address larger tasks than purely mental processing or simply using pieces of paper. Third, working programs allow large-scale empirical testing. Among other things, this allows estimating average case performance, something that is hard to obtain by theoretical analysis.

1.2.1 Chapter Summaries

The remainder of this chapter, Section 1.3, presents an introduction to explanation-based learning, which the acquainted reader can skip. It contains a historical overview, a description of standard explanation-based generalization, and a discussion of major research questions in EBL. Additional overviews of explanation-based learning appear in [DeJong88, Ellman89].

Chapter 2 presents PHYSICS 101, a complete problem-solving system that learns in mathematically-based domains. PHYSICS 101 analyzes the elimination of *obstacles* in mathematical calculations. Obstacles are variables that preclude the direct evaluation of the problem's unknown; canceling these variables allows the determination of the value of the unknown. One important feature of analyzing variable cancellation is that the generalization of number is properly motivated. Generalization occurs by performing the general versions of these cancellations in the general case. Throughout this chapter, an example involving the acquisition of the concept of momentum conservation is used. Appendix A presents additional examples that further illustrate PHYSICS 101.

Chapter 3 provides a description of the BAGGER system and an extension of it called BAGGER2. In these domain-independent approaches, the *form* of the explanation motivates generalizing its structure. The presence of certain repeated patterns in an explanation triggers number generalization. Examples from circuit implementation and tower building tasks demonstrate how these systems learn. Appendix B presents additional examples of BAGGER's operation, while Appendix C contains all of the rules initially provided to BAGGER and BAGGER2.

Chapter 4 contains an empirical analysis of explanation-based learning. Primarily it compares the performance of BAGGER to an implementation of a standard explanation-based generalization algorithm and to a problem-solving system that does not learn. In addition to investigating the value of generalizing the structure of explanations, the experiments address a number of other issues in explanation-based learning. This chapter also reports information relevant to designing a practical explanation-based learning system. Appendix D contains additional statistics gathered in this empirical study.

Chapter 5 concludes this book. This chapter first reviews the major contributions of the reported research. Next, it presents related approaches to generalizing the structure of explanations and compares them to this work. Finally, it presents several open research issues and proposes approaches to their solution.

1.2.2 Relevance to Research Areas Outside Machine Learning

The results obtained in the development of PHYSICS 101, BAGGER, and BAGGER2 are applicable to several research areas in addition to machine learning. The remainder of this section describes the relevance of these systems to psychological modeling of learning, construction of intelligent tutoring systems, improvement of computer systems that perform symbolic mathematics, and development of automatic programming systems.

Psychological Modeling

PHYSICS 101 is intended to be a psychologically plausible model of problem solving and learning in mathematically-based domains [Shavlik85b, Shavlik86a, Shavlik87c]. It is proposed that focusing on obstacle cancellation provides a way of understanding much of human mathematical reasoning. This work investigates the transition from novice to expert problem solver [Chi81, Chi82, Larkin80]. The understanding and learning models proposed in PHYSICS 101 are particularly relevant for modeling the performance of humans with strong mathematical abilities when they are learning concepts in a new mathematically-based domain, such as physics. Developing a deep understanding in many domains is predicated on the ability to comprehend the constraints inherent in mathematical formalisms that model the domain.

Intelligent Tutoring Systems

The application of techniques developed in artificial intelligence to the educational process is a promising endeavor [Sleeman82, Wenger87]. PHYSICS 101 is relevant to intelligent computer-aided instruction in two ways [Shavlik87a]. One, a model of a learning mechanism is proposed. This model predicts which types of sample problem solutions are difficult to understand and to generalize. The results of this work can be used to judge the pedagogical usefulness of various sample solutions. Two, the data structures and algorithms in the model's computer implementation might form the foundations of practical intelligent tutors for mathematically-based domains.

Symbolic Mathematics Systems

Symbolic mathematics systems, such as MACSYMA [Mathlab83], MAPLE [Geddes82], REDUCE [Hearn84], and SMP [Wolfram83], perform remarkable feats. Unfortunately these systems neither help in formulating an approach to a problem, improve their performance with experience, automatically adapt to the idiosyncrasies of individual users, nor provide comprehensible explanations of their problem-solving steps. Largely this is because the bulk of their mathematical knowledge is implicitly encoded within their algorithms (see [Fateman85] for a discussion of this). PHYSICS 101 is given descriptions of problems and, whenever possible, produces a solution, explaining how and why its solution works. When the system cannot solve a problem, it asks to observe a solution performed by its human user. The solution produced is analyzed and, if proved correct, generalized. The generalized problem-solving technique is then added to the system's knowledge base, thereby improving its future problem-solving performance. A learning system such as PHYSICS 101 can be

6

incorporated into systems that perform symbolic mathematical computations to construct an expert aid for workers in mathematically-based domains [Shavlik86b]. By initially observing the use of composite concepts — those derivable from a domain's first principles — to efficiently solve problems, these concepts can be acquired by the system and used to rapidly solve similar problems in the future.

Automatic Programming

Automatic ways of generating software are clearly needed [Business Week88]. Software development techniques have not kept up with the rapid rate of improvements in computer hardware, a problem that will only worsen as parallel architectures become more prevalent. Several problems have hampered progress in automatic programming. One, search for an acceptable algorithm is combinatorially explosive. Two, utilizing domain-specific knowledge is hard. Three, specifying the desired behavior of the resulting program completely and unambiguously is a complicated task. Explanation-based learning systems such as BAGGER and BAGGER2 can be extended to address these issues. As will be seen in Section 3.3, BAGGER2 in particular produces results that can easily be interpreted as simple programs.

An explanation-based learning approach to automatic programming could proceed as follows [Maclin89]. Rather than providing a specification and then having the system design the *entire* algorithm, a human (who need not know how to program) could outline solutions to specific cases. The system would explain and then generalize these solutions into algorithms that apply to these specific cases and to related cases. There are several advantages of this approach. One, a specific problem is simpler to understand than is a general problem and explanation-based learning provides a way of producing a general algorithm from the understanding of a specific problem's solution. Two, articulating a specific problem and solution constitute a natural way for a user to present an algorithm. Three, an explanation-based approach incorporates a method of including and using domain-specific knowledge in a domain-independent way. See [Hill87, Prieditis88, Steier87, Van Harmelen88, and Section 5.2.3 of this book] for other views on the relationship between EBL and automatic programming.

1.3   Explanation-Based Learning

In explanation-based learning, knowledge about a domain is used to construct an explanation of how a specific problem can be solved.[4] The resulting explanation is then generalized so that conceptually similar problems can be solved quickly in the same manner.

---

[4] The notion of a *problem* should be taken rather broadly. EBL can be used to justify why a specific example is a member of some concept, explain why a sequence of actions produces a desired state in the world, and analyze why one operator should be preferred over another.

1.3.1 A Brief History

The view that analyzing the solution to a single, specific problem may lead to a useful general problem-solving technique can be traced back to the STRIPS system [Fikes72]. This influential system learned *macro-operators* by generalizing an operator sequence that satisfied some goal in the blocks world. Additional early work, either intentionally within the emerging paradigm of explanation-based learning, or research that can now be viewed as being in the spirit of EBL, includes [DeJong81, DeJong83b, Lewis78, Mitchell83a, Neves81, Silver83, Soloway78, Sussman75, Waterman70, Winston83]. All of this work investigated having a computer system apply its understanding of a domain to the process of learning by generalizing solutions to single examples.

This approach to learning can be contrasted to the more traditional approach of analyzing descriptions of a number of positive, and possibly negative, instances of some concept. In this paradigm, learning usually occurs by extracting the commonalities among the positive examples to produce a description of the concept. Care must be taken to avoid including any of the negative instances in the acquired concept. This type of learning has been termed *empirical* or *similarity-based learning* [Lebowitz86]. Examples of research investigating this approach to machine learning include [Hunt66, Michalski80b, Mitchell78, Quinlan79, Rendell83, Schank82, Vere78, Winston75]. Reviews, comparisons, and critiques can be found in [Angluin83, Bundy85, Dietterich82, Dietterich83, Michalski83, Mitchell82, Schank86]. Connectionist approaches to learning [Hinton89, Rumelhart86] can also be viewed as belonging to this paradigm.

The main difference between the similarity-based and explanation-based approaches is that the similarity-based approaches do not use knowledge about a domain to justify which of the features of an example explain why it is or is not a member of the concept being learned. This can be a strength if this knowledge is not available [Dietterich86]. However, often the knowledge is available. Research in explanation-based learning is investigating how to take advantage of this additional knowledge, mitigating the need for a large number of examples and avoiding the combinatorially expensive process of searching through a large space of possible concept descriptions.

Following the initial work on explanation-based learning, a second wave of research tested and extended the emerging methodologies in more complicated domains: mathematics [Mahadevan85, O'Rorke84, Porter85, Utgoff86], circuit design [Ellman85, Mitchell85], natural language [Mooney85, Pazzani85], robotics [Segre85], physics [Shavlik85b], chemistry [Rajamoney85], and game playing [Minton84]. More recently, the fundamental underpinnings of explanation-based learning have become apparent and a third wave of research has focussed on developing domain-independent explanation-based generalization algorithms [Anderson86, Cohen88, DeJong86b, Hirsh87, Kedar-Cabelli87, Mitchell86, Mooney86, O'Rorke87b, Rosenbloom86, Shavlik87b]. Initially the attempts to produce explanation-based generalization algorithms were influenced by the notions of *goal regression* [Waldinger77] and *weakest preconditions* [Dijkstra76]. However, more recently the simpler notion of *unification* [Nilsson80] has been seen as sufficient [Hirsh87, Kedar-Cabelli87, Mooney86].

1.3.2 The Standard Method

Figure 1.2 schematically compares the operation of standard EBL algorithms and a structure-generalizing EBL algorithm. Both techniques assume that, in the course of solving a problem, the solver interconnects a collection of pieces of general knowledge (e.g., inference rules, rewrite rules, or plan schemata), using unification to insure compatibility. The generalizers then produce an *explanation structure* [Mitchell86] from the specific problem's explanation. To build the explanation structure, they first strip away the details of the specific problem and then replace each instantiated rule in the explanation with a copy of the original general rule. If the same general rule is used multiple times, its variables are renamed each time it appears in the explanation structure. This prevents spurious equalities among variables in the explanation structure. At this point the two approaches differ.

The structure-generalizing algorithms presented in this book extend the EGGS algorithm [Mooney86], a standard domain-independent explanation-based generalization algorithm. EGGS determines the most general unifier that lets the solver validly connect the explanation structure's general pieces of knowledge and produces a new composite knowledge structure

Standard EBL

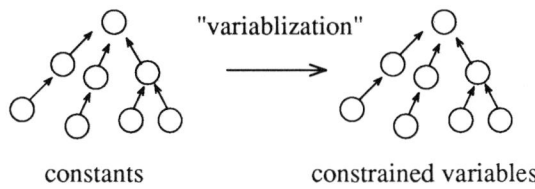

constants   constrained variables

Structure-Generalizing EBL

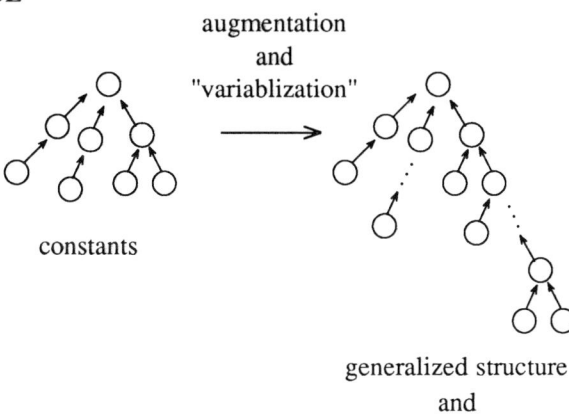

constants

generalized structure
and
constrained variables

Figure 1.2   Generalizing the Structure of Explanations

which contains the unifications that must hold in order to combine the knowledge pieces in the given way. If one assumes tree-structured explanations, then satisfaction of the leaf nodes implies that the root (goal) node will also be satisfied. There is no need to reason again about combining the pieces of knowledge to achieve the goal. The problem solver may have performed a substantial amount of work constructing the original solution, following many unsuccessful paths and then backtracking. The new knowledge structure can lead more rapidly to solutions in the future, because it avoids the unsuccessful paths and eliminates the need to rederive the intermediate conclusions. However, note that a standard generalizer does not change the graphical structure of the explanation. If some process is repeated three times in the specific problem's explanation, it will be repeated exactly three times in the rule the standard generalizer acquires. The other domain-independent explanation-based generalization algorithms operate basically the same way. See [Mooney86, Mooney89c] for further comparison.

In contrast, a system that generalizes explanation structures also determines the necessary unifications, but, importantly, it also reformulates the explanation structure so that additional pieces of knowledge are incorporated. Unlike the result of standard explanation-based learning, the generalized structure in the lower right corner of Figure 1.2 represents a *class* of potential explanation structures and not a single fixed structure.

The remainder of this subsection briefly presents Mooney's EGGS algorithm and a sample application of it. The reader is referred to [Mooney89c] for additional details, including a correctness proof. Table 1.1 contains the EGGS algorithm, using the unification notation in [Nilsson80].[5] The variable γ contains the unifications necessary such that all the portions of the explanation structure can be consistently connected; initially γ is null. EGGS traverses the

---

Table 1.1 The EGGS Generalization Algorithm
(Figure 3.12 of [Mooney89c] - reprinted with permission)

let γ be the null substitution { }
for each equality between expressions x and y in the explanation structure
do
    let θ be the MGU of $x\gamma$ and $y\gamma$
    let γ be $\gamma\theta$
for each expression x in the explanation structure **do**
    replace x **with** $x\gamma$

---

[5] The notation $x\,\gamma$ denotes the result of applying the substitutions specified by γ to the expression x. The result of combining two substitutions $\gamma\,\theta$ is the substitution obtained by applying θ to γ and then adding all unifications for variables appearing in θ but not in γ.

explanation structure and computes the most general unifier (MGU) wherever two terms are equated, subject to the constraint that the MGU is consistent with all previous unifications. Lastly, it applies the final substitution list to the entire explanation structure.

Figure 1.3 contains an example. A simple domain theory appears at the top of this figure. Leading question marks indicate variables, which are all universally quantified. Basically, this domain theory says that: if one knows someone nice, then he or she likes that person; animate objects know themselves; humans are animate; friendly people are considered nice; happy people are considered nice.[6] In the specific training example, one is told that John is a happy human and asked to show that John likes himself; this is easily accomplished using the domain theory, as shown in Figure 1.3's upper graph. The next task is to convert this explanation into an explanation structure. Recall that this involves replacing each instantiated rule in the explanation with a copy of the original general rule. Figure 1.3 uses Mooney's notation of triple parallel lines to indicate where the consequent of one rule supports an antecedent of another. The specifics of the problem are *not* part of the explanation structure, but are shown in italics in Figure 1.3's lower graph for clarity. Applying EGGS to this explanation structure produces the result that all variables must be identical. Extracting the leaves and root of this structure after EGGS runs produces the general rule that says "happy people like themselves."

Standard explanation-based generalization algorithms do alter their explanation structures by pruning portions of the structure considered easily recomputable (or *operational*, a term defined in the next subsection). If one assumes the predicate *knows* is easily satisfied, everything below *knows(?x, ?y)* can be pruned from Figure 1.3 before applying EGGS. In this case, EGGS produces the rule below, which says if you know someone who is happy, you like him or her:

$$knows(?x,?w) \land happy(?w) \rightarrow likes(?x,?w).$$

However, the simple and insufficient technique of pruning is the only way standard EBL methods generalize their explanations. For instance, pruning will not support generalizing number, except by pruning away portions of the explanations where number generalization should occur.

1.3.3 Additional Research Issues

In addition to the need for generalizing explanation structures, this book addresses several other research issues in explanation-based learning. This subsection introduces these issues.

Constructing Explanations

The process of constructing explanations of how to solve specific problems can be

---

[6] This domain theory may not accurately reflect the real world, but that is a different issue in EBL. This book does not address the issue of dealing with incorrect domain theories; see Section 5.3.5 for a brief discussion of this important topic.

Initial Domain Theory

$$\text{knows}(?x, ?y) \wedge \text{nice-person}(?y) \rightarrow \text{likes}(?x, ?y)$$
$$\text{animate}(?z) \rightarrow \text{knows}(?z, ?z)$$
$$\text{human}(?u) \rightarrow \text{animate}(?u)$$
$$\text{friendly}(?v) \rightarrow \text{nice-person}(?v)$$
$$\text{happy}(?w) \rightarrow \text{nice-person}(?w)$$

Specific Example

Given human(John) $\wedge$ happy(John), show that *likes(John, John)*.

Explanation of How to Solve this Problem

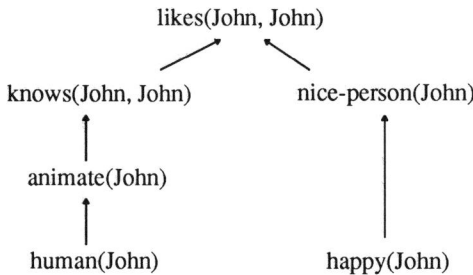

The Explanation Structure for this Problem (within the box)

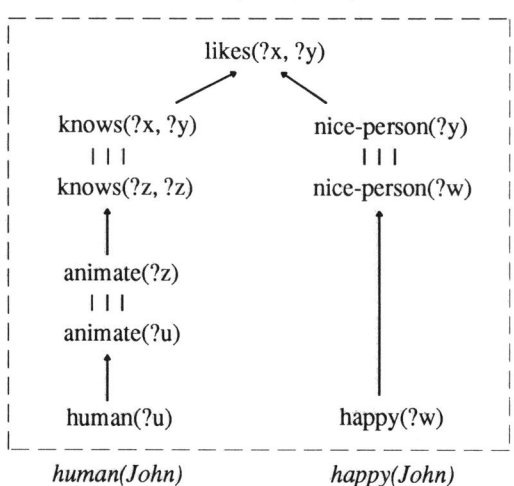

The Necessary Unifications

All variables must match ?z.

The General Rule EGGS Produces

$$\text{human}(?z) \wedge \text{happy}(?z) \rightarrow \text{likes}(?z, ?z)$$

Figure 1.3   A Sample Application of EGGS

computationally intractable [Mitchell86]. Without an explanation to generalize, EBL cannot, of course, learn anything. A common approach to this issue is to construct approximate explanations, refining them on the basis of further experience [Bennett89, Chien89, Tadepalli89]. Chapter 4 presents empirical evidence for the claim that EBL systems should learn by *observing* external agents solve problems [DeJong83a]. In this approach, a learner does not solve complicated problems on its own, but rather waits until it sees another agent solve the problem. Explaining the solution steps of another is usually substantially easier than generating these steps on one's own [DeJong86a, Mooney89c, Section 4.3.4 of this book]; hence, previously intractable problems can be addressed.

Learning apprentices are one approach to learning by observation. Learning apprentices have been defined [Mitchell85] as

> *interactive* knowledge-based consultants that directly assimilate new knowledge by observing and analyzing the problem-solving steps contributed by their users in their *normal* use of the system.

The incorporation of learning apprentices in practical problem solvers [Hill87, Minton88a, Mitchell85, O'Rorke87b, Segre88b, Shavlik87e, Wilkins88] is an active area of research in machine learning. Chapter 4 presents empirical results relevant to the design of learning apprentices.

Selecting Good Explanations

An important issue in explanation-based learning, one that has received little attention, is the question of how representative a sample problem is of future problems likely to be encountered. Most research assumes that each sample problem is not anomalous, and, hence, its generalization is worth saving because it will prove applicable to similar problems in the future. Often the criterion for learning is simply that the system could not solve the sample problem on its own or that solving it required more than one rule. However care must be taken to prevent a system from being overloaded with acquired concepts that will rarely be used [Minton85]. This issue of deciding when to learn is exacerbated when generalizing the structure of explanations, because the final result is, roughly speaking, conceptually further away from the specific example. It is not appropriate to generalize structure whenever possible. The systems described in this book conservatively estimate when generalizing the structure of explanations is appropriate. Determining the appropriateness of generalizing structure is a theme interwoven throughout this book and is also seen as an important open research issue.

The Utility of Learning

One major issue in EBL is that, as a system learns more rules, its problem-solving performance can *decrease*. One reason this occurs is that a problem solver can spend substantial time trying to apply learned rules that appear promising, but ultimately fail [Fikes72, Markovitch89, Minton85, Mooney89a]. A second potential performance degradation can occur when a new broadly-applicable rule, which can require substantial time to instantiate, blocks access to a more restricted, yet often sufficient, rule whose preconditions are easier to evaluate [Shavlik87c, Section 2.4.3 of this book]. Minton defines the *utility* problem as insuring that EBL systems generate new knowledge whose benefits outweigh its costs [Minton88b]. Chapter 4's experiments address the utility of learning.

Operationality versus Generality

Acquiring the definition of a new general concept is only half of the problem faced by a machine learning system. To contribute usefully to improved problem solving, the system must be able later to apply the new concept effectively [Braverman88b, DeJong86b, Hirsh88, Keller88b, Mitchell86, Segre87, Shavlik87c]. That is, the concept must be *operational* [Mostow83] in addition to being widely applicable.

The relationship between operationality and generality generally involves the following two considerations.[7] A rule whose relevance is easy to determine may only be useful in an overly-narrow range of problems. Conversely, a broadly-applicable rule may require extensive work before a problem solver can recognize its appropriateness.

One can view the process of generalizing explanation structures in terms of operationality versus generality. Rules produced by generalizing explanation structures will subsume several rules acquired by an EBL system that does not generalize its explanation structures. Often a problem solver must perform less work to instantiate one of the latter rules; however, since there are more of them to consider and they are less widely applicable, it make take longer overall to solve a problem. One question is whether it is better to learn the more general rule or whether it would be better to individually learn the subsumed rules as they are needed. Experiments in Chapter 4 empirically address this question; the results demonstrate the value of generalizing explanation structures.

Even when generalizing explanation structures, questions arise about operationality and generality. Section 4.3.3 and Appendix B.2.2-3 discuss this topic from the perspective of the BAGGER system. Section 2.4.3 discusses how PHYSICS 101 forms specializations called *special-cases*; this process guarantees improved operationality and yields new rules with potentially high utility.

---

[7] See [Keller88a, Keller88b, Segre88a] for additional views on this relationship.

2 Learning in Mathematically-Based Domains

All the mathematical sciences are founded on relations between physical laws and laws of numbers, so that the aim of exact science is to reduce the problems of nature to the determination of quantities by operations with numbers.

James Clerk Maxwell

2.1 The PHYSICS 101 System

Mathematically-based domains present several unique challenges and opportunities for machine learning. Many scientific and technical domains — physics, electronics, chemistry, economics — share the common formalism of mathematics, and much of the reasoning in these fields involves understanding the constraints inherent in mathematical descriptions. Mathematical models of real-world situations are constructed, and these mathematical abstractions are used to predict the behavior of the domain being modeled. Hence, solving quantitative problems in these domains requires a competence in symbolic mathematical manipulation. Furthermore, since mathematics is the underlying formal language, many important domain concepts can be adequately captured only through a mathematical specification. Thus, concept learning in these domains is also rooted in mathematics.

The research reported is this chapter focuses on learning new concepts from examples in mathematically-oriented domains, using the explanation-based learning paradigm. A computer system has been constructed that embodies the theories of learning and problem solving developed. The fully-implemented system is intended to model, in a psychologically plausible manner, the acquisition of concepts taught in a first-semester college physics course [Shavlik85b, Shavlik86a, Shavlik87c] — hence, it is named PHYSICS 101. The model assumes competence in mathematics at the level of someone who has completed a semester of calculus.

The focus of the implementation is not physics *per se*. Very little knowledge about physics is in the system. In fact, all of its initial physics knowledge is contained in a half-dozen formulae, which are listed later in this section. None of the system's algorithms utilize knowledge about physics, except that which is captured in these initial physics formulae. Rather, the focus is on mathematical reasoning, and the domain of physics is used as a test bed, since it is an elegant domain that stresses the use of complicated mathematics.

The explanation-based learning is particularly appropriate to mathematically-oriented domains, because EBL supports the construction of large concepts by analyzing how one can piece together smaller concepts in order to solve a specific problem. Combining small concepts to form larger ones is the basis of progress in mathematical domains.

As is typical in the explanation-based learning paradigm, PHYSICS 101 acquires structured knowledge chunks. In this chapter, these chunks of knowledge are termed *schemata* [Chafe75], and are similar in spirit to *scripts* [Cullingford78, Schank77], *frames* [Charniak76, Minsky75], and *macro-operators* [Fikes72]. New schemata are built by usefully organizing other schemata.

2.1.1 The Learning Model

The model of learning used in the PHYSICS 101 system is inspired by intuitions concerning the importance of concrete experiences when acquiring abstract concepts. In complex domains like physics, people seem to understand general rules best if they are accompanied by illustrative examples. As a result, a large part of most physics texts is taken up by examples and exercises. Indeed, there is psychological evidence that a person who discovers a rule from examples learns it better than one who is taught the rule directly [Egan74] and that illustrative examples provide an important reinforcement to general rules [Bransford76, Gick83].

Figure 2.1 illustrates the model of human learning incorporated in PHYSICS 101. After a physical situation is described and a problem is posed,[1] the learner attempts to solve the problem. Focus in this research is on the process of learning during a successful solution; particularly on learning from a teacher's example. When the student cannot solve a problem, he or she requests a solution from his or her instructor. The solution provided must then be

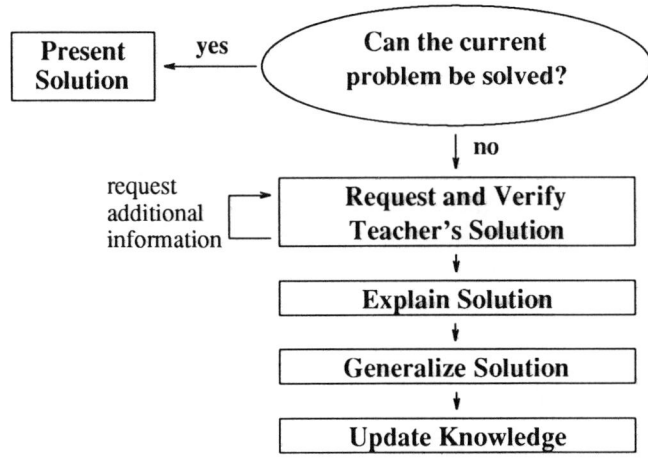

Figure 2.1   An Overview of the Learning Model

---

[1] Problems are expressed in the language of mathematics, not in ordinary English. The important problem of translating "word problems" into mathematical descriptions is not addressed. However, it has been addressed in the work of others [Bundy79, Novak76, Palmer83].

16

verified; additional details are requested when steps in the teacher's solution cannot be understood. The process by which the student understands an example is divided into two phases. First, using his current knowledge about mathematics and physics, the student verifies that the solution is valid. At the end of this phase the student knows that his instructor's solution solves the current problem, but he does not have any detailed understanding of *why* his teacher chose these steps to solve the problem. During the second phase of understanding, the student determines a reason for the structure of each expression in the teacher's solution. Especially important is understanding new formulae encountered in the solution. After this phase the student has a firm understanding of how and why this solution solved the problem at hand. In the third and final phase he is able to profitably generalize any new principles that were used in the solution process, thereby increasing his knowledge of classical physics.

2.1.2 Terminology

The following definitions are used to describe PHYSICS 101:

(1) A *problem* is a set of variables, with specifications of some of the properties of these variables, together with a mathematical expression (called the *unknown*) for which the value of some property is desired. (A single, isolated variable is the simplest form of an unknown.) The properties of expressions can include such things as their value at specific points or their dependence on some other variable, such as time.

(2) An *unacceptable* variable is one whose value for the desired property of the unknown is also not known (at least is not *explicitly* known). For example, if it is desired to know the value of the variable X at time t, and the value of Y at time t is not known, then Y is an unacceptable variable in this problem.

(3) When they appear in a calculation, unacceptable variables are called *obstacles*.

(4) An *equation schema* is an inference rule which specifies a conjunction of antecedents (the preconditions) and a consequent (an equation). The equation can be used to rewrite terms in some expression. For example, the precondition of the equation $\frac{x}{x} = 1$ is that x be non-zero.

(5) *Problem-solving schemata* describe strategies used to solve problems. They guide the problem solver in its task of applying equation schemata in order to solve the problem.

(6) *Background knowledge* consists of equation schemata describing general mathematical laws (e.g., equations of algebra and calculus), equation schemata describing domain-specific properties (e.g., *force = mass × acceleration*), problem-solving schemata, and miscellaneous inference rules. The domain-specific equations specify the variables known to the system (e.g. force, mass, and acceleration) that are not mentioned in the problem description.

(7) A *primary obstacle set* for a problem is a group of unacceptable variables which, if the values of their specified properties were known, would permit the system to solve

17

the problem (that is, determine the value of the unknown's property). Initially, a problem's obstacle set contains those variables in the initial expression that are unacceptable. If this set is empty, the problem is solved. As obstacles from the set are assigned values for the requested property, they are eliminated from the primary obstacle set.

(8)   The *problem-solving task* consists of rewriting obstacles using equation schemata, under the guidance of problem-solving schemata, until the primary obstacle set is empty.

The notion of *obstacle* is related to that of *impasse* [Brown80]. The difference is that obstacles are inherent in problem descriptions while impasses arise during the process of problem solving. Additional reasoning may lead to a way to resolve the impasse, and if so, problem solving can continue. Obstacles may lead to impasses if the problem solver does not know how to surmount them, but this is not necessary. Obstacles continue to exist in completed solutions and provide a focus in which the steps in a solution can be explained.

2.1.3   Other Approaches to Learning in Mathematical Domains

There is a substantial literature describing computer models of learning in mathematical domains. In this section, these systems are described and compared to the approach taken in PHYSICS 101.

BACON [Langley81, Langley87], ABACUS [Falkenhainer86], and COPER [Kokar86] empirically learn equations by analyzing multiple data measurements and discovering regularities. AM [Lenat76] discovers interesting concepts in mathematics, using heuristics to guide its searching. The LEX [Mitchell83b] and META-LEX [Keller87a, Keller87b] systems learn heuristics under which an integration operator is useful. *Version spaces* [Mitchell78] are used in LEX to delimit plausible versions of the heuristic. This is done by considering positive and negative examples of application of the operator. META-LEX works by generating simplifications of its inference rules, then testing their effectiveness in improving the performance of problem solving. DARWIN [Araya84] uses experimentation, in place of a domain model, to determine when a special-case physics solution technique is applicable. It generates and tests variations on a problem description in order to construct a description of the class of problems soluble by the special-case technique used to solve the original problem. PET [Porter86] uses *experimental goal regression* to learn mathematics. This technique also achieves its power through directed experimentation.

Unlike PHYSICS 101, these systems are inductive [Angluin83, Michalski83]. They learn new concepts that are consistent with the examples presented to or generated by them, by analyzing the similarities and differences among the examples. Confidence in the accuracy of the acquired results grows as more examples are seen. With only a few examples to analyze, irrelevant characteristics may appear relevant (because, for example, they appear in all of the positive examples seen) or necessary characteristics may appear unnecessary (because, for instance, they do not appear in any negative examples). PHYSICS 101, being explanation-based, produces intertwined descriptions of the role of each aspect of a problem. These explanation structures allow the system to produce, from a small number of examples, new concepts that are as certain as the underlying concepts from which the explanation is constructed. The explanation-based approach allows PHYSICS 101 to incorporate into new concepts descriptions of the effects of problem characteristics not seen in the example from which it learns. For example, although it experiences an example involving momentum conservation, PHYSICS 101 learns the more general equation describing how external forces affect momentum.

There have been a number of other explanation-based approaches to learning in mathematical domains. LEX2 [Mitchell83a] is an explanation-based version of LEX. LP [Silver86] analyzes worked mathematics problems and learns information that constrains, but does not eliminate, search through its operator space. ALEX [Neves85] learns to solve simple algebraic equations by examining solved problems. LA [O'Rorke87b] learns new schemata for use in natural deduction proofs. Finally, Bennett's system [Bennett87] learns approximations that transform intractable problems into soluble ones. However, none of these systems generalize the structure of their explanations.

Using analogy to learn new concepts in mathematical domains is another heavily investigated approach. Forbus and Gentner [Forbus86] describe an approach to learning *qualitative* physics using analogical reasoning. PHINEAS [Falkenhainer87] implements some of the ideas in their proposal. Aspects of geometry and algebra are analogically learned in the PUPS [Anderson87] system. The NLAG system [Greiner88] learns about hydraulics using its knowledge of electricity.

In analogical learning, new knowledge is acquired by mapping old knowledge from a well-understood domain to a novel situation. Learning from analogies can involve aspects of the similarity/difference-based and explanation-based approaches to learning. Similarity between the current problem and previous problems helps in the selection of candidate analogs and in the construction of mappings between the two situations. Successful analogies may lead to the construction of abstractions of the two situations [Gick83, Winston82], which can be performed in a similarity or explanation-based fashion. One way analogy differs from the approach taken in explanation-based systems is that attention is not focused on combining pieces of knowledge into larger knowledge chunks (schemata). Also, using analogy, no learning takes place the first time a problem is solved. Instead, an analogous problem must be encountered before the solution to the first problem contributes to the acquisition of knowledge. Finally, none of these systems address generalizing number.

2.2 Solving Problems

This section discusses PHYSICS 101's problem solver, including how acquired equation schemata are used in future problem solving. The problem solver serves two basic purposes in the system. One, it attempts to solve new problems; two, when it cannot solve a new problem, it performs the calculations that justify the steps in the solution provided by the system's teacher. Readers only interested in PHYSICS 101's learning algorithms can skip to Section 2.3.

PHYSICS 101 contains a schema-based problem solver which searches through the space of mathematical expressions. (Three strategies, which are explained later, substantially constrain this search.) The problem solver is provided a goal description — a mathematical expression called the *unknown* and a description of the property of this unknown whose value is desired. For example, the unknown may be a single variable whose value is sought or it may be an algebraic expression where the goal is to determine the expression's time-dependence. The goal description can either come from the teacher, requesting information about some situation, or it can come from the system's understander module, in its efforts to justify a teacher-provided solution step. Following receipt of the goal description, the problem solver first chooses an initial equation and then successively applies legal transformations to the current right-hand side of the equation, substituting subexpressions for other subexpressions and occasionally backtracking, until an expression satisfying the goal description is reached. A successful solution pathway is sketched in Figure 2.2; observe that more than one substitution is allowed during the transformation from one equation to the next.

Figure 2.3 contains an overview of the operation of the problem solver after it is given a description of the current problem. Solving a problem involves three main stages. First, the solver chooses some equation schema that appears relevant to the problem and then algebraically manipulates the equation so that all the *obstacles* appear on the right-hand side. Next, it transforms the right-hand side expression until all of the obstacles are eliminated. If the problem solver cannot do this, it chooses an alternative starting equation; when no alternatives exist the solver requests and analyzes a solution from the system's teacher, which may lead to new equation schemata being added to the database of schemata. If it produces an acceptable equation (i.e., an obstacle-free one), in the last stage of problem solving the solver extracts the answer to the problem from the acceptable equation.

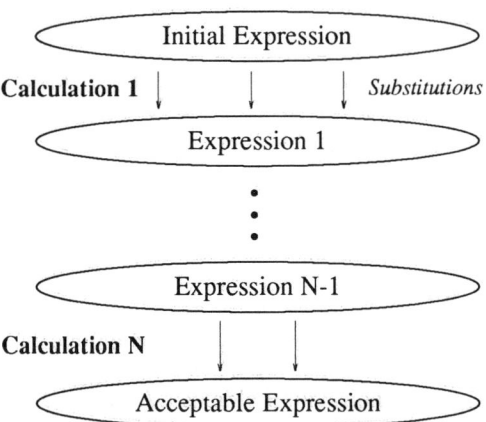

Figure 2.2   The Structure of a Successful Calculation Sequence

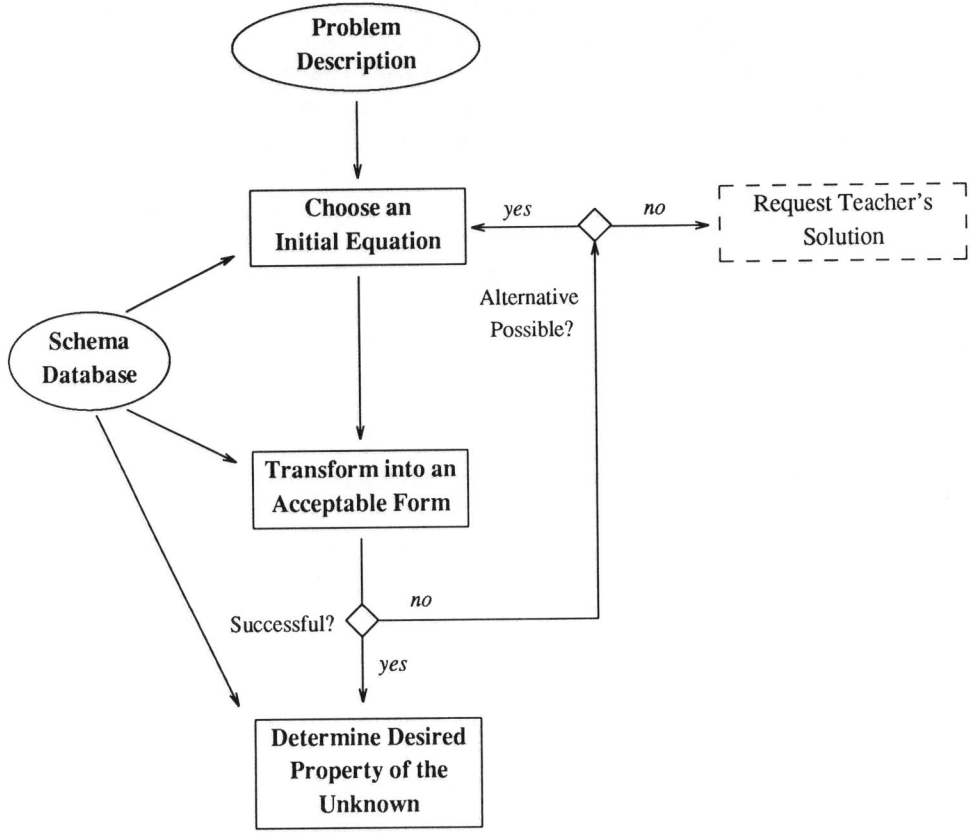

Figure 2.3   Overview of the Problem Solver

A simple example illustrates these phases. Assume the problem is to determine the value of variable x, given the values of variables a, b, and c. Also assume the system possesses equation schemata containing the following equations.

$$y = ax + b \quad \text{and} \quad y = 10c$$

Initially the system will choose the equation on the left and reverse it so that the obstacle y is on the right. Next, it will transform this unacceptable expression by using the equation $y = 10c$, producing $ax + b = 10c$, an acceptable equation. Finally, the value of x is extracted.

Later sections describe the methods by which PHYSICS 101 chooses an equation with which to work and how it searches the space of mathematical expressions in the hopes of eliminating the obstacles. First, though, there is a presentation of the initial knowledge of the system and a brief description of schema-based problem solving.

2.2.1 Initial Knowledge of the System

PHYSICS 101 possesses a large number of mathematical problem-solving techniques. For example, it can symbolically integrate expressions, cancel variables, perform arithmetic, and replace terms by utilizing known formulae. Figure 2.4 contains a portion of the system's hierarchy of calculation techniques. A calculation step may either rearrange the entities in the current expression, simplify the current expression, or replace terms in the expression by substituting formulae. Rearrangement involves such things as moving constants into and out of integrals and derivatives. Simplification involves algebraic cancellation, numerical calculation, and the solving of calculus. The formulae that may be used to replace variables existing in an expression are determined by the domain being investigated.

Table 2.1 contains some of the general mathematical rewrite rules known to the system. Note some formulae belong to more than one category, depending on use. (Terms beginning with a question mark are universally quantified variables.)

Table 2.2 contains the initial physics formulae provided to the system, along with the conditions on their applicability. The first two formulae in Table 2.2 define the physical concepts of velocity (*V*) and acceleration (*A*). An object's velocity is the time rate of change of its position (*X*) and its acceleration is the time rate of change of its velocity. Newton's Second and Third Laws are also included. (Newton's First Law need not be included because it is a special case of his second law.) The second law states that the net force (*F*) on an

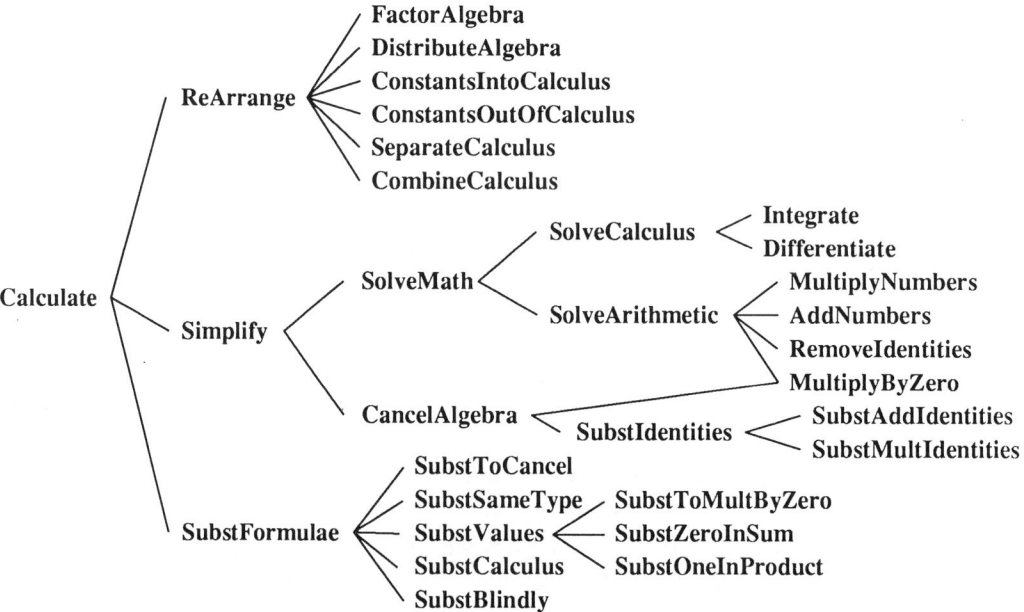

Figure 2.4   Some of the System's Mathematical Techniques

Table 2.1 Sample Mathematical Rewrite Rules

$?expression - ?expression = 0$

   Problem-Solving Schema: SubstAddIdentities

$?expression + 0 = ?expression$

   Problem-Solving Schema: RemoveIdentities

$?expression \, / \, ?expression = 1$

   Problem-Solving Schema: SubstMultIdentities
   Preconditions: NOT(ZeroValued($?expression$))

$1 * ?expression = ?expression$

   Problem-Solving Schema: RemoveIdentities

$\int (?independent * ?expression) \, d\,?x = ?independent \int ?expression \, d\,?x$

   Problem-Solving Schema: ConstantsOutOfCalculus
   Preconditions: IndependentOf($?independent$, $?x$)

$\int (?expression_1 + ?expression_2) \, d\,?x = \int ?expression_1 \, d\,?x + \int ?expression_2 \, d\,?x$

   Problem-Solving Schema: SeparateCalculus

$\int ?expression_1 \, d\,?x + \int ?expression_2 \, d\,?x = \int (?expression_1 + ?expression_2) \, d\,?x$

   Problem-Solving Schema: CombineCalculus

$\dfrac{d}{d\,?x} ?expression^{?n} = ?n \, ?expression \, \dfrac{d}{d\,?x} ?expression^{?n-1}$

   Problem-Solving Schema: Differentiate
   Preconditions: Number($?n$)

$\int ?independent \, d\,?x = ?independent * ?x + constant$

   Problem-Solving Schema: Integrate
   Preconditions: IndependentOf($?independent$, $?x$)

Table 2.2   The Initial Physics Formulae of the System

$$V_{?i,\,?c}(t) = \frac{d}{dt} X_{?i,\,?c}(t)$$

    Preconditions: Member($?i$,*ObjectsInWorld*) $\wedge$ IsaComponent($?c$)

$$A_{?i,\,?c}(t) = \frac{d}{dt} V_{?i,\,?c}(t)$$

    Preconditions: Member($?i$,*ObjectsInWorld*) $\wedge$ IsaComponent ($?c$)

$$F_{net,\,?i,\,?c}(?t) = M_{?i} * A_{?i,\,?c}(?t)$$

    Preconditions: Member($?i$,*ObjectsInWorld*) $\wedge$ IsaComponent($?c$) $\wedge$ IsaTime($?t$)

$$F_{net,\,?i,\,?c}(?t) = F_{ext,\,?i,\,?c}(?t) + F_{int,\,?i,\,?c}(?t)$$

    Preconditions: Member($?i$,*ObjectsInWorld*) $\wedge$ IsaComponent($?c$) $\wedge$ IsaTime($?t$)

$$F_{int,\,?i,\,?c}(?t) = \sum_{\substack{j \in ObjectsInWorld \\ j \neq ?i}} F_{j,\,?i,\,?c}(?t)$$

    Preconditions: Member($?i$,*ObjectsInWorld*) $\wedge$ IsaComponent($?c$) $\wedge$ IsaTime ($?t$)

$$F_{?j,\,?i,\,?c}(?t) = -F_{?i,\,?j,\,?c}(?t)$$

    Preconditions: Member($?i$,*ObjectsInWorld*) $\wedge$ Member($?j$, *ObjectsInWorld*) $\wedge$

                                     $?i \neq ?j \wedge$ IsaComponent($?c$) $\wedge$ IsaTime($?t$)

---

object equals its mass (M) times its acceleration (A). The net force is decomposed into two components: the external force (F_{ext}) and the internal force (F_{int}). External forces result from any external fields (e.g., gravity) that act upon objects. Object $?i$'s internal force is the sum of the forces the other objects in the world[2] exert on object $?i$. These *inter-object* forces are constrained by Newton's Third Law, which says that every action has an equal and opposite reaction.

Position, velocity, acceleration, and force are spatial *vectors*. Hence one of their arguments ($?c$) indicates which vector component is being discussed (x, y, or z). All of these physical variables are functions of time. Mass, however, is a time-independent scalar. It is only indexed by the physical object whose mass is being specified.

When a problem is described, the number of objects in the world is specified. At this time, the system expands any summations ($\sum$'s) and any products ($\prod$'s) in its known formulae.

---

[2] The term *world* is used to refer to physical systems and situations. The term *system* is reserved for referring to computer programs.

For instance, if there are three objects in a world, the second from last equation in Table 2.2 becomes:

$$F_{int,?i,?c}(?t) = F_{?j1,?i,?c}(?t) + F_{?j2,?i,?c}(?t)$$

> **Preconditions:**
> Permutation($\{?i, ?j1, ?j2\}$, *ObjectsInWorld*) $\wedge$ IsaComponent($?c$) $\wedge$ IsaTime($?t$)

Expanded equations are produced because of their greater psychological plausibility as a model of learning by a college freshman.

World-specific equations can also be provided when a new problem is posed. For example, it may be stated that the external force on object k is $M_k g X_{k,y}$. While formulae of these types may be used in solutions to specific examples, they could unnecessarily constrain generalization, since they do not hold in *all* worlds.

2.2.2 Schema-Based Problem Solving

A schema-based problem solver, such as PHYSICS 101, attacks problems by combining known problem-solving schemata in order to achieve a desired goal. Schemata of this type specify the goal they achieve, the preconditions that must be true for the schema to be applicable, and either the intermediate subgoals that must be met or the actual solution steps. This means that schemata can either decompose a problem or actually solve it. If no known schemata apply, the system is not able to solve the problem.

To illustrate these ideas, consider someone with the goal of buying a new suit. The preconditions for the *clothes-buying* schema would include such things as having enough money to buy a suit, time to go to a clothing store during its business hours, and a means of transportation. The plan would include traveling to the store, choosing a suit, paying for it, and returning. Other schemata might contain the details of how these steps could be performed.

A major claim of schema-based problem solvers is that intelligence consists of a large collection of general schemata together with the ability to recognize when to apply each, rather than the ability to construct novel, creative solutions to a problem. This view entails very little searching. Instead, power comes from the number and generality of a system's schemata. Having the right knowledge chunks is essential to effective problem-solving.

A major goal of schema-based problem solvers is to minimize the combinatorially-explosive nature of search-based problem solving. Schemata package together a collection of interrelated problem-solving operators in order to guide the search through the problem space. One schema can move the solver through several states in the problem space without intervening search. This is illustrated in Figure 2.5 where a portion of a search tree is drawn. A single schema may contain the composition of the operators indicated by bold lines, allowing directed traversal through this subtree.

Completeness is usually sacrificed in schema-based problem solving. That is, the problem solver does not fully search the entire problem space. The hypothesis is that, although it cannot solve as many problems as a complete solver, the constrained solver will perform substantially better on the problems it can solve. The loss of completeness is unavoidable,

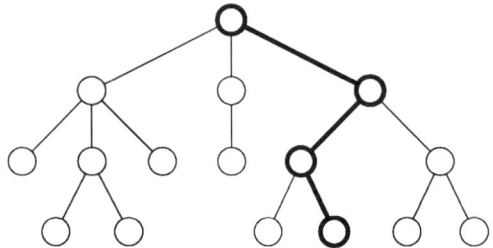

Figure 2.5   Traversing a Search Tree with a Schema

since on problems of nontrivial size, an exhaustive search is not computationally feasible. One strength of explanation-based learning is that it can be used to produce new schemata for problem solving, as will be seen later in this chapter, thereby bringing more problem classes within the scope of the constrained problem solver.

2.2.3   Choosing the Initial Equation

An important part of solving a mathematical problem is determining an equation with which to begin. This can be viewed as characterizing the problem [Chi81, Larkin80]. For example, a new physics problem can be viewed as one to be attacked using conservation of momentum, conservation of energy, or by resorting to "first principles" (Newton's Laws). This section describes the process by which PHYSICS 101 chooses the initial equation, from which it attempts to solve the problem.

If the *unknown* is more complicated than simply an isolated variable, the solver enters its next phase (Section 2.2.4), where it attempts to eliminate the obstacles in the unknown. However, when the unknown is simply an isolated variable, the solver chooses an initial equation that involves this variable. After choosing an equation, it algebraically rearranges the equation so that all of the obstacles appear on the right-hand side. If it cannot accomplish this, the solver chooses another initial equation. An alternative to this approach would be to try to rewrite the equation so that only the unknown appears on the left-hand side of the equation. However, choosing an equation, and then rearranging it so that all the obstacles are on the right-hand side, simplifies problem solving because some acceptable variables may remain on the left-hand side.

The solver only considers those equations containing the unknown as candidate initial expressions. PHYSICS 101's equation schemata are divided into two groups: those specifying the initial equations provided to the system (the *first principles*) and those acquired through learning (the *derived schemata*). Furthermore, the derived schemata are subdivided into two groups: special and general cases. Special cases result from merging a problem-solving technique with a general equation schema, thereby producing a more efficient but less general schemata. This process is described more fully in Section 2.4. Since the derived schemata combine other equations in previously useful ways, the system attempts to use them first. If the current problem is closely related to a previously-experienced one, then the generalized solution to that problem will lead to a rapid solution of the current problem.

Candidate equations are evaluated in the following order (recall that at each step only those equations containing the unknown are considered):

(1) *The special-case derived schemata.* The problem solver determines if the preconditions of these schemata are satisfied by the current problem description. Special-case equations are preferred over general ones, as the special-case schemata contain a substantial amount of compiled problem solving. If one of the special cases applies, it is likely it will lead to rapid solution of the problem.

(2) *The general-case derived schemata.* The system determines if the preconditions of these schemata are true in the current situation. More problem solving may be needed here than when a special case is used, but there should be substantial savings over resorting to first principles.

(3) *The special-case derived schemata — revisited.* This time the solver uses a version of the closed-world hypothesis [Reiter78] to make assumptions. Making assumptions can transform an intractable problem (due to complicated mathematics beyond the scope of the problem solver) or insoluble problem (due to insufficient data) into one that can be solved. Assumption-making is done in the following manner. The system first checks each precondition of the current special-case schema. If any precondition can be proven false (i.e, its negation can be proven), the solver rejects the current schema; otherwise it accepts it. This means that the system assumes that any precondition that cannot be shown to be false is true. For example, one precondition of some derived schema may state that every external force must be zero. If the solver discovers a non-zero external force, it cannot use the schema. However, if nothing is known about the external forces, the schema can be used. If PHYSICS 101 makes the closed-world assumption, when providing the final answer, it also lists the assumptions made (those preconditions that cannot be proved true or false, and are assumed to be true).[3]

(4) *The first principles.* Assumptions are not made about first principles. All of their preconditions must be provably true.

The issue of making consistent assumptions during mathematical problem solving is an important research issue. However, the topic of assumption-making is only briefly investigated in PHYSICS 101. This research ignores issues involved in ensuring that assumptions made in one step of problem solving are consistent with the rest of the steps. Because special-case schemata contain compiled problem-solving knowledge, when they are chosen as the initial equation they usually lead to a solution after only a small amount of algebraic manipulation. For this reason, not checking consistency is less likely to lead to problems. However, this is not the case when the solver uses general-case schemata and first

---

[3] Although making assumptions may lead to incorrect answers during problem solving (due to the assumptions being wrong), any learning that results from analyzing the solution will not produce incorrect results. This is because Physics 101 incorporates the assumptions made into the learned schema as preconditions.

principles; hence, assumption-making is not performed when checking the preconditions of these schema types.

The problem of proving preconditions can be formidable. For example, determining if an external force is zero may require reasoning about all the consequences of Newton's Laws. In PHYSICS 101, the module that proves preconditions is very limited. It does not combine equations in order to answer queries. It only retrieves assertions made when the problem is described, performs arithmetic, and interprets the connectives and quantifiers of predicate calculus (e.g., *and, or, not, implies, for all,* and *there exists*).

Once it chooses an equation, the solver algebraically manipulates the equation to bring all of the obstacle variables to the right-hand side. This is done in a manner similar to Bundy's *attraction, collection,* and *isolation* methods [Bundy81, Bundy83]. If this process fails, the solver rejects the equation. These same techniques are used to extract the answer to the problem from the final, obstacle-free equation.

2.2.4 Transforming an Expression into an Acceptable Form

The problem-solving model used to transform the chosen initial equation into an acceptable form, i.e., one without obstacles, is discussed in this section. It is intended to be a psychologically plausible model of problem solving [Shavlik86a].

A novice human problem solver attacks a problem in one of two ways. He may immediately notice a way to progress toward the solution. Alternatively, he may flounder around performing legal, but aimless, operations in an attempt to transform the problem into a familiar form. An expert, on the other hand, can perform in a qualitatively different manner. If the solution is not immediately apparent, he can focus his efforts in a much more guided way. Instead of simply thrashing around, an expert has an appreciation of what kinds of transformations are likely to change the current problem into a soluble problem.

Consider the problem of evaluating the expression

$$M_1 V_1 + M_2 V_2$$

when the values of M_1 and M_2 are known, but those of V_1 and V_2 are not. This expression cannot be evaluated directly. A valid approach might be to substitute equivalent expressions for the unknowns. A novice might perform the unappealing substitutions of Figure 2.6. While these transformations are valid, they are unlikely to yield a solution. An expert will appreciate this, and be more likely to perform the pleasing problem transformations of Figure 2.6. In this example, there is something about the parallel structure of the problem that makes a parallel substitution more appealing. Yet parallel substitutions are not always aesthetically appealing. For example, consider the substitutions of Figure 2.7. In this example, parallel substitution using Newton's Third Law (every action has an equal and opposite reaction) misses a useful variable cancellation. If one only uses a single instantiation of this formula, the two forces can be eliminated from the calculation.

Three qualitatively different strategies for problem solving appear in the PHYSICS 101 problem-solving model; attention is selectively focused according to one of these strategies. *Strategy 1* is hill climbing. The problem solver focuses attention on this strategy as long as some schema moves it closer to its goal. Occasionally the problem solver will reach a local

28

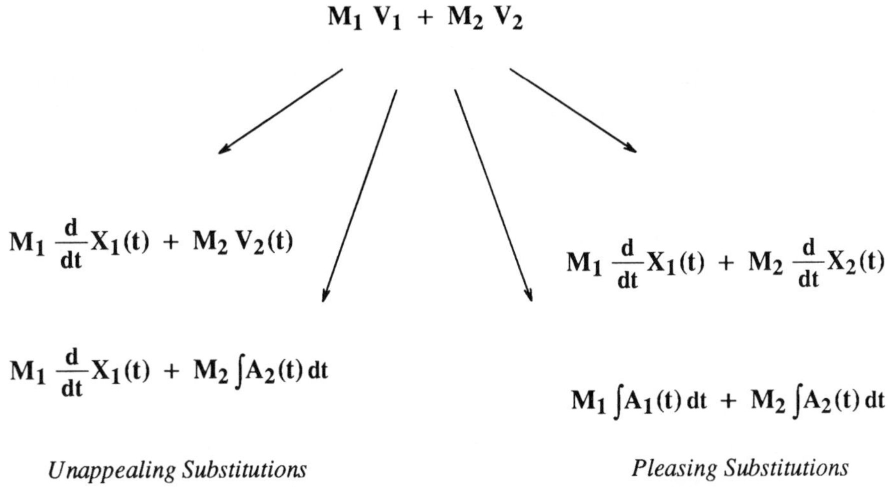

$$M_1 \, V_1 \; + \; M_2 \, V_2$$

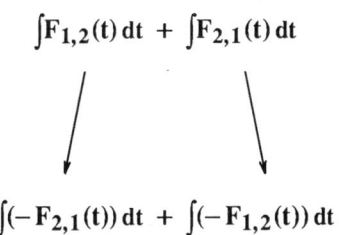

$$M_1 \frac{d}{dt} X_1(t) \; + \; M_2 \, V_2(t) \qquad\qquad\qquad M_1 \frac{d}{dt} X_1(t) \; + \; M_2 \frac{d}{dt} X_2(t)$$

$$M_1 \frac{d}{dt} X_1(t) \; + \; M_2 \int A_2(t) \, dt$$

$$M_1 \int A_1(t) \, dt \; + \; M_2 \int A_2(t) \, dt$$

Unappealing Substitutions   *Pleasing Substitutions*

Figure 2.6   Sample Mathematical Substitutions

maximum; there will be no way to move closer to the goal. At these times, the problem solver must diverge from its goal, in the hopes of transforming the current situation into one where hill climbing can again occur. There are two qualitatively different ways by which the problem solver re-focuses its attention during this divergent phase. First, it attempts to transform the current situation in some seemingly useful way. Characteristics that are believed to be of general or domain-specific problem-solving importance (e.g., symmetry) are to be maintained or introduced; introduction of troublesome characteristics is to be avoided. Such motivated diversions compose *Strategy 2*. As a last resort, the problem solver merely selects an arbitrary legal schema. This can lead to aimless floundering, due to the large number of possible combinations of operator sequences. This unmotivated application of schemata is termed *Strategy 3*.

$$\int F_{1,2}(t) \, dt \; + \; \int F_{2,1}(t) \, dt$$

$$\int (-F_{2,1}(t)) \, dt \; + \; \int (-F_{1,2}(t)) \, dt$$

Figure 2.7   Inappropriate Parallel Substitutions

Figure 2.8 schematically presents an overview of the three strategies. Strategy 1 is used as long as progress toward the goal is achieved. When a local maximum is reached without satisfying the goal, a place to jump in the space is needed. Strategy 2 preserves important characteristics of the current state. It is likely that under Strategy 2 the problem solver transfers to a new high spot in the problem space. When Strategy 2 cannot contribute to the solution, Strategy 3 leads to an arbitrary location. Most likely this will be further from the goal, but progress to the goal can commence again.

Under each of the strategies, the problem solver can use both derived schemata and the first principles. In this phase of problem solving, these two categories are not treated differently and assumptions are not made. The next subsections give examples of the use of these three strategies in PHYSICS 101.

Strategy 1 — Definite Progress

PHYSICS 101's problem-solving goal is to produce an expression that only contains variables that satisfy some property (e.g., being constant with respect to time, having a known value, etc.). In this case, the hill-climbing measure is the number of variables in the expression that do *not* satisfy the property. That is, this number is the size of the obstacle set.

PHYSICS 101 contains two basic techniques for reducing the number of undesirable variables. In the first technique, undesirable variables can be replaced using known equations if these formulae only introduce acceptable terms or lead to the cancellation of unacceptable ones (obstacles). An example of this technique appears in Table 2.3 (discussed below). In the second technique, the solver can use values of variables if doing so reduces the hill-climbing measure. For instance, if the current expression is $A * B * C$, and A's value is zero, both B and C can be canceled by replacing A with its numerical value. Similarly, given the expression $A * B * C - B * C$, where A equals one, a numerical replacement can lead to a reduction in obstacles.

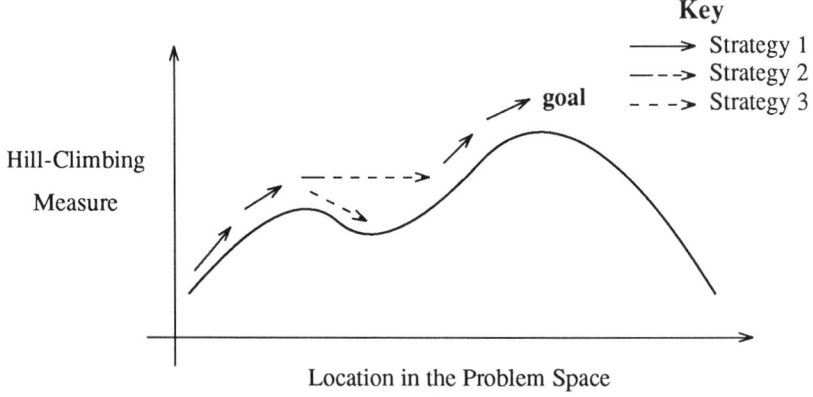

Figure 2.8   The Problem-Solving Model as Hill Climbing

A problem-solving schema applied under Strategy 1 is illustrated in Table 2.3. The goal is to evaluate the top expression, but the values of the two inter-object forces ($F_{1,2}$ and $F_{2,1}$) are not known. A "substitute-to-cancel-obstacles" schema can detect that the two inter-object forces cancel due to Newton's third law. The schema first applies Newton's third law to replace one of the inter-object forces. It then brings these potential canceling terms into a position where cancellation can take place. This requires that the two integrals be combined. Finally, the two troublesome variables can be eliminated to produce zero units of force.

Strategy 2 — Motivated Diversions

There are five techniques used in PHYSICS 101 that follow the second strategy. They are presented below, in the order in which they are preferred by the system.

(1) *Elimination of acceptable variables.* Even when it is not possible to reduce the number of unacceptable terms in an expression, it is a good idea to cancel terms, even acceptable ones. Eliminating these terms may allow productive cancellations that had been prevented by their presence. For example, suppose the problem solver possesses the following formulae, and A and C are acceptable.

$$A = B\ /\ C \quad \text{and} \quad B = -D$$

If the current expression is $A * C + D$, the problem solver cannot reduce the number of obstacles. However, if it uses the first of the above formulae, some terms can be canceled, although the number of obstacles is momentarily increased.

Table 2.3 Example of an Operator Applied under Strategy 1

Consider the Expression

$$\int F_{1, 2, z}(t)\, dt + \int F_{2, 1, z}(t)\, dt$$

Choose a Variable-Cancelling Substitution

$$\int (-F_{2, 1, z}(t))\, dt + \int F_{2, 1, z}(t)\, dt$$

Bring Cancellers Together

$$\int (-F_{2, 1, z}(t) + F_{2, 1, z}(t))\, dt$$

Cancel Variables

$$\int 0\, \frac{kg\ m}{s^2}\, dt$$

---

(2)   *Elimination of integrals and derivatives.* Performing calculus is harder than performing algebra. When it is not possible to eliminate terms, it is often a good idea to eliminate calculus structure. An example where PHYSICS 101 removes calculus from an expression is shown in Table 2.4; the labels on the left refer to Table 2.4's problem-solving techniques. Here the program detects that it can eliminate the derivative because it knows the derivatives of all the terms being differentiated. Applying this operator adds four steps to the calculation sequence. After this schema is applied, direct progress toward the goal state can be made. (Continuing the calculation in Table 2.4 leads, as discussed in Appendix A, to the principle of conservation of energy.)

(3)   *Preservation of expression type.* Assume the system has the following two equations.

$$(i) \ A = (D * E) \qquad (ii) \ A = (F + G)$$

If the current expression is $A * B * C$, Equation (i) would be preferred as this would maintain the property that the expression is a product of terms. Conversely, given $A + B + C$, the second equation is preferred, because after substitution the expression continues to be a sum of terms. There is a strong reason for preserving expression type, one involving more than aesthetics. In the first example the system can produce

$$D * E * B * C \quad or \quad (F + G) * B * C.$$

In the result on the left, all the terms are equally accessible. Future substitutions

---

Table 2.4   An Application of the Substitute-Calculus Schema

$$\frac{d}{dt} (\frac{1}{2} M_1 V^2_{1,y}(t) + M_1 g X_{1,y}(t))$$

$$SeparateDerivatives \quad = \frac{d}{dt} (\frac{1}{2} M_1 V^2_{1,y}(t)) + \frac{d}{dt} (M_1 g X_{1,y}(t))$$

$$ConstsOutOfDerivatives \quad = \frac{1}{2} M_1 \frac{d}{dt} V^2_{1,y}(t) + M_1 g \frac{d}{dt} X_{1,y}(t)$$

$$Differentiate \quad = \frac{2}{2} M_1 V_{1,y}(t) \frac{d}{dt} V_{1,y}(t) + M_1 g \frac{d}{dt} X_{1,y}(t)$$

$$RemoveIdentities \quad = 1 M_1 V_{1,y}(t) \frac{d}{dt} V_{1,y}(t) + M_1 g \frac{d}{dt} X_{1,y}(t)$$

$$= M_1 V_{1,y}(t) \frac{d}{dt} V_{1,y}(t) + M_1 g \frac{d}{dt} X_{1,y}(t)$$

---

involving B, for example, can cancel D or E. (Recall that elimination of undesirable variables is the mechanism that leads to the goal state.) The right-hand result requires that a replacement for B cancel F and G together.

(4) *Preservation of structural symmetry.* When similar additive or multiplicative structure is present, the same general rule should be used repeatedly whenever possible. For example, given the following expression, substitutions involving all three of the A's or all three of the B's would be favored.

$$A_1 B_1 + A_2 B_2 + A_3 B_3$$

This heuristic suggests why transformations on the left side of Figure 2.6 are unpleasing. It would be better to replace both of the velocities either by the derivatives of position or by the integrals of acceleration. A mixture is not appealing.

(5) *Creation of a Same Type Expression.* It generally is a good policy to reason with variables rather than numbers. This is especially important if the solution is to be analyzed in order to determine its generality. However, if the replacement of a variable with its value creates a "same type" expression, the replacement should occur under Strategy 2. For example, consider the expression below, where $C = 0$.

$$A (B + C) D$$

Replacing C with zero and simplifying creates a multiplicative expression. The variable B would become accessible to combination with variables A and D. Similarly, an additive expression can often be produced when the value of some variable, embedded in a multiplicative subexpression, is 1.

Strategy 3 — Floundering Around

In Strategy 3, PHYSICS 101 looks for a legal substitution and applies it. Only one substitution is made in the current equation, in order to minimize this undirected perturbation of the calculation. Also, if after using Strategy 3, Strategies 1 and 2 are still not applicable, the current search path terminates. That is, Strategy 3 is not used in successive calculation steps. This is done to prevent the problem solver from traversing the entire (possibly infinite) search space and is one of the principle reasons the solver is incomplete. Upon failing to produce a solution on its own accord, PHYSICS 101 requests one from its teacher. If a new schema results from analyzing the solution, the system will be able to solve the current intractable problem, and related problems, in the future.

Choosing Among Alternatives

When several schemata are seen as being equally viable, the problem solver must choose which to apply. Under Strategy 3 the choice is made arbitrarily. For the other two strategies the choice is made using the second strategy. For example, if there are a number of ways to cancel two obstacles, a way that preserves the symmetry of the situation is preferred. When the second strategy does not distinguish a single choice, the schema that introduces the smallest number of new variables is used. If there still is no clear favorite, a random choice is made. Choice points are maintained for decisions made under Strategies 1 and 2. The system backtracks to the most recent choice point when no further progress can be made along the current search path.

The system does not record *all* possible choices; rather *only* those possibilities suggested by the highest ranking strategy are kept. That is, if there are multiple choices under Strategy 2, PHYSICS 101 never considers Strategy 3 at that point, even if all of the alternatives under Strategy 2 fail. This contributes to the efficiency of the problem solver; it is also a source of incompleteness.

Relation to other Mathematical Reasoning Research

Other mathematical reasoning research can be viewed in terms of these strategies. Bundy's meta-level solution methods [Bundy81, Bundy83] follow Strategy 1. He considers solving complicated equations containing a single unknown variable (there may be multiple occurrences of the unknown, however). His *attraction*, *collection*, and *isolation* methods always bring one closer to the goal of having the only occurrence of the unknown isolated on the left-hand side of an equation. The mathematical problem-solving methods learned by Silver's LP program [Silver86] follow Strategy 2. LP acquires information that constrains the choice of applicable operators; its learned operators are not guaranteed to bring the problem solver closer to a final solution. The LEX system of Mitchell [Mitchell83b] acquires heuristics that estimate when it is wise to apply an integration operator. It learns how operators previously used only under Strategy 3 can be applied by Strategy 2. The later LEX2 system [Mitchell83a] learns under what conditions a specific integration operator will lead to a solution. This can be viewed as learning how to apply, under Strategy 1, an operator previously used only under Strategy 3.

Several other approaches to learning about problem solving can be analyzed with respect to these categories. Iba's [Iba85] approach to determining useful subsequences of operators (those from which macro-operators should be constructed) is to use a ''peak-to-peak'' heuristic. These peaks are local maxima of the evaluation function used to guide the search for the solution to the current problem, and sequences are segmented at the peaks. The resulting macro-operators fall under Strategy 1 if they move from one peak to a higher one. If the result is an operator sequence that leads away from the goal, it falls under Strategy 2, because it is probably better to jump to another relatively high point than to make an arbitrary move. Minton, in his MORRIS system [Minton85], also focuses on deciding which macro-operators to learn. One type, called *T-macros*, are learned when an operator sequence first appears to be moving away from the goal, but by the end of the sequence has achieved progress toward the goal. These macro-operators fall under Strategy 1.

Finally, these three strategies can be viewed in terms of simulated annealing problem-solving models [Hinton86, Kirkpatrick83]. Progress using Strategy 1 involves the movement toward a problem space minima. Strategy 2 is analogous to slightly increasing the system ''temperature'' when stuck at a local minima that is not a goal state. Here it is desired that the problem solver does not drift too far in the problem space. Strategy 3 potentially involves much greater increases in system temperature, and, hence, much greater jumps in the problem space.

The second strategy illustrates an essential difference between novice and expert problem solvers [Chi81, Chi82, Larkin80, Schoenfeld82]. It is easy to recognize definite progress toward a goal and it is easy to recall which operators can be legally applied. Expertise involves knowing which characteristics of a situation should be preserved (or created) when no way to definitely progress toward the goal is known.

2.3   Building Explanations

Explanation-based learning systems generalize the explanations of solutions to specific sample problems and save the results, in the hope they will help solve future problems. This section addresses the construction of explanations in mathematically-based domains. The focus is on understanding solutions, presented by a teacher, to problems the system could not solve on its own.[4] During this understanding process, the system may need to fill gaps in the teacher-provided solution. The teacher must provide enough guidance so that the system's limited problem solver can successfully solve the problem. If the provided solution can be sufficiently-well understood, a new schema may result, and the next time the system faces a problem related to the current one it may be able to solve it without the need for external assistance.

Understanding a teacher-provided solution involves two phases. First, the system attempts to verify that each of the instructor's solution steps mathematically follows. If successful, in the second phase the mathematical reasoning component of PHYSICS 101 builds an explanation of *why* the solution works. A sample collision problem illustrates these two phases.

2.3.1   A Sample Problem

In the one-dimensional problem shown in Figure 2.9, there are three balls moving in free space, without the influence of any external forces. (Nothing is specified about the forces between the balls. Besides their mutual gravitational attraction, there could be a long-range electrical interaction and a very complicated interaction during the collision.) In the initial state (state A) the first ball is moving toward the other two, which are stationary. Some time later (state B) the second and third balls are recoiling from the resulting collision. The task is to determine the velocity of the first ball after the collision.

PHYSICS 101 cannot solve this problem with only the schemata shown in Figure 2.4. Initially, it tries the formula $V = \frac{d}{dt}X$, which leads nowhere, then attempts the solution steps presented in Table 2.5. PHYSICS 101's problem solver is incomplete, as previously described. One source of incompleteness is that the problem solver never performs two unmotivated ("blind") substitutions consecutively (as described in Section 2.2.4). The problem solver possesses no motivated strategy to lead it past line 2 in Table 2.5, and asks for a solution from

---

[4] Although the emphasis is on teacher-provided solutions, much of the discussion in this section also applies to the explanation of the system's own problem solving. It may take a substantial amount of work for Physics 101 to solve a problem, even without needing external help, and this effort can be reduced in the future by creating a new schema from the analysis of its labors.

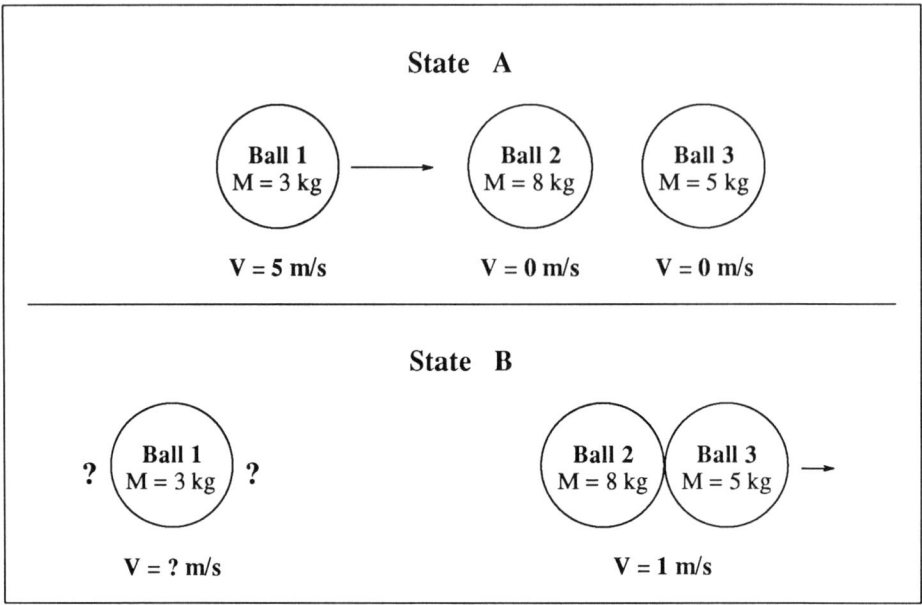

Figure 2.9   A Three-Body Collision Problem

its teacher.

The teacher's solution to the collision problem can be seen in Table 2.6. Without explicitly stating it, the teacher invokes the principle of conservation of momentum, as the momentum $(M \times V)$ of the balls at two different times is equated. This equation is not a variation of any formula known to the system (Table 2.2). It needs a physically consistent mathematical derivation if PHYSICS 101 is to accept the solution provided.

Table 2.5 The Failed Solution Attempt

$$V_{1,x}(t)$$

(1) SubstSameType $= \int A_{1,x}(t)\,dt$

(2)   SubstBlindly $= \int \dfrac{F_{net,\,1,\,x}(t)}{M_1}\,dt$

Table 2.6 The Teacher's Solution

$$M_1 V_{1,x}(A) + M_2 V_{2,x}(A) + M_3 V_{3,x}(A) = M_1 V_{1,x}(B) + M_2 V_{2,x}(B) + M_3 V_{3,x}(B)$$

$$(3\,kg)(-5\frac{m}{s}) = 8\,kg\, V_{1,x}(B) + (3\,kg)(1\frac{m}{s}) + (5\,kg)(1\frac{m}{s})$$

$$-15\frac{kg\,m}{s} = 8\,kg\, V_{1,x}(B) + 8\frac{kg\,m}{s}$$

$$V_{1,x}(B) = -2.88\frac{m}{s}$$

2.3.2 Verifying a Teacher's Solution

In order to accept a teacher's answer, the system must verify each of the steps in the solution. Besides being mathematically correct, the calculations must be consistent with its domain-specific knowledge. To be valid, each of the solution steps must be assigned to one of the following four classifications.

(1)   Instantiation of a known formula: *force = mass × acceleration* is an example of this type.

(2)   Definition of a new variable in order to shorten later expressions: *resistance = voltage / current* would fall in this category.

(3)   Rearrangement of a previously-used formula. These equations are mathematical variants of previous steps. The replacement of variables by their values also falls into this category.

(4)   Statement of an unknown relationship among known variables. These steps require full justification, which the system performs symbolically by reasoning about algebra and calculus. Only the steps in this category are candidates for generalization.

PHYSICS 101 possesses several methods for verifying equations falling into Category 4. Two are suggested when the two sides of an equation only differ in the time at which they are evaluated (a condition satisfied by the initial equation in Table 2.6). One method this suggests is to determine if the common form underlying each side of the equation is constant with respect to time. This can be done by seeing if the common form's derivative is zero. The second suggested method is to determine how the underlying form explicitly depends on time. If time can be made explicit, it is easy to see if it is valid to equate the expression at two different times. This method can handle more situations than the first, and is the one used by PHYSICS 101 to understand the teacher's solution.

Figure 2.10 illustrates three possible forms of the underlying time-dependent expression. The expression could be periodic, and hence could be equated at times separated by some number of periods. Alternatively, the expression could be parabolic. Here there would be

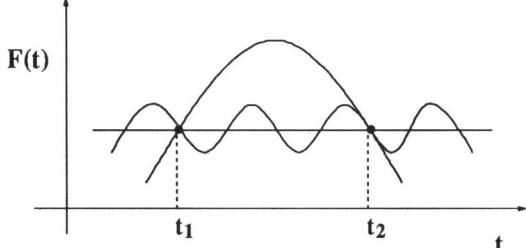

Figure 2.10   Equating an Expression at Two Times

some quadratic relationship between times where it is valid to equate the expression. A third possibility is that the expression is constant with respect to time. In this last case, it is valid to equate the expression at *any* two times.

Once the system selects a method for verifying a new equation, it must perform the mathematics necessary to determine any additional information required by the method. For example, it may need to determine the derivative of an expression or legally eliminate all the terms whose time-dependence is not known. In this phase, PHYSICS 101 is a mathematical problem solver and uses the techniques presented in the previous section.

The actual calculations of the system appear in Table 2.7. The goal is to convert, via a series of equality-preserving transformations, the top expression into an equivalent expression whose time dependence is explicit. Once this is done, the system can determine if Table 2.6's first equation is valid. (The top expression in Table 2.7 is called the *left-hand side* of the calculation, while the other expressions are termed *right-hand sides*.)

PHYSICS 101 produces the annotations to the left of the expressions in Table 2.7. These annotations indicate which of its problem-solving schemata (Figure 2.4) PHYSICS 101 uses to perform each calculation step. In the first step, the formulae substitutions are not chosen in support of a variable cancellation, but are chosen in accordance with the problem solver's Strategy 2.[5] In the next step, the solver chooses the formulae substitutions because the mass terms can be canceled. Before this cancellation can take place, however, the canceling terms must be brought together. The calculation continues in a like manner until the solver eliminates all the unknowns. Then it substitutes the known values and solves the ensuing arithmetic and calculus. Since the initial expression in Table 2.7 is constant, it can be equated at any two times.

---

[5] Initially, the system chooses to replace the velocities by the derivatives of the positions. This leads nowhere and the system backtracks. No other backtracking occurs during the calculation of Table 2.7. The system is guided by the goal of canceling variables, which greatly reduces the amount of unnecessary substitution during problem solving.

Table 2.7 Verifying the First Equation in Table 2.6

$$M_1 V_{1,x}(t) + M_2 V_{2,x}(t) + M_3 V_{3,x}(t)$$

(1) SubstSameType $= M_1 \int A_{1,x}(t)\, dt + M_2 \int A_{2,x}(t)\, dt + M_3 \int A_{3,x}(t)\, dt$

(2) SubstToCancel $= M_1 \int \dfrac{F_{net,\,1,x}(t)}{M_1}\, dt + M_2 \int \dfrac{F_{net,\,2,x}(t)}{M_2}\, dt + M_3 \int \dfrac{F_{net,\,3,x}(t)}{M_3}\, dt$

(3) ConstsOutCalculus $= \dfrac{M_1}{M_1} \int F_{net,\,1,x}(t)\, dt + \dfrac{M_2}{M_2} \int F_{net,\,2,x}(t)\, dt + \dfrac{M_3}{M_3} \int F_{net,\,3,x}(t)\, dt$

(4) SubMultIdentities $= 1 \int F_{net,\,1,x}(t)\, dt + 1 \int F_{net,\,2,x}(t)\, dt + 1 \int F_{net,\,3,x}(t)\, dt$

(5) RemoveIdentities $= \int F_{net,\,1,x}(t)\, dt + \int F_{net,\,2,x}(t)\, dt + \int F_{net,\,3,x}(t)\, dt$

(6) SubstSameType $= \int (F_{ext,\,1,x}(t) + F_{int,\,1,x}(t))\, dt + \int (F_{ext,\,2,x}(t) + F_{int,\,2,x}(t))\, dt$

$\qquad\qquad\qquad + \int (F_{ext,\,3,x}(t) + F_{int,\,3,x}(t))\, dt$

(7) SubstSameType $= \int (F_{ext,\,1,x}(t) + F_{2,1,x}(t) + F_{3,1,x}(t))\, dt$

$\qquad\qquad\qquad + \int (F_{ext,\,2,x}(t) + F_{1,2,x}(t) + F_{3,2,x}(t))\, dt$

$\qquad\qquad\qquad + \int (F_{ext,\,3,x}(t) + F_{1,3,x}(t) + F_{2,3,x}(t))\, dt$

(8) SubstToCancel $= \int (F_{ext,\,1,x}(t) + F_{2,1,x}(t) + F_{3,1,x}(t))\, dt$

$\qquad\qquad\qquad + \int (F_{ext,\,2,x}(t) - F_{2,1,x}(t) + F_{3,2,x}(t))\, dt$

$\qquad\qquad\qquad + \int (F_{ext,\,3,x}(t) - F_{3,1,x}(t) - F_{3,2,x}(t))\, dt$

(9) CombineCalculus $= \int (F_{ext,\,1,x}(t) + F_{2,1,x}(t) + F_{3,1,x}(t) + F_{ext,\,2,x}(t) - F_{2,1,x}(t) + F_{3,2,x}(t)$

$\qquad\qquad\qquad + F_{ext,\,3,x}(t) - F_{3,1,x}(t) - F_{3,1,x}(t))\, dt$

(10) SubAddIdentities $= \int (F_{ext,\,1,x}(t) + 0\,\frac{kg\,m}{s^2} + 0\,\frac{kg\,m}{s^2} + F_{ext,\,2,x}(t) + 0\,\frac{kg\,m}{s^2} + F_{ext,\,3,x}(t))\, dt$

(11) AddNumbers $= \int (F_{ext,\,1,x}(t) + F_{ext,\,2,x}(t) + F_{ext,\,3,x}(t) + 0\,\frac{kg\,m}{s^2})\, dt$

(12) RemoveIdentities $= \int (F_{ext,\,1,x}(t) + F_{ext,\,2,x}(t) + F_{ext,\,3,x}(t))\, dt$

(13) SubstValues $= \int (0\,\frac{kg\,m}{s^2} + 0\,\frac{kg\,m}{s^2} + 0\,\frac{kg\,m}{s^2})\, dt$

(14) AddNumbers $= \int 0\,\frac{kg\,m}{s^2}\, dt$

(15) Integrate $= constant_1$

2.3.3 Explaining Solutions

At this point, the system has ascertained that its teacher's use of a new equation is indeed valid. One can view Table 2.7 as an explanation structure; underlying the calculation are a large number of equation schemata, along with their associated preconditions. These schemata justify the transformations from one line to the next. Between each pair of consecutive expressions are the equation schemata (and their preconditions) used to rewrite one expression into the next. This is illustrated in Figure 2.11. The left side of this figure shows the general structure existing between consecutive expressions, while the right half presents a simple, concrete example.

However, although Table 2.7 constitutes a perfectly acceptable explanation of the solution to the specific example of Figure 2.9, the underlying explanation does not directly suffice to produce the maximally general concept. Applying a standard explanation-based generalization algorithm does produce a generalization of the specific solution (see Section 2.4.2); it generalizes a number of attributes of the problem. For example, its result does not only apply to colliding balls — it applies to situations involving any type of physical object. Nor does the problem have to be in the x-direction, since none of the schemata used to tie the calculation together constrain the component of the variables. A third property generalized is that the external forces need not individually be zero. All that Step 15 of Table 2.7 requires is that the external forces sum to zero. However, since the standard method does not generalize the explanation structure, one unfortunate aspect of the specific example remains; the new law only applies to physical situations involving *three* objects. Without that property, adding the $M V$ terms of three objects will not lead to the complete

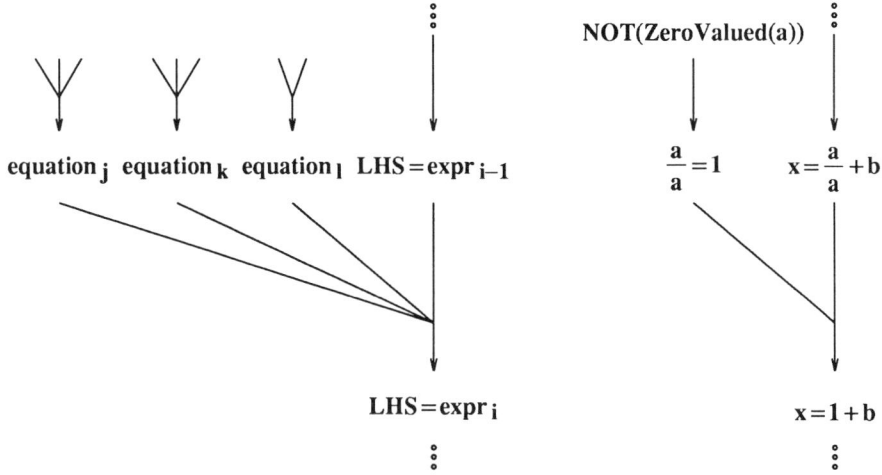

Figure 2.11   The Underlying Structure of a Calculation

cancellation of internal forces of the objects. The preconditions of the new schema would insist on a three-object world without external forces, because only then will the sum of three momentum terms always be constant across time. Unfortunately this result is not broadly applicable. Such a system would need to learn separate rules when it encountered a four-object system, a five-object system, etc.

In order to produce the proper generalization to N, the system must determine a reason for including each variable in the teacher's initial equation. This will determine which variables are required in its general form.

In the explanation process, PHYSICS 101 determines how the value of the desired property of the current problem's *unknown* is obtained. As stated earlier, the problem's unknown is the expression about which the value of some property is being sought; in the sample problem, V_1 is the unknown and its value in state B is being sought. During this process, the system determines the role of each variable in the initial expression of the calculation.

During a calculation one of three things can happen to a variable:

(1)   its value can be substituted,

(2)   it can be symbolically replaced during a formulae substitution, or

(3)   it can be *canceled.*

Understanding and generalizing variable cancellation drives PHYSICS 101. The system can identify the first five of the following six types of variable cancellations:

additive identity
>   These are algebraic cancellations of the form $x - x = 0$. Line 10 in Table 2.7 contains two additive cancellations.

multiplicative identity
>   These are algebraic cancellations of the form $x / x = 1$. Line 4 in Table 2.7 involves two multiplicative cancellations.

multiplication by zero
>   These are cancellations that result from an expression (which may contain several variables) being multiplied by zero. None appear in Table 2.7.

integration (to a number)
>   This type of cancellation occurs when variables disappear during symbolic integration. When integration produces *new* variables (other than the integration constant), this calculation is viewed as a substitution involving the original terms. No cancellations of this type appear in Table 2.7.

differentiation (to a number)
>   This is analogous to cancellation during integration.

assumed ignorable
>   A term can be additively ignored because it is assumed to be approximately equal to zero or multiplicatively ignored because it is assumed to be approximately equal to one.

2.3.4 Understanding Obstacles

Recall that *obstacles* are those expressions appearing in a calculation whose values are not known. *Primary obstacles* are obstacles descended from the unknown. In the momentum problem the only primary obstacles not replaced in a formula substitution are $F_{2,1}$ and $F_{3,1}$. If the value of the desired property of each of the primary obstacles were known, the value of the unknown's desired property would be specified. The system ascertains how these obstacles are eliminated from the calculation. Canceling obstacles is seen as the essence of the solution strategy, because when all the obstacles have been canceled the value of the unknown's desired property can easily be calculated.

Figure 2.12 illustrates the concept of primary obstacles. The goal in this sample problem is to determine the value of V_1. Since this is not known, the problem is transformed to that of finding A_1 (for simplicity, the integral sign is ignored here). However, the value of A_1 is not known either. This leads to the substitution of $F_{net,1}$ divided by M_1. The mass is known, but the net force is not. The net force is then decomposed into two components - a known external force and an unknown internal force. Finally, the internal force is further decomposed into its constituents. These two inter-object forces are the obstacles to knowing the value of $V_{1,x}$. PHYSICS 101 needs to determine how the solution in Table 2.7 circumvents the need to know the value of these two variables.

Figure 2.13 contains the *cancellation graph* for the three-body collision problem. This data structure is built by the system during the development of an understanding of the specific solution. (Algorithmic details of the cancellation graph construction process appear in the next subsection.) The graph holds the information that explains how the specific example's obstacles are eliminated from the calculation. The system uses this information to guide the generalization process described in the next section.

To reason about a calculation, PHYSICS 101 must be able to distinguish different instances of the same variable. For example, the M_1 introduced in line 2 of Table 2.7 plays a different role than the M_1 appearing in the left-hand side of the equation. The system marks variables

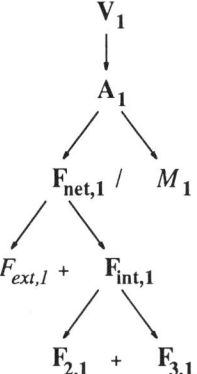

Figure 2.12   Decomposing the Unknown

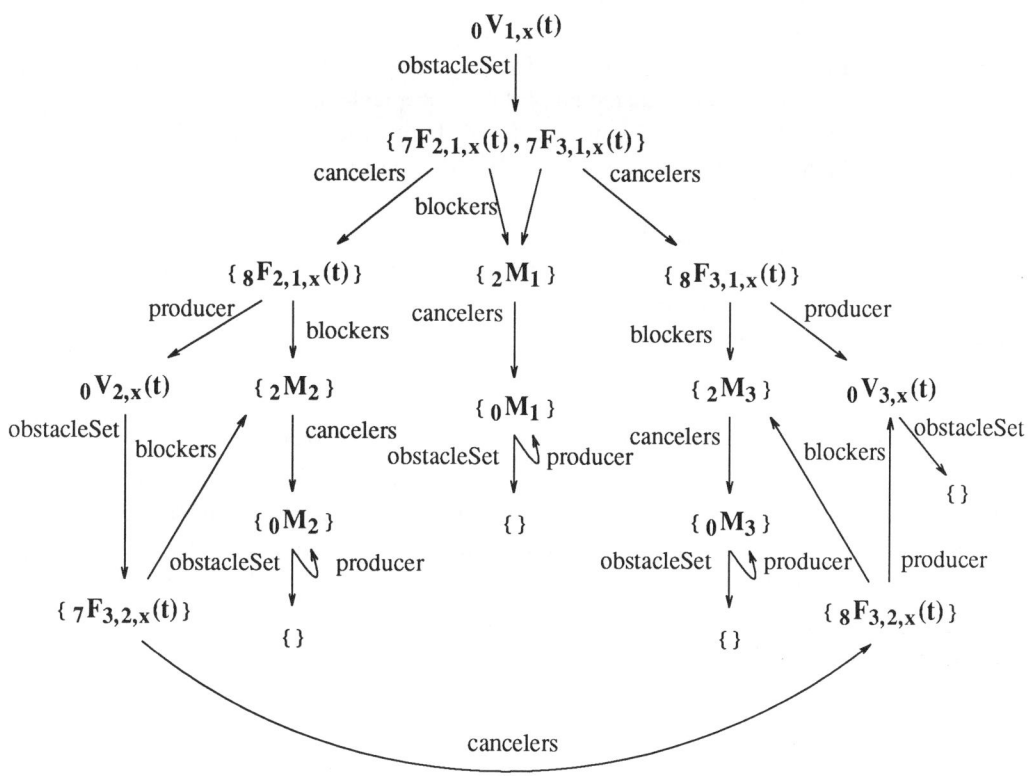

Figure 2.13   The Cancellation Graph

with the solution step in which they first appear. This information is recorded in Figure 2.13's cancellation graph (and in subsequent cancellation graphs) by the subscript preceding a variable; variables originating in the left-hand side are prefixed with zeroes.

To understand the calculation, the system first determines that the primary obstacles $F_{2,1,x}$ and $F_{3,1,x}$ are eliminated by being *additively canceled*. Although canceled additively, these variables descended from a multiplicative expression $(A = \frac{F}{M})$. Hence, the system must determine how they are *additively isolated*. Multiplication by M_1 performed this task; so the system has an explanation of the M_1 term in the left-hand side expression of Table 2.7.

The next thing to do is to determine how the terms that additively cancel $F_{2,1,x}$ and $F_{3,1,x}$ are introduced into the calculation. $F_{2,1,x}$ is canceled by a force descended from $V_{2,x}$. $F_{2,1,x}$, too, must first be additively isolated. PHYSICS 101 discovers that the left-hand side's M_2 performs this isolation. The system now has explanations for the M_2 and the $V_{2,x}$ terms in the left-hand side. Similar reasoning determines the role of M_3 and $V_{3,x}$.

Cancellation of the primary obstacles requires the presence of additional variables on the left-hand side of the equation. These extra terms may themselves contain obstacle variables; these are called *secondary obstacles*. The system must also determine how these obstacles are eliminated from the calculation. The elimination of the secondary obstacles may in turn require the presence of additional variables in the left-hand side expression, which may introduce additional secondary obstacles. This recursion must terminate, however, as the calculation is known to have eliminated all of the unacceptable terms.

Canceling the inter-object forces involving ball 1 introduced one secondary obstacle — $F_{3,2,x}$. This secondary obstacle was additively canceled by a force descended from $V_{3,x}$. Canceling this secondary obstacle produced no new obstacles.

Once the system determines how all of the obstacles in the calculation are canceled, generalization can occur. At this time, PHYSICS 101 can also report any variables in the left-hand side of a calculation that are irrelevant to the determination of the value of the unknown. Those variables not visited during the construction of the cancellation graph are not necessary, even though they are present in the teacher's solution.

2.3.5 Constructing the Cancellation Graph — Algorithmic Details

This section presents the cancellation graph construction algorithm and illustrates it with an algebraic example. The cancellation graph algorithm analyzes the completed calculations and ascertains why they achieve their goal. Hence, the algorithm can also be applied to analyzing complete calculations produced by an external agent, as well as internally produced calculations.

The algorithm is expressed here in a pseudo-code, designed for readability. (The actual implementation is written in INTERLISP.) In this algorithm, the notation *record.field* is used to represent a given field of a record, and back arrows ($\leftarrow$) indicate value assignment. The construct

for each *element* **in** *set* **unless** *test* **do** *statement*

means that *element* is successively bound to each member of *set* and, unless *test* is true, *statement* is evaluated.

Tables 2.8 and 2.9 contain the algorithm for constructing cancellation graphs, while Table 2.10 lists the fields referenced and describes their setting when the algorithm commences. (Fields ending with question marks are boolean-valued.) Further details on these fields are provided as the algorithm is discussed.

These graphs record the roles played by each of the variables in the calculation. A sample problem is used to illustrate the algorithm; it is contained in Table 2.11, and its cancellation graph appears in Figure 2.14. The features of this specific cancellation graph are explained as the algorithm is described. Recall that the first expression in a sequence of calculation steps is called the *left-hand side* of the calculation, while the subsequent expressions are termed *right-hand sides*.

In the sample calculation, Greek letters are used for variables that cannot appear in the final right-hand side of the calculation. For example, it may be that the final right-hand side can only contain variables whose value is known or variables that are time-independent. The goal is to rewrite the left-hand side, via a series of equality-preserving transformations, into an expression containing no Greek letters. The equation schemata used to produce each new expression are shown in the right column. A mixture of domain-specific and general

Table 2.8   Building the Cancellation Graph — Part I

procedure   CheckForObstacles (variable)

    if variable.notChecked? **then**

        variable.notChecked? ← *false*

        variable.obstacleSet ← FindObstacleSet({variable})

        AnalyzeObstacles(variable.obstacleSet)

procedure   FindObstacleSet (variables)

    answer ← { }   /* *answer* is a local variable. */

    for each variable **in** variables **unless** variable.eliminated?

        do if variable.replaced?

            then answer ← answer ∪ FindObstacleSet(variable.descendants)

          else if variable.unacceptable?

            then answer ← answer ∪ {variable}

    return answer

procedure   AnalyzeObstacles (obstacleSet)

    for each obstacle **in** obstacleSet **do** Eliminate(obstacle)

    for each obstacle **in** obstacleSet **do** CheckForSecondaryObstacles(obstacle)

procedure   Eliminate (variable)

    variable.eliminated? ← *true*

    AnalyzeBlockers(variable.blockers)

    AnalyzePartners(variable.partners)

    AnalyzeCancelers(variable.cancelers)

---

algebraic rewrite rules are used. β is the variable about which some information is sought, i.e., it is the problem's unknown. In this example, subscripts are used to differentiate various instantiations of the *same* variable (e.g., b_1 and b_2). In other words, b_1 and b_2 both refer to the variable b.

Table 2.9 Building the Cancellation Graph — Part II

procedure AnalyzeBlockers (blockers)

    for each blocker **in** blockers **unless** blocker.eliminated? **do** Eliminate(blocker)

procedure AnalyzePartners (partners)

    for each partner **in** partners **unless** partner.eliminated?

        do partner.eliminated? ← *true*

           AnalyzeBlockers(partner.blockers)

procedure AnalyzeCancelers (cancelers)

    for each canceler **in** cancelers

        do canceler.eliminated? ← *true*

           AnalyzeBlockers(canceler.blockers)

procedure CheckForSecondaryObstacles (variable)

    for each blocker **in** variable.blockers **do** CheckForSecondaryObstacles(blocker)

    for each partner **in** variable.partners

        do CheckForObstacles(partner.producer)

           for each blocker **in** partner.blockers **do** CheckForSecondaryObstacles(blocker)

    for each canceler **in** variable.cancelers

        do CheckForObstacles(canceler.producer)

           for each blocker **in** canceler.blockers **do** CheckForSecondaryObstacles(blocker)

CheckForObstacles(unknown)   /* Construct the cancellation graph. */

This sample calculation illustrates the major components and attributes of cancellation graphs. The graph specifies the role of each variable in the left-hand side of the calculation. Combined together in the given manner, these variables support the answer to the question about the unknown. One important feature is that unnecessary variables (e.g., α in Table 2.11) do not appear in the graph.

Table 2.10 Fields Used in the Cancellation Graph Algorithm

Field	Initial Setting
notChecked?	initially *true*, reset in algorithm when checked for obstacles
obstacleSet	initially *{}*, set in algorithm
unacceptable?	*true* if this variable cannot appear in the final right-hand side of the calculation
eliminated?	initially *false*, set in algorithm
replaced?	*true* if replaced by a rewrite rule during the calculation
descendants	variables introduced when this variable rewritten
blockers	set of variables preventing cancellation of this variable
partners	set of variables in the canceled expression in addition to this variable
cancelers	set of variables that canceled this variable
producer	variable in the left-hand side of the calculation that produced this variable

The first step in building a cancellation graph is to create the *primary obstacle set* for the problem's unknown. An obstacle set for a collection of variables consists of those variables possessing the following properties:

(1)   they are in the given collection or descended (via rewriting with equation schemata) from a member of it,

(2)   they cannot appear in the final right-hand side of a calculation,

(3)   they are canceled in the calculation, and

(4)   they are not marked earlier in the algorithm as being eliminated from consideration.

The function *FindObstacleSet* assumes that the provided calculation is successful. This means that if an unacceptable variable is not replaced, it must be canceled, since there can be no unacceptable variables in the final right-hand side of a calculation.

The only member of the sample problem's primary obstacle set is δ_1. It appears in line 2 and is canceled in line 7 of Table 2.11. The only other descendant of the unknown β is c_2, and because it is not an obstacle c_2 can appear in the final expression of the calculation. The next things to do are to see how the obstacle is canceled and then determine if there are any undesirable side effects of doing this. If there are side effects, one must determine how they are circumvented in the specific example.

Table 2.11 A Sample Calculation	
Calculation Steps	Rewrite Rules Used
$\alpha\left((a-b_1)\dfrac{\beta}{c_1}+d\right)g$	β is the unknown
(1) $= f\left((a-b_1)\dfrac{\beta}{c_1}+d\right)g$	$\alpha = f$
(2) $= f\left((a-b_1)\dfrac{\delta_1\,c_2}{c_1}+d\right)g$	$\beta = \delta c$
(3) $= f\left((a-b_1)\delta_1+d\right)g$	$?x/?x = 1$ $?x\,1 = ?x$
(4) $= f\left((\epsilon_1+b_2-b_1)\delta_1+d\right)g$	$a = \epsilon+b$
(5) $= f\left(\epsilon_1\,\delta_1+d\right)g$	$?x-?x = 0$ $?x+0 = ?x$
(6) $= f\left(\epsilon_1\,\delta_1+\gamma_1-\epsilon_2\,\delta_2\right)g$	$d = \gamma-\epsilon\,\delta$
(7) $= f\,\gamma_1\,g$	$?x+?y = ?y+?x$ $?x-?x = 0$ $?x+0 = ?x$
(8) $= \dfrac{f\,\gamma_1\,h}{\gamma_2}$	$g = \dfrac{h}{\gamma}$
(9) $= f\,h$	$?x/?x = 1$ $1\,?x = ?x$

PHYSICS 101 analyzes an obstacle set once it is constructed, and determines how each element of this set is eliminated from the calculation. This involves three steps.

(1) Determining how those variables blocking the cancellation are eliminated. *Blockers* are variables preventing additive or multiplicative access (depending on the manner of cancellation) to an obstacle.

(2) Determining how the obstacle's cancellation partners are brought into position for the cancellation. *Partners* are variables that must be present in combination with the obstacle in order for the obstacle to be canceled.

(3) Determining how the cancelers of the obstacle are brought into position. *Cancelers* are the variables that directly cancel an obstacle.

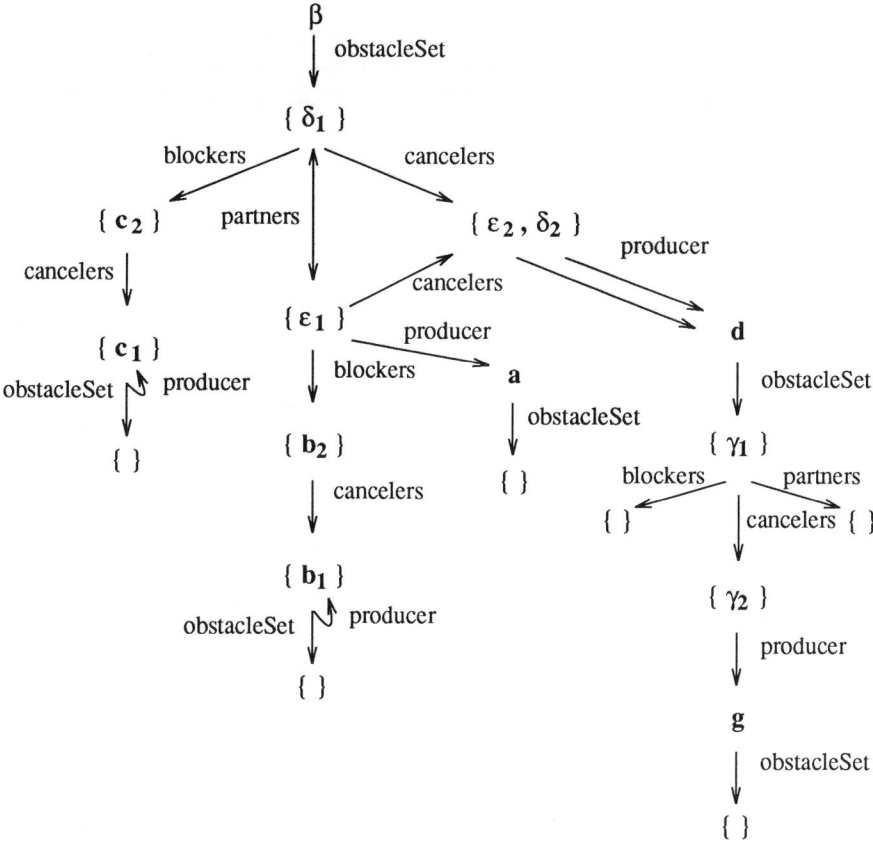

Figure 2.14 The Cancellation Graph for the Calculation in Table 2.11

Analyzing the Blockers of the Obstacle

The first step is to determine how the obstacle is isolated for cancellation. When introducing an obstacle into a calculation (via the application of equation schemata), additional variables are often unavoidably also introduced. Some of these may be blocking the cancellation of the obstacle, and, if so, the system must ascertain how these *blockers* are eliminated.

The blockers of an obstacle depend on the manner in which the obstacle is canceled. This is illustrated in Table 2.12. The *blocker sets* for various expressions and cancellation types are shown. The first column contains the expression descended from the producer of the obstacle, while the second column contains the full expression containing the obstacle that is canceled when the obstacle is eliminated. For example, if the equation schemata used to cancel the obstacle a_1 specifies $\dfrac{a_1+b_1}{a_2+b_2} = 1$, then the canceled expression is $a_1 + b_1$. (In this case b_1 is the only cancellation partner and $\{a_2,b_2\}$ is the canceler set.) In the last two

Table 2.12 Blockers of Obstacle a			
Expression Descended from a's Producer	Full Canceled Expression	Obstacle Cancellation Type	
		Additive	Multiplicative
(1) $a + b + c$	a	$\{\ \}$	$\{\,b,\,c\}$
(2) $a\,b\,c$	a	$\{b,\,c\}$	$\{\ \}$
(3) $a\,(b{+}c)\,d$	a	$\{\,b,\,c,\,d\}$	$\{\ \}$
(4) $(a{+}b)\,c{+}d$	a	$\{\,c\}$	$\{\,b,\,d\}$
(5) $(a\,b{+}c)\,d$	a	$\{\,b,\,d\}$	$\{\,c\}$
(6) $a + b + c$	$a + b$	$\{\ \}$	$\{\,c\}$
(7) $a + b + c$	$a + x$	$\{\ \}$	$\{\,b,\,c\}$
(8) $a + b + c$	$a\,x$	$\{\,b,\,c\}$	$\{\,b,\,c\}$

columns are the blocker sets as a function of the cancellation type.

In Table 2.12's first example, obstacle a is *additively isolated* and *multiplicatively blocked*, while in the second and third examples the opposite is true. The fourth and fifth lines are examples of expressions that are blocked for both types of cancellation. The last three examples illustrate the effect of a more complicated canceled expression. As shown in line 6, variables in the canceled expression are not blockers. Line 7 shows that an additive cancellation partner does not effect a sum of variables, while a multiplicative cancellation partner means that the sum of variables must be reduced to a single term (line 8).

In the calculation of Table 2.11, the obstacle δ_1 is additively canceled (line 7) and has a multiplicative cancellation partner (ε_1). The variable c_2 is the only member of δ_1's blocker set.

Analyzing the Partners of the Obstacle

Next, the understander analyzes the cancellation partners of the obstacle. This entails determining how the blockers of each partner are eliminated. By eliminating these blockers, the partners are positioned so they can participate in the cancellation with the obstacle. In Table 2.11, the only blocker of ε_1 is b_2.

Analyzing the Cancelers of the Obstacle

Finally, the cancellation of the obstacle must be understood. This requires determining how the blockers of the cancelers are eliminated in order to properly position the cancelers so they can eliminate the obstacle. The expression $-\varepsilon_2\,\delta_2$ canceled the only member of β's obstacle set in line 7 of Table 2.11. No variables blocked this cancellation.

Checking for Secondary Obstacles

Once all the members of an obstacle set are eliminated, the understander checks (in the procedure *CheckForSecondaryObstacles*) to see if this process lead to the existence of additional (secondary) obstacle sets. Canceling an obstacle requires the presence of its partners and cancelers, as well as those variables that canceled the blockers of the obstacle, the blockers of its partners, and the blockers of its cancelers. Hence, additional variables must be present in the left-hand side of the calculation. These *producer* variables are checked to see if their presence means additional obstacle sets are present in the calculation. If so, the understander analyzes these secondary obstacle sets in the same manner as the primary obstacle set.

Notice that eliminating the secondary obstacles can also require additional variables in the left-hand side of the calculation. These variables may also have obstacles sets (again called secondary sets) that need to be eliminated. Since the successful calculation contained a finite number of calculation steps (and, hence, a finite number of potential obstacle variables), the algorithm always terminates.

There are several cancelers in the calculation of Table 2.11: c_1, b_1, ε_2, and δ_2. The first two of these appear in the left-hand side of the calculation (and, hence, are their own producers). The third and fourth cancelers are produced by d. The obstacle set of d only contains γ_1, which is introduced in line 6. Although not acceptable in the final right-side of the calculation, variables ε_2 and δ_2 are not members of this obstacle set because when this set is constructed these variables are already eliminated. The variable g in the left-hand side of the calculation produces the canceler of γ_1 and the obstacle set for g is the empty set.

The producers of cancellation partners are also checked to see if they have obstacle sets. The variable a produced ε_1, the cancellation partner of δ_1. The obstacle set of a is also empty.

Notice that all of the variables, other than α, in the left-hand side of the calculation in Table 2.11 appear in Figure 2.14. This graph records the role of each variable in the determination of the desired property of the unknown. The variable α does not appear in the cancellation graph because it serves no purpose in the achievement of the goal. One of the important features of the cancellation graph process is that it detects irrelevant variables in the left-hand expression.

2.4 Generalizing Solutions

Once the solution to a problem is understood, PHYSICS 101 must generalize it so that similar problems can be easily solved in the future. This involves generalizing the structure of the specific problem's solution, as well as generalizing the constants in the specific example. Before presenting PHYSICS 101's generalization method, standard explanation-based generalization is considered.

2.4.1 The Result of Standard Explanation-Based Learning

Standard explanation-based learning generalization algorithms (e.g., [Mitchell86, Mooney86]) can be applied to the explanation structure underlying a calculation. The result obtained by doing this with the calculation of Table 2.7 appears in Table 2.13.

These standard methods generalize a number of characteristics of the sample problem. For example, the x-component of the velocities need not be used, and the learned technique applies to any vector component. Also, because of the equation schemata used, the masses of the three objects must be non-zero and constant with respect to time. The cancellations of the inter-object forces (line 10 of Table 2.7) leads to the requirement that the general objects be distinct. The property of the specific example that each external force is zero is generalized. In the general case these forces need not *individually* be zero; what is needed is that they *sum* to zero. Line 15 of Table 2.7 causes this constraint because the integration rule used requires that the integrand be zero.

However, because the standard methods do not generalize the *structure* of the explanation, the result they obtain only applies to situations where there are *three* objects in the problem's world. A separate rule must be learned for situations containing four objects, five objects, etc. In addition, the acquired schema is not relevant when the external forces do not sum to zero. No appreciation of the effect of external forces on a system's momentum is obtained. By recognizing and analyzing obstacle cancellations, then reconstructing the explanation in the general case, PHYSICS 101 overcomes these shortcomings.

As will be seen, in PHYSICS 101 generalization occurs by reconstructing the specific calculation in the general case, thereby generalizing the structure of the specific example. There are three reasons why the underlying structure of the generalized calculation can differ from that of the specific calculation.

(1)   One cause of altering structure is the fact that some equation schemata are marked ''problem-specific.'' Schemata that replace variables (e.g., F_{ext}) with their values in a

---

Table 2.13   The Result of Standard Explanation-Based Learning

Equation

$$M_{?i_1} V_{?i_1, ?c}(?t) + M_{?i_2} V_{?i_2, ?c}(?t) + M_{?i_3} V_{?i_3, ?c}(?t) \ = \ constant$$

Preconditions

IsaComponent($?c$) $\wedge$ IsaTime($?t$) $\wedge$

NOT(ZeroValued($M_{?i_1}$)) $\wedge$ NOT(ZeroValued($M_{?i_2}$)) $\wedge$ NOT(ZeroValued($M_{?i_3}$)) $\wedge$

IndependentOf($M_{?i_1}$, t) $\wedge$ IndependentOf($M_{?i_2}$, t) $\wedge$ IndependentOf($M_{?i_3}$, t) $\wedge$

$?i_1 \neq ?i_2 \wedge ?i_1 \neq ?i_3 \wedge ?i_2 \neq ?i_3 \wedge$ Permutation($\{?i_1, ?i_2, ?i_3\}$, *ObjectsInWorld*) $\wedge$

ZeroExpression(ValueOf($F_{ext, ?i_1, ?c}$) + ValueOf($F_{ext, ?i_2, ?c}$) + ValueOf($F_{ext, ?i_3, ?c}$))

---

specific problem are the simplest type of problem-specific schemata. More complicated examples are also possible. For example, the formula $F_{net} = M A$ holds in all physics problems, while $F = M g$ is only applicable to certain problems. Problem-specific equations are not used when generalizing a calculation (they may be used, though, when building special cases). The obstacle graph helps determine how the calculation can be reconstructed without using equation schemata of this type. How this is done is explained later, and a sample problem where this occurs appears in Appendix A.2.

(2)   Another cause of altering an explanation's structure is mentioned in the previous section. Any variables appearing in the left-hand side of a specific calculation, but not appearing in the calculation's cancellation graph, do not appear in the generalized calculation. The generalization algorithm never considers these unnecessary variables nor their descendants.

(3)   The third cause is the primary reason for the proper generalization of the momentum example. As described earlier, in specific problems "expanded" versions of equations are used. However, in the general calculation the unexpanded forms are used. For example, the general equation

$$A (x) = \prod_{i=1}^{N} B (x, y_i) \quad \textit{expands to} \quad A (x) = B (x, y_1) B (x, y_2) B (x, y_3) B (x, y_4)$$

in a problem where $N=4$. This is what facilitates the generalization of number. Notice, though, that simply replacing an expanded equation by a general equation containing a Σ or a $\prod$ does not produce the proper generalization. As in the momentum example, the occurrence of a summation deep within the calculation leads to the summation of some previously ungrouped terms (i.e., the $M_i V_i$'s). Focusing on obstacles and their elimination motivates this global regrouping.

To produce the desired result, the left-hand side of the acquired equation must contain the sum of the $M V$ terms for each object in the situation. There must be proper motivation for this regrouping of an expression a large distance away from the expression where the inter-object forces cancel. Simply replacing equations in the specific calculation with their general versions and then applying standard explanation-based constraint propagation will not result in the correct regrouping of the left-hand side. The necessary regrouping will also not occur if the problem solver uses the general formulae, rather than the expanded versions, when constructing the original justification of the teacher's solution step. Focusing on the cancellation of obstacles *does* provide the necessary guidance, by determining the role of these $M V$ terms in the specific example and then extending the role to the general case.

2.4.2   Using the Cancellation Graph to Guide Generalization

PHYSICS 101 performs generalization by using its explanation of the specific solution (the *cancellation graph*) to guide the determination of the problem's unknown in the general case. This entails reconstructing the specific solution in its general form under the guidance of the cancellation graph. In other words, the structure of the explanation of the specific problem's solution is generalized. This section presents the algorithm and uses the three-body collision example to illustrate the generalization process.

Tables 2.14 and 2.15 present the algorithm for reconstructing the calculation. This algorithm is very similar to that used for building the cancellation graph. Obstacles and their blockers, partners, and cancelers are again the focus. Basically, the algorithm works as follows. First, it uses the general version of the unknown as the initial left-hand side of the calculation, and then applies the general versions of the equation schemata used in the specific calculation until it introduces the primary obstacles in their general form.[6] Next, the algorithm eliminates the general versions of any blockers, which may lead to the introduction of more general variables in the left-hand side of the calculation. Following this, it introduces any partners of the obstacle, also in their general form, and eliminates their blockers. It then introduces the general versions of the cancelers and eliminates their general blockers. After this, it records the cancellation and eliminates the obstacles and their cancelers from the calculation. Finally, the method recursively analyzes secondary obstacles.

Introducing a variable involves finding its *producer* in the general case, inserting the producer into the left-hand side of the calculation, then performing the general versions of the substitutions performed in the specific calculation until the general version of the variable appears in the general calculation.

The producer in the general case may not always be the general version of the specific calculation's producer. Usually the general producer is the general version of the specific producer. However, this is not the case when the obstacle is produced because a *problem-specific* equation is used. When a problem-specific equation is used, the system finds the producer of a variable by tracing backwards through the application of equation schemata, starting at the one that directly introduced the variable, until the problem-specific equation is found. The producer is the variable, introduced at this step, that is an ancestor of the variable being introduced. For example, if the following three equations are used to produce δ, where the first equation is problem-specific, then the general producer of δ is β.

$$\alpha = \beta$$

$$\beta = \chi$$

$$\chi = \delta$$

If the producer does not appear in the left-hand expression of the specific calculation, the method must determine the producer's proper form in the left-hand side. This entails passing the producer backwards through all the calculation steps between the one in which the producer is introduced and the initial step. The only time the producer is altered is when it is involved in calculus. When this occurs, the system determines the expression that will be

---

[6] The unexpanded forms of equations are used. Recall that in solving the specific problem, indefinite summations (Σ) and products (Π) are expanded into ordinary sums and products.

Table 2.14   Building the General Version of the Calculation — Part I

procedure   AnalyzeGeneralObstacles (variable)
    for each obstacle **in** variable.obstacleSet
      do IntroduceIntoGeneralCalculation(obstacle)
    for each obstacle **in** variable.obstacleSet
      unless OR(obstacle.notUsed?, obstacle.eliminated?)
      do EliminateInGeneral(obstacle)
    for each obstacle **in** variable.obstacleSet
      unless OR(obstacle.notUsed?, obstacle.eliminated?)
      do EliminateSecondaryObstacles(obstacle)

procedure   EliminateInGeneral (variable)
    EliminateGeneralBlockers(variable.blockers)
    IntroduceGeneralPartners(variable.partners)
    IntroduceGeneralCancelers(variable.cancelers)
    RecordGeneralCancellation(variable.generalVersion)

procedure   EliminateGeneralBlockers (blockers)
    for each blocker **in** blockers **unless** blocker.eliminated?
      do EliminateInGeneral(blocker)

procedure   IntroduceGeneralPartners (partners)
    for each partner **in** partners **unless** partner.eliminated?
      do IntroduceIntoGeneralCalculation(partner)
          EliminateGeneralBlockers(partner.blockers)

procedure   IntroduceGeneralCancelers (cancelers)
    for each canceler **in** cancelers
      do IntroduceIntoGeneralCalculation(canceler)
          EliminateGeneralBlockers(canceler.blockers)

Table 2.15   Building the General Version of the Calculation — Part II

procedure   EliminateSecondaryObstacles (variable)

   for each blocker **in** variable.blockers **do** EliminateSecondaryObstacles(blocker)

   for each partner **in** variable.partners

      do AnalyzeGeneralObstacles(partner.producer)

         for each blocker **in** partner.blockers **do** EliminateSecondaryObstacles(blocker)

   for each canceler **in** variable.cancelers

      do AnalyzeGeneralObstacles(canceler.producer)

         for each blocker **in** canceler.blockers **do** EliminateSecondaryObstacles(blocker)

procedure   IntroduceIntoGeneralCalculation (variable)

         \<described in text>

procedure   RecordGeneralCancellation (generalVariable)

         \<described in text>

AnalyzeGeneralObstacles(unknown)   /* Reconstruct the calculation. */

SimplifyCalculation()   /* Simplify the new calculation. */

---

converted into the producer by this calculus.[7] For example, if after differentiating, the producer P' results, then the system must solve the following for P, the new producer.

$$\frac{d}{d\,?x} P = P'$$

The result is $P = \int P'\, d\,?x$; the reverse transformation holds for integration. An example of this appears in Appendix A.2, where a problem-specific equation is used in a calculation.

Once the producer of a variable is determined, the next step is to merge it into the current left hand-side of the general calculation. This depends on how it relates to other producers in the current left-hand side. For example, if there are none, it becomes the original left-hand side. If it is the producer of an additive partner, it is added to the producer of the other variable in the partnership. Similarly, if it produces a multiplicative canceler, it divides the

---

[7] There is one exception to this method for determining producers. Because it is desired that the unknown appear in the left-hand expression, if the specific producer of an obstacle is the unknown, then the general producer is the general version of the unknown, regardless of the equation schemata used to produce the obstacle. This means that a problem-specific equation may be used in the general calculation, and a precondition of the resulting schema is that this problem-specific equation hold in the current situation.

related producer.

After adding the producer of a variable to the general calculation, the system applies, in their general form, the equation schemata that convert the producer into the variable of interest. While this is occurring, it maintains the necessary unifications among predicate calculus variables in the equation schema and its preconditions, using the explanation-based EGGS [Mooney86] algorithm.

Whenever adding the general version of an equation to the general calculation, the system maintains pointers between the variables in the general calculation and their specific calculation counterparts. This is illustrated in Figure 2.15 for a sample substitution where the internal force on an object is replaced by the sum of inter-object forces. In addition to pointing to each of its specific versions, each variable in the general calculation records its *range*. The range of a variable defines allowable values for subscripts. For instance, the range of $F_{j, ?i, ?c}$ in Table 2.2 specifies that j ranges over the elements of *ObjectsInWorld*, except for $?i$.

If there is no specific counterpart for a general variable, the specific example did not address all of the issues inherent in the general calculation. In particular, it did not address

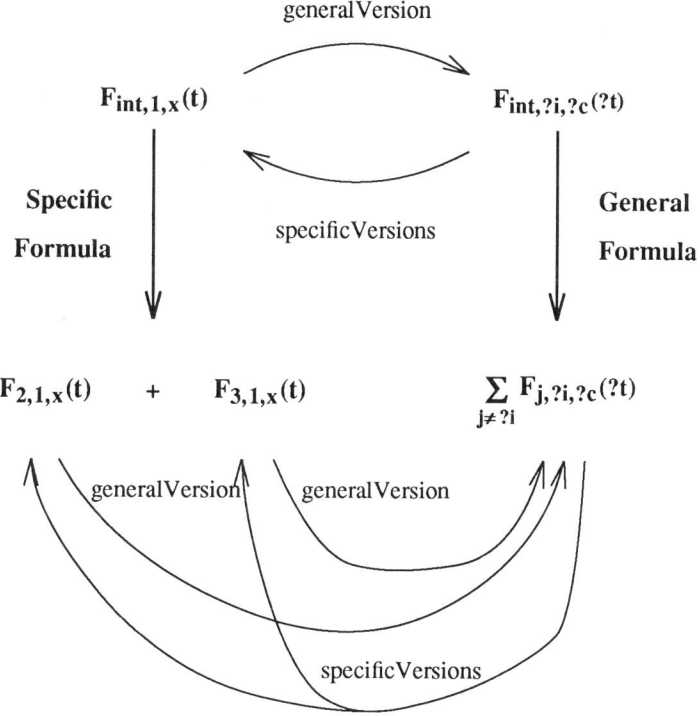

Figure 2.15   Mapping Between Specific and General Variables

how this variable should be handled. Since there is no indication whether or not this general variable is acceptable, generalization terminates and the system learns no general equation schema. An example of this appears in Appendix A.5, which discusses a two-body collision problem.

Variable ranges are used to determine the necessary range of the producers of cancelers. If X_j ranges over the elements of *ObjectsInWorld*, except for i, then the producer of its canceler receives the same range. Hence, if it is an additive cancellation and P is the producer of X's canceler, then $\displaystyle\sum_{\substack{j \varepsilon\, ObjectsInWorld \\ j \neq i}} P_j$ is merged into the left-hand side of the calculation. For a multiplicative cancellation $\displaystyle\prod_{\substack{j \varepsilon\, ObjectsInWorld \\ j \neq i}} P_j$ is used.

Once a variable and its cancelers are present in the general calculation, the system records the cancellation. This involves altering the ranges of the variables involved in the cancellation and removing the canceled possibilities. The necessary unifications are also recorded. If the range of a subscript becomes empty, PHYSICS 101 marks the general variable as eliminated. To illustrate this, assume that the range of one instantiation of the variable X_j is the singleton i, while the range of its canceler is from 1 to n. After recording the cancellation, the first instantiation is canceled and the second has the new range of 1 to n except i.

After recording the cancellation, the system determines whether or not it introduced any secondary obstacles by the elimination of the blocking or obstacle variable. If so, it analyzes . these secondary obstacles in a recursive manner. Finally, it algebraically simplifies the resulting calculation, and performs any remaining arithmetic. Preconditions of the equation schemata used in the general calculation are collected, with all predicate calculus variables in their constrained form, and PHYSICS 101 constructs a new equation schema.

In the remainder of this subsection, the momentum example is used to illustrate the steps in PHYSICS 101's generalization process. The system starts with the generalized unknown, $V^{?n}{}_{?s,\, ?c}(?arg)$. It then performs the general versions of the specific formulae substitutions that produced the first of the primary obstacles. This can be seen, for the collision problem, in Table 2.16.[8]

While applying the general equation schemata, the system maintains a global unification list, again using the EGGS algorithm. This process determines how the terms in the new general formulae used must relate to ones already in the general calculation. For example, $?arg$ in the generalized unknown is constrained to be t and $?n$ is constrained to be 1, since the first step of Table 2.16 applies the second equation of Table 2.2 to the generalized unknown. Unifications that are needed to satisfy the preconditions of the equation schemata are also maintained.

---

[8] The calculations that follow are verbatim transcriptions of actual outputs of the implemented system. The numbers associated with each line refer to the calculation steps of Table 2.7.

Table 2.16   Introduction of the Primary Obstacles

$$V_{?s,\ ?c}(t)$$

$$(1) \quad = \int A_{?s,\ ?c}(t)\, dt$$

$$(2) \quad = \int \frac{F_{net,\ ?s,\ ?c}(t)}{M_{?s}}\, dt$$

$$(3) \quad = \frac{1}{M_{?s}} \int F_{net,\ ?s,\ ?c}(t)\, dt$$

$$(6) \quad = \frac{1}{M_{?s}} \int (F_{ext,\ ?s,\ ?c}(t) + F_{int,\ ?s,\ ?c}(t))\, dt$$

$$(7) \quad = \frac{1}{M_{?s}} \int (F_{ext,\ ?s,\ ?c}(t) + \sum_{\substack{j\in\ ObjectsInWorld \\ j\neq ?s}} F_{j,\ ?s,\ ?c}(t))\, dt$$

Recall from the previous section that the inter-object forces are *additively* canceled in the specific case. Hence, the next generalization step is to additively isolate each inter-object force. $M_{?s}$ is introduced into the left-hand side of the general calculation in order to accomplish this isolation. Table 2.17 presents this generalization step.

At this point, the system has isolated, for an additive cancellation, the general versions of the primary obstacles. To perform this cancellation, those terms that will cancel the intra-object forces must be introduced into the general calculation. The system determines that in the specific solution each inter-object force acting on ball 1 is canceled by the equal-but-opposite inter-object force specified by Newton's Third Law.

In the general case, *all* of the other objects in a situation exert an inter-object force on Object $?s$. *All* of these inter-object forces need to be canceled. In the specific case, $M_2 \times V_2$ produced and isolated the additive canceler of $F_{2,\,1}$ while $M_3 \times V_3$ produced and isolated the additive canceler of $F_{3,\,1}$. So to cancel Object $?s$'s inter-object forces, an $M_j \times V_j$ term must come from every other object in the situation. Table 2.18 presents the introduction of the summation that produces the terms that cancel Object $?s$'s inter-object forces. Notice how the goal of cancellation motivates generalizing the number of objects involved in this expression.

Once all the cancelers of the generalized primary obstacle are present, the primary obstacle itself can be canceled. This is shown in Table 2.19, which is a continuation of Table 2.18 (the last line of Table 2.18 is repeated in Table 2.19).

Table 2.17   Introduction of $M_{?s}$ to Additively Isolate the Primary Obstacles

$$M_{?s}\, V_{?s,\,?c}(t)$$

$$(1) \quad = M_{?s} \int A_{?s,\,?c}(t)\, dt$$

$$(2) \quad = M_{?s} \int \frac{F_{net,\,?s,\,?c}(t)}{M_{?s}}\, dt$$

$$(3) \quad = \frac{M_{?s}}{M_{?s}} \int F_{net,\,?s,\,?c}(t)\, dt$$

$$(4) \quad = 1 \int F_{net,\,?s,\,?c}(t)\, dt$$

$$(5) \quad = \int F_{net,\,?s,\,?c}(t)\, dt$$

$$(6) \quad = \int (F_{ext,\,?s,\,?c}(t) + F_{int,\,?s,\,?c}(t))\, dt$$

$$(7) \quad = \int \Big(F_{ext,\,?s,\,?c}(t) + \sum_{\substack{j\in ObjectsInWorld \\ j\neq ?s}} F_{j,\,?s,\,?c}(t)\Big)\, dt$$

Now that the primary obstacles are canceled, the system checks to see if any secondary obstacles have been introduced. As can be seen in Table 2.17, the inter-object forces *not* involving object *?s* still remain in the expression; these are secondary obstacles. Figure 2.16 graphically illustrates these remaining forces in a situation containing N objects. All of the forces acting on Object *?s* have been canceled, while a force between Objects j and k still appears whenever neither j nor k equal *?s*. This highlights an important aspect of generalizing to N. Introducing more entities may create new interactions that do not appear and, hence, are not addressed in the specific example. (This issue is further elaborated in the discussion of the BAGGER system and in the concluding chapter.)

PHYSICS 101 cannot eliminate the remaining inter-object forces if the specific example only involves a two-object collision. The system does not detect that the remaining forces all cancel one another, since in the two-object example there is no hint of how to deal with these secondary obstacles. A collision involving three or more objects must be analyzed by the system to properly motivate this cancellation. More details on the reasons for this are given in Appendix A.5. In the three-body collision problem, the system continues as shown in Table 2.20.

Table 2.18 Introduction of the Cancelers of the Primary Obstacles

$$M_{?s}\, V_{?s,\ ?c}(t) + \sum_{\substack{j \in ObjectsInWorld \\ j \neq ?s}} M_j\, V_{j,\ ?c}(t)$$

(1) $$= M_{?s} \int A_{?s,\ ?c}(t)\, dt + \sum_{j \neq ?s} M_j \int A_{j,\ ?c}(t)\, dt$$

(2) $$= M_{?s} \int \frac{F_{net,\ ?s,\ ?c}(t)}{M_{?s}}\, dt + \sum_{j \neq ?s} M_j \int \frac{F_{net,\ j,\ ?c}(t)}{M_j}$$

(3) $$= \frac{M_{?s}}{M_{?s}} \int F_{net,\ ?s,\ ?c}(t)\, dt + \sum_{j \neq ?s} \frac{M_j}{M_j} \int F_{net,\ j,\ ?c}(t)\, dt$$

(4) $$= 1 \int F_{net,\ ?s,\ ?c}(t)\, dt + \sum_{j \neq ?s} 1 \int F_{net,\ j,\ ?c}(t)\, dt$$

(5) $$= \int F_{net,\ ?s,\ ?c}(t)\, dt + \sum_{j \neq ?s} \int F_{net,\ j,\ ?c}(t)\, dt$$

(6) $$= \int (F_{ext,\ ?s,\ ?c}(t) + F_{int,\ ?s,\ ?c}(t))\, dt + \sum_{j \neq ?s} \int (F_{ext,\ j,\ ?c}(t) + F_{int,\ j,\ ?c}(t))\, dt$$

(7) $$= \int (F_{ext,\ ?s,\ ?c}(t) + \sum_{j \neq ?s} F_{j,\ ?s,\ ?c}(t))\, dt + \sum_{j \neq ?s} \int (F_{ext,\ j,\ ?c}(t) + \sum_{k \neq j} F_{k,\ j,\ ?c}(t))\, dt$$

Table 2.19 Cancellation of the Primary Obstacles

(7) $$= \int (F_{ext,\ ?s,\ ?c}(t) + \sum_{j \neq ?s} F_{j,\ ?s,\ ?c}(t))\, dt + \sum_{j \neq ?s} \int (F_{ext,\ j,\ ?c}(t) + \sum_{k \neq j} F_{k,\ j,\ ?c}(t))\, dt$$

(9) $$= \int (F_{ext,\ ?s,\ ?c}(t) + \sum_{j \neq ?s} F_{j,\ ?s,\ ?c}(t) + \sum_{j \neq ?s} [F_{ext,\ j,\ ?c}(t) + \sum_{k \neq j} F_{k,\ j,\ ?c}(t)])\, dt$$

(10) $$= \int (F_{ext,\ ?s,\ ?c}(t) + 0\, \frac{kg\, m}{s^2} + \sum_{j \neq ?s} [F_{ext,\ j,\ ?c}(t) + \sum_{k \neq j,\ ?s} F_{k,\ j,\ ?c}(t)])\, dt$$

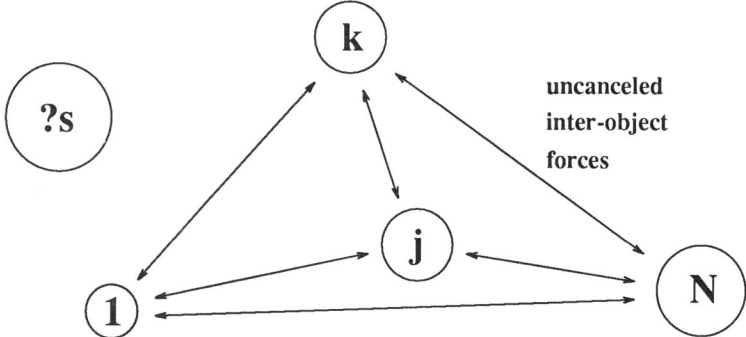

Figure 2.16 The Remaining Inter-Object Forces

uncanceled
inter-object
forces

Table 2.20 Cancellation of the Secondary Obstacles

$$(10) \quad = \int (F_{ext,\ ?s,\ ?c}(t) + 0\ \frac{kg\ m}{s^2} + \sum_{j \neq ?s} [F_{ext,\ j,\ ?c}(t) + 0\ \frac{kg\ m}{s^2}])\ dt$$

$$(11) \quad = \int (F_{ext,\ ?s,\ ?c}(t) + \sum_{j \neq ?s} F_{ext,\ j,\ ?c}(t))\ dt$$

Once all possible obstacle cancellations of the cancellation graph have been produced, PHYSICS 101 produces the final result. It collects the preconditions of each equation schema, uses the global unification list to determine the final form of each variable in these preconditions, and simplifies the final result. This process produces the restrictions that the masses of the objects be constant over time (since each was factored out of a temporal integral — see Table 2.7) and that the objects cannot have zero mass (since their masses appear in the denominator of expressions). The final result appears in Table 2.21. The system records the new equation, along with its preconditions. In addition, it records the terms canceled in the general calculation. Although not implemented in PHYSICS 101, the eliminated terms could be used to help index the acquired formula. For example, when the inter-object forces are not specified, this equation schema could be suggested as possibly being appropriate.

In addition to not being restricted to situations containing three objects, the newly-acquired formula is not restricted to situations where the external forces are all zero. Instead, PHYSICS 101 has obtained an appreciation of how the external forces affect momentum. This process also determines that there is no constraint that restricts this formula to the x-direction; it applies equally well to the y- and z-components of V. Hence, the acquired formula is a vector law. Notice that those physics variables whose values are used in the specific solution (e.g., the F_{ext}) remain in the general formula. The final equation is added to PHYSICS 101's

Table 2.21 The Final Result

Equation

$$\frac{d}{dt} \sum_{i \in ObjectsInWorld} M_i V_{i, \, ?c}(t) = \sum_{i \in ObjectsInWorld} F_{ext, \, i, \, ?c}(t)$$

Preconditions

IsaComponent($?c$) $\wedge$

$\forall \, i \in ObjectsInWorld$ NOT(ZeroValued(M_i)) $\wedge$

$\forall \, i \in ObjectsInWorld$ IndependentOf(M_i, t)

Eliminated Terms

$\forall \, i \, \forall \, j \neq i \; F_{i, \, j, \, ?c}(t)$

---

collection of general formulae. (If PHYSICS 101 generalizes the two-body collision it would produce an expression still containing those inter-object forces that do not involve object i. However, this formula would not be kept; see Appendix A.5 for further discussion.)

The new formula says: *The rate of change of the total momentum of a collection of objects is completely determined by the sum of the external forces on those objects.* Other problems, which involve any number of bodies under the influence of external forces, can be solved by the system using this generalized result. For example, it can be used to solve the three-dimensional collision problem involving four objects, where there are external forces due to gravity, that is shown in Figure 2.17.

2.4.3 Learning Special-Case Schemata

One would expect that acquired schemata should be as general as possible so that they might each cover the broadest class of future problems. Indeed, explanation-based learning research has been primarily aimed at the acquisition of such maximally general schemata. However, an intermediate level of generalization is often appropriate. The class of intermediate generality schemata improves the performance of a system's problem solver by supplying "appropriately general" schemata instead of forcing the system to rely on its maximally general schemata. Storing both the maximally general schemata and the intermediate level schemata results in much improved efficiency with no loss of generality. This section describes how PHYSICS 101 produces intermediate-level schemata, which are called *special cases*.

A major issue in explanation-based learning concerns the relationship between *operationality* and *generality* (see Section 1.3.3). A schema whose relevance is easy to determine may only be useful in an overly-narrow range of problems. Conversely, a

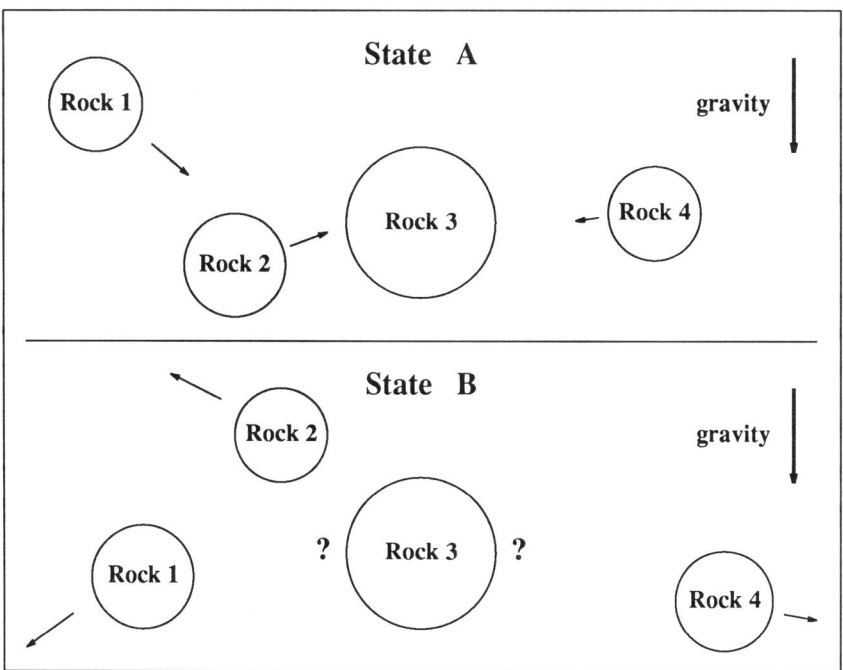

Figure 2.17   A Three-Dimensional Collision Problem in a Gravitational Field

broadly-applicable schema may require extensive work before a problem solver can recognize its appropriateness. Most approaches to selecting the proper level of generality involve pruning easily-reconstructable portions of the explanation structure. PHYSICS 101 produces operational rules by constraining a general schema in such a way that its relevance is easily checked. Special cases are the result of composing the new, general equation schema with a problem-solving schema. A successful composition results in a specialization which is guaranteed to work using the composed problem-solving technique. This frees the problem solver from performing the planning that would otherwise be required to elaborate the general schema to fit the current problem-solving episode. The system can, of course, always resort to its collection of maximally general schema when no special case is appropriate.

PHYSICS 101's special-case algorithm is presented in Table 2.22. As in the basic model (Figure 2.1), in the extended model a known problem-solving schema is initially used to understand a solution to a specific problem. The explanation-based analysis of the solution may lead to the construction of a new broadly-applicable schema. Interestingly, the generalization process often produces a new schema that, in its fullest form, is not directly usable by the originally applied problem-solving schema. For example, the acquired momentum law describes how the external forces affect a physical system's momentum. It is *not* a conservation law, although the original calculation involved the problem-solving

Table 2.22   The Algorithm for Constructing Special-Case Equations

Let *primary* = the primary problem-solving schema used in the specific example
    equation = the newly-acquired equation schema
      facts = specific facts about the current example

Step 1:   Satisfy the preconditions of *primary* using *equation* and *facts*, producing a proof tree.

Step 2:   Traverse the proof tree, locating subtrees whose root is a new equation (i.e., one not already known to the system).

Step 3:   Generalize the resulting subtrees using a standard EBL algorithm, extracting the general version of the new special-case equation and its preconditions.

---

schema for conserved quantities. Constraining the general result so that the originally-used problem-solving schema does apply produces a special case. In the special-case schema, the constrained schema, its constraints, and the original problem-solving schema are packaged together to produce a specialized equation schema.

In the approach taken, automatically acquiring schemata of the intermediate level of generality requires that the system's schemata be organized into two classes:

(1)   Schemata that represent general problem-solving knowledge, which apply across many application domains (e.g., a schema for utilizing a conserved quantity to solve a problem). In PHYSICS 101, these are the *problem-solving schemata.*

(2)   Schemata that represent declarative knowledge of the domain of application (e.g., Newton's laws). In PHYSICS 101, these are the *equation schemata.*

People with mature problem-solving backgrounds possess the first type of schema and are told schemata of the second type when introduced to a new domain. Through study they acquire a large collection of schemata that combine aspects of both types, thereby increasing their problem-solving performance in the domain. Combining general problem-solving techniques with domain specific knowledge produces schemata that, when applied, leads to the rapid solution of new problems. This performance is modeled in the PHYSICS 101 system. (This general idea of combining problem-solving knowledge and domain knowledge also appears in some second-generation expert systems [Van de Velde89].)

Special case concepts maintain pointers to the general concepts from which they arose and the properties that distinguish the special cases from their general cases are recorded. As described in Section 2.2, the system first checks these special-case cues when selecting an appropriate schema during problem solving. If no special case is applicable, it then accesses the general concepts. Besides constructing them when acquiring a general case, PHYSICS 101 can create a new special case whenever it uses the general case to solve a later problem.

In addition to improving a problem solver's efficiency, special cases also indicate good assumptions to make. For instance, if the values of the external forces are not known, assume they are zero, as this will allow solution to an otherwise impossible problem. Physics problems often require one to assume things like "there is no friction," "the string is massless," "the gravity of the moon can be ignored," etc. Problem descriptions given in textbooks contain cues such as these, and students must learn how to take advantage of them. Facts in the initial problem statement suggest possible problem-solving strategies, while any additional requirements of the special case situations indicate good assumptions to make (provided they do not contradict anything else that is known).

To see an example of special case construction, consider the three-body collision problem again. The schema used to solve this problem is shown in Table 2.23. This schema makes use of conserved quantities during problem solving. It says that one way to solve for an unknown is to first find an expression containing the unknown that is constant with respect to some variable. Next, instantiate this expression for two different values of the variable, create an equation from the two instantiated expressions, and solve the equation for the unknown. If the values of all but one variable at these two points are known, simple algebra can be used to easily find the unknown.

Recall that the result in Table 2.21 is *not* a conservation law. It describes how the momentum of a system evolves over time. Although this new formula applies to a large class of problems, recognizing its applicability is not easy. The external forces on the system must be summed and a possibly complicated differential equation needs to be solved. Applying this law requires more than using simple algebra to find the value of the unknown.

Table 2.23   Conserved Quantity Schema

Preconditions

CurrentUnknown(?*unknown*) ∧ ConstantWithRespectTo(?*expression*, ?*x*) ∧
SpecificPointOf(?x_1, ?*x*) ∧ SpecificPointOf(?x_2, ?*x*) ∧ ?x_1 ≠ ?x_2 ∧
?*leftHandSide* = InstantiatedAt(?*expression*, ?x_1) ∧
?*rightHandSide* = InstantiatedAt(?*expression*, ?x_2) ∧
?*equation* = CreateEquation(?*leftHandSide*, ?*rightHandSide*) ∧
ContainedIn(?*unknown*, ?*equation*)

Schema Body

SolveForUnknown(?*equation*, ?*unknown*)

Figure 2.18 contains a portion of the proof that demonstrates that the originally-used problem-solving schema (Table 2.23) can be used with the new general formula. (Arrows run from the antecedents of an inference rule to its consequents.) In order for the conserved quantity schema to be applicable to this new formula, it must be the case that momentum be constant with respect to time. This means that the derivative of momentum must be zero, which leads to the requirement that the external forces sum to zero. This requirement is satisfied in the specific solution because each external force is individually zero, and the system uses this property to characterize the special case. When this occurs, the momentum of a world can be equated at *any* two distinct states. The special case schema for momentum conservation appears in Table 2.24.

The intermediate level schemata generated by PHYSICS 101 are similar in scope of applicability to those that human experts appear to possess. The conservation of momentum problem results in a special-case schema characterized by the absence of external forces and the specification of a *before* and *after* situation. These features are those cited by experts as the relevant cues for the principle of conservation of momentum (see Table 12 of [Chi81]).[9]

Although the motivation for this intermediate level of generalization is computational, the use of this level helps to reconcile the approach with a variety of psychological evidence showing that problem solvers use highly specific schemata [Hinsley77, Schoenfeld82, Sweller85]. Much of expertise consists of rapidly choosing a tightly-constrained schema appropriate to the current problem. However, the difference between the knowledge of an expert and a novice cannot be explained on the basis of number of schemata alone. The scope and organization of these schemata have been shown in psychological experiments to

$$\text{ConstantWithRespectTo}\left(\sum_i M_i V_{i, ?c}(t) \, , \, t \right)$$

$$\uparrow$$

$$\frac{d}{dt} \sum_i M_i V_{i, ?c}(t) = 0 \, \frac{kg\ m}{s^2}$$

$$\uparrow$$

$$\frac{d}{dt} \sum_i M_i V_{i, ?c}(t) = \sum_i F_{i, ext, ?c}(t) \qquad \sum_i F_{i, ext, ?c}(t) = 0 \, \frac{kg\ m}{s^2}$$

$$\nearrow \qquad\qquad\qquad\qquad \uparrow$$

IsaComponent(?c) $\wedge$ $\qquad\qquad\qquad\qquad$ $\forall i \ F_{i, ext, ?c}(t) = 0 \, \frac{kg\ m}{s^2}$
$\forall i \in ObjectsInWorld$ NOT(ZeroValued(M_i)) $\wedge$
$\forall i \in ObjectsInWorld$ IndependentOf(M_i , t)

Figure 2.18   Satisfying the Second Precondition of the Conserved Quantity Schema

---

[9] It should be noted that it was not the explicit intent to model this psychological data. Rather, computational efficiency considerations led to a system that produced results matching this empirical data.

Table 2.24   The Special-Case Momentum Law

Equation

$$\sum_{i \in ObjectsInWorld} M_i\, V_{i,\,?c}(t) = constant$$

Preconditions

IsaComponent($?c$) $\wedge$

$\forall\, i \in ObjectsInWorld$ NOT(ZeroValued(M_i)) $\wedge$

$\forall\, i \in ObjectsInWorld$ IndependentOf(M_i , t)

Special Case Conditions

$\forall\, i \in ObjectsInWorld$ $F_{ext,\,i,\,?c}(t) = 0$

Problem Solving Schema Used

conserved-quantity-schema

---

be qualitatively different [Chi81, Larkin80, Schoenfeld82]. In representing a problem, novices make great use of the specific objects mentioned in the problem statement, while experts first categorize according to the techniques appropriate for solving the problem.

Throughout this book it is claimed that most explanation-based generalization algorithms do not perform enough generalization. In particular, they do not generalize number. However, in this section it is argued that specialized concepts have value. There are two answers to this apparent contradiction. One, special cases are motivated and their restricted applicability is not merely a result of an algorithmic limitation. (Plus, the general cases are also learned and can be used in future problem solving.) Two, determining the proper amount to generalize is an important unsolved problem and is only partially addressed by the work on PHYSICS 101. More work is needed on understanding this major issue in explanation-based learning.

2.4.4   Performance Analysis

PHYSICS 101's problem solving improvement after learning is analyzed in this section. Performance on several collision problems, differing as to the number of physical objects involved, is measured before and after learning the concept of momentum conservation. The goal in each case is to determine the velocity of one of the objects after the collision. In all of the problems, there are no external forces, and sufficient, randomly-generated mass and velocity values are provided to make each problem soluble; nothing is stated about the inter-object forces. As mentioned earlier, the standard system cannot solve collision problems before learning due to the incompleteness of its problem solver. However, to gather the data presented below, the problem solver was slightly extended. This was done by allowing as many "blind" substitutions as necessary. Ordinarily a search path terminates when two of these unmotivated substitutions occur consecutively.

Figure 2.19 graphs the time to solve problems as a function of the number of objects in the situation. The solid line represents the system's performance without learning, while the dashed line represents its performance after learning. Without benefit of learning, the system uses only its mathematical knowledge and the equations of Figure 2.2. It uses the special-case law for momentum conservation to solve the problem after learning. All points result from averaging five measurements, and the choice of the number of objects is made randomly in order to reduce the effect of inter-sample dependencies. (The standard deviation for each point is less than 10% of the solution time.) It takes about 280 seconds to learn the general momentum evolution law and its special-case concept of momentum conservation from the teacher's solution to the three-body collision problem.

This graph demonstrates the value of a system that can generalize number. From one sample solution, a new concept is acquired that enables the system to rapidly solve collisions involving any number of objects. If PHYSICS 101 did not possess this capability, that is, if it used standard explanation-based learning techniques, it would still gain the speedup of a factor of 10 on three-body collisions. However, it would require another sample solution when it experienced collisions involving different numbers of objects. Also, if the system acquired separate rules for each number of objects in a collision, a significant amount of problem-solving time could be wasted determining which, if any, is applicable to a new problem. Further empirical study of the advantages of generalizing the structure of explanations appear in Chapter 4, which investigates the performance of the BAGGER system.

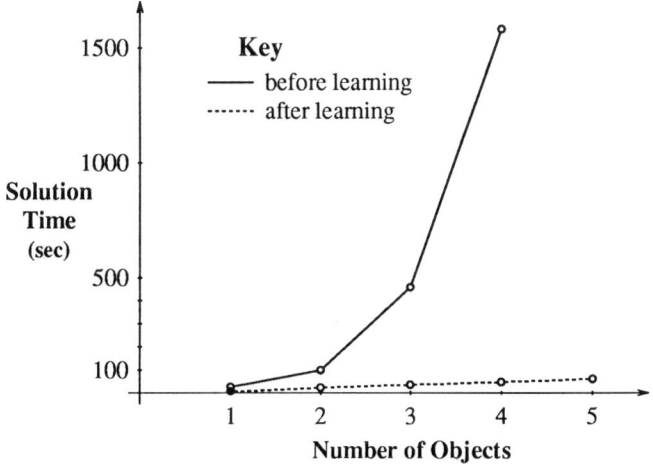

Figure 2.19   Performance on N-Body Collision Problems

2.5 Summary

PHYSICS 101 is a mathematical reasoning system that performs explanation-based learning in mathematically-oriented domains. This system's reasoning processes are guided by the manner in which variables are canceled in a specific problem. Attention focuses on how *obstacles* are eliminated in the specific problem. Obstacles are variables that preclude the direct evaluation of the unknown. Canceling these variables allows the determination of the value of the unknown. The explanation of a specific calculation closely guides the construction of a general version of the calculation, from which a new general concept is extracted. New schemata are only learned when the system can eliminate all of the obstacles in the general version of a problem.

PHYSICS 101 presents a novel perspective on the process of explanation-based generalization. Rather than directly using the explanation of the specific problem's solution, as is done in more standard algorithms, the explanation of a specific calculation closely guides the construction of a general version of the calculation, from which a new general concept may be extracted. The new calculation is often substantially more general, in terms of its structure as well as its variables, than the specific calculation. Special cases of the generalized calculation, which can be more efficiently used during problem solving, are also constructed.

Because explanation-based learning requires extensive domain knowledge, it clearly is not appropriate for all learning in a new domain. However, it may still be applicable to initial concept acquisition in a novel domain. This is possible if the domain can be viewed from the perspective of a known formalism for which one possesses abstract problem-solving knowledge. Such is the case with physics, which mathematics elegantly formalizes. Thus, a learner without extensive knowledge of physics can utilize his or her knowledge of mathematics in an explanation-based fashion to acquire physics concepts. The foundation of mathematics underlies many other application domains besides physics. In such domains, one can achieve a kind of domain independence by formalizing mathematical reasoning and strictly separating the learner's initial application domain knowledge from its mathematical knowledge. This is a major lesson from PHYSICS 101; explanation-based learning research can at times transcend individual domains, and instead leverage formalisms that apply to a number of domains. Just as PHYSICS 101's mathematical construct of a cancellation graph leads to powerful concepts in physics, additional constructs in mathematics and other formalisms may prove fruitful for acquiring new concepts in many domains.

3 A Domain-Independent Approach

3.1 The BAGGER System

In Chapter 2's PHYSICS 101, the need for generalizing the structure of an explanation is motivated by an analytic justification of an example's solution and general domain knowledge. In the momentum problem, information localized in a single physics formula leads to a global restructuring of a specific solution's explanation. PHYSICS 101 reasons about the use of mathematical formulae. Its generalization algorithm takes great advantage of the properties of algebraic cancellation and is based on the assumption that the general version of these cancellations should be represented in the general concept acquired.

However, as discussed in the introduction, the need to generalize the structure of explanations is ubiquitous. It occurs in many domains besides those that involve mathematics. This chapter presents a second approach to the problem of generalizing explanation structures. In this approach, the *form* of the explanation motivates generalizing its structure. The explanation-based generalization algorithm developed is domain-independent — no special characteristics of any particular domain are used as the foundation of the method.

Observations of repeated rule or operator applications indicate that generalizing the number of rules in the explanation may be appropriate. However, such observations alone are insufficient. Number generalization is desirable only if there exists a certain recursive structural pattern, in which each application achieves preconditions for the next. In stacking blocks, for example, the same sort of repositioning of blocks occurs repeatedly, each building on the last. This chapter adopts the vocabulary of predicate calculus to investigate this notion of structural recursion. The desired form of recursion is manifested as repeated application of inference rules in such a manner that a portion of each consequent is used to satisfy some of the antecedents of the next application. This means that number generalization will not occur solely because some rule appears repeatedly in an explanation. Instead, the repetitions must be in a goal-subgoal relationship.

The BAGGER system (Building Augmented Generalizations by Generating Extended Recurrences) attempts to construct concepts that involve generalizing to N. The fully-implemented BAGGER system analyzes explanation structures and detects extendible repeated, interdependent applications of rules. When any are found, it extends the explanation so that an arbitrary number of repeated applications of the original rule are supported. It then generalizes the final structure and produces a new rule, which embodies a crucial shift in representation, as will be seen. This chapter also presents an extension of BAGGER, called BAGGER2, that is capable of capturing a larger class of number-generalized concepts.

3.1.1   Some Sample Learning Episodes

Several examples are briefly presented in this section to illustrate the operation of BAGGER. Details for each example appear later in this chapter or in Appendix B.

One problem solution analyzed by BAGGER is shown in Figure 3.1. The goal is to place a properly-supported block so that its center is above the dotted line and within the horizontal confines of the line. BAGGER is provided low-level domain knowledge about blocks, including how to transfer a single block from one location to another and how to calculate its new horizontal and vertical position. Briefly, to move a block it must have nothing on it and there must be a free space at which to place it. The system produces a situation calculus proof validating the actions shown in Figure 3.1, in which three blocks must be moved to build the tower.

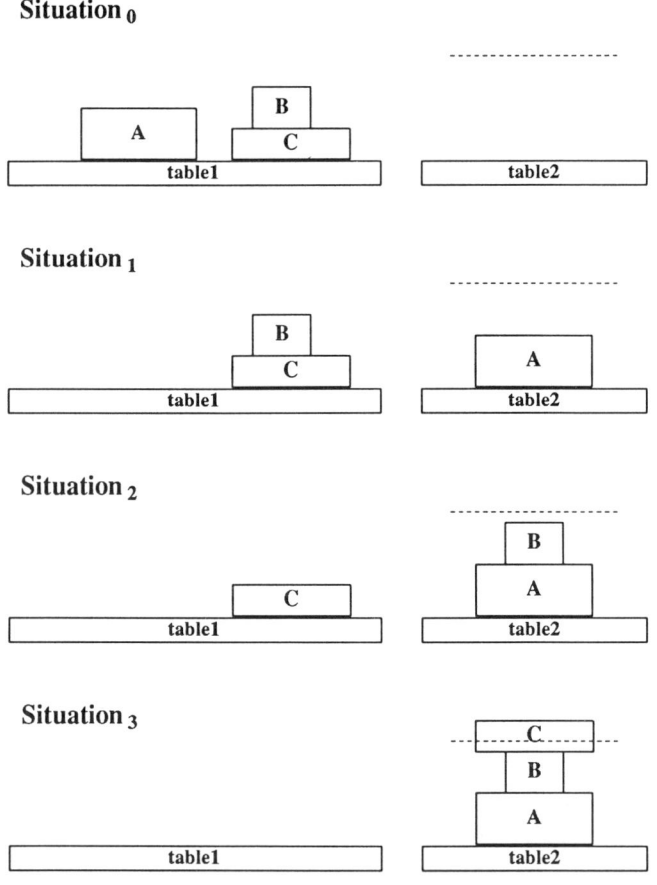

Figure 3.1   Constructing a Three-Block Tower

If a standard explanation-based generalization algorithm is applied to the resulting proof, a plan for moving *three* blocks will result. They need not be these same three blocks — any three distinct ones will suffice. Nor is it is necessary that the first block moved be placed on a table; any flat, clear surface is acceptable. Finally, the height of the tower need not be the same as that in the specific example. Given appropriately sized blocks, towers of any height can be constructed. Standard algorithms generalize many characteristics of the problem. However, the fact that exactly three blocks are moved would remain.

If one considers the universe of all possible towers, as shown in Figure 3.2, only a small fraction of them would be captured by the acquired rule. Separate rules would need to be learned for towers containing two blocks, five blocks, etc. What is desired is the acquisition of a rule that describes how towers containing any number of blocks can be constructed.

By analyzing the proof of the construction of the three-block tower, BAGGER acquires a general plan for building towers by stacking *arbitrary* numbers of blocks, as illustrated in Figure 3.3. This new plan incorporates an indefinite number of applications of the previously known plan for moving a single block.

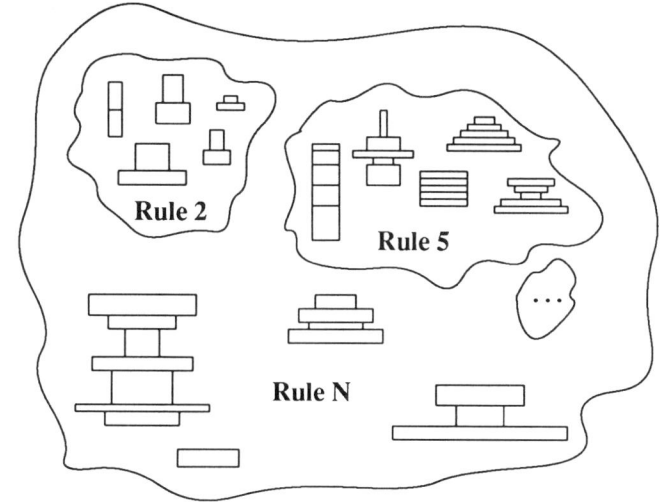

Figure 3.2   Universes of Constructible Towers

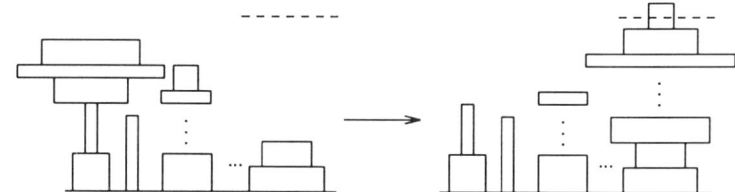

Figure 3.3   The Effects of a General Plan for Constructing Towers

In another example, the system observes three blocks being removed from a stack in order to satisfy the goal of having a specific block be clear. Extending the explanation of these actions produces a plan for unstacking any number of blocks in order to clear a block within the stack. Figure 3.4 illustrates this general plan's effects. The plan includes the system's realization that the last unstacked block is currently clear and thus makes a suitable site on which to place the next block to be moved. This knowledge is incorporated into the plan and no problem solving need be performed to find destinations once the first free location is found.

Unlike many other block-manipulation examples, in these examples it is *not* assumed that blocks can support only one other block. This means that moving a block does not necessarily clear its supporting block. Another concept learned by BAGGER, by observing two blocks being moved from the top of a table, is a general plan for clearing an object directly supporting any number of clear blocks. This plan is illustrated in Figure 3.5.

The domain of digital circuit design also contains many examples where a fixed number of rule applications should be generalized into an arbitrary number. By observing the repeated application of DeMorgan's Law to implement a three-input AND by negating the output two cascaded OR gates, BAGGER produces a general version of DeMorgan's Law which can be used to implement N cascaded AND gates using N OR gates and negating the final output. This example appears in Figure 3.6.

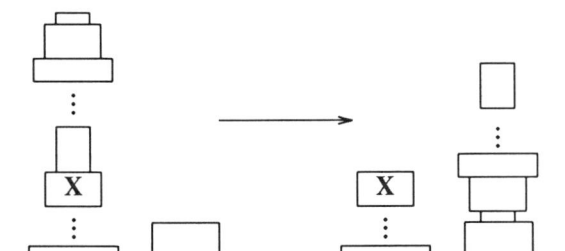

Figure 3.4   The Effects of a General Plan for Unstacking Towers

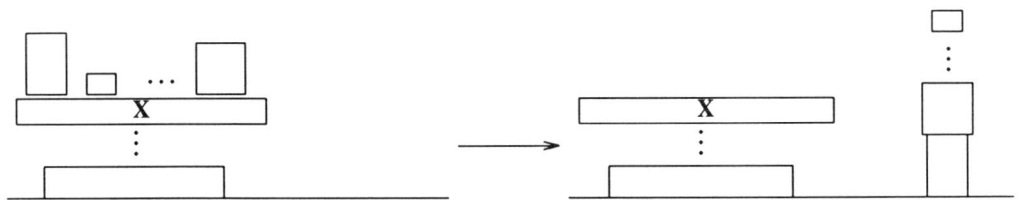

Figure 3.5   The Effects of a General Plan for Clearing Objects

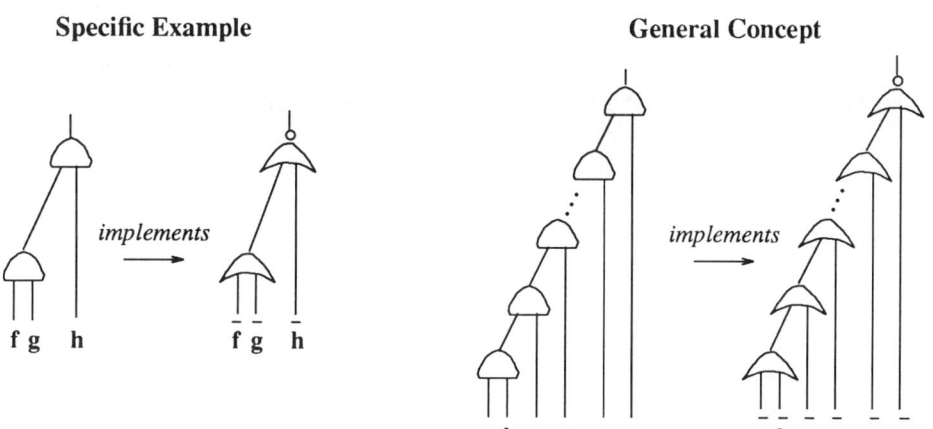

Specific Example   **General Concept**

implements   *implements*

f g   h   f g   h   a b c d ···y z   a b c d ···y z

Figure 3.6   A Circuit Implementation Example

3.1.2 Situation Calculus

Most of BAGGER's examples use situation calculus [McCarthy63] to represent actions, in the style of Green [Green69]. In this formalism, predicates and functions whose values may change over time possess an extra argument that indicates the situation in which they are being evaluated. For example, rather than using the predicate *On(x,y)* to indicate that *x* is on *y*, the predicate *On(x,y,s)* is used to indicate that *x* is on *y* in Situation *s*. In this framework, operators are represented as functions that map from one situation to another situation. For instance, the term *Do(Transfer(A,B,s0))* represents the situation that results from the initial situation upon transferring Block *A* to Block *B*.

As an example, consider the following situation calculus rule.

$$AchievableState(Do(Transfer(?x, ?y), ?s)) \rightarrow On(?x, ?y, Do(Transfer(?x, ?y), ?s))$$

This rule formalizes one effect of a transfer. It says that if one can legally achieve the situation represented by the term *Do(Transfer(?x,?y),?s))*, then in this situation *?x* is on *?y*. A separate rule would define legal transfers.

Problem solving with BAGGER's situation calculus rules can be viewed as transforming and expanding situations until one is found in which the goal is known to be achieved. The BAGGER system has two types of inference rules: *intersituational* rules which specify attributes that a new situation will have after application of a particular operator, and *intrasituational* rules which can embellish BAGGER's knowledge of a situation by specifying additional conclusions that can be drawn within that situation.

Each intersituational inference rule specifies knowledge about one particular operator. However, operators are not represented by exactly one inference rule. A major inference rule specifies most of the relevant problem-solving information about an operator. But it is augmented by many lesser inference rules which capture the operator's frame axioms and other facts about a new situation. This paradigm contrasts with the standard STRIPS [Fikes71]

75

formalism.[1] The inference rules of a STRIPS-like system are in a one-to-one correspondence with the system's operators. Each inference rule fully specifies an operator's add- and delete-lists. These lists provide all of the changes needed to transform the current situation into the new situation. Any state not mentioned in an add- or delete-list is assumed to persist across the operator's application. Thus, the new situation is completely determined by the inference rule. In the BAGGER system this is not the case. Many separate inference rules are used to fully characterize the effect of an operator.

The advantage of the STRIPS approach is that the system can always be assured that it has represented all that there is to know about a new situation. However, this can also be a disadvantage. A STRIPS-like system must always muddle through all there is to know about a situation, no matter how irrelevant many facts may be to the current problem. Conversely, the advantages of BAGGER's approach are that the inference rules are far less complex and therefore more manageable, the system's attention focusing is easier because it does not bog down in situations made overly-complex by many irrelevant facts, and a programmer can more easily write and update knowledge about operators. Furthermore, STRIPS-style operators do not allow disjunctive or conditional effects in their add- or delete-lists, which reduces their expressive power.

A potential disadvantage of BAGGER's approach is that to completely represent the effects of applying an operator in a particular situation, the system must retrieve all of the relevant inference rules. However, this is not a task that arises in BAGGER's problem solving. Indeed, there has been no attempt to guarantee the completeness of the system's inferential abilities. This means that there may be characteristics of a situation which BAGGER can represent but cannot itself infer.

3.1.3 Sequential Rules

Like its standard inference rules, number-generalized rules in the BAGGER system are usually represented in situational calculus. The previous section discusses two types of inference rules: intra and intersituational rules. To define number-generalized rules, the intersituational rules are further divided into two categories: simple intersituational rules and *sequential* intersituational rules (or simply *sequential rules*). Sequential rules apply a variable number of operators. Thus, within each application of a sequential rule many intermediate situations may be generated. The actual number of intermediate situations depends on the complexity of the problem to be solved. The rule for building towers is an example of a sequential rule. This rule (Figure 3.3) is able to construct towers of any number of blocks in order to achieve a specified goal height (the dotted line). The rule itself decides how many blocks are to be used and selects which blocks to use from among those present in the current situation.

---

[1] Fahlman [Fahlman74] and Fikes [Fikes75] augmented the standard STRIPS model by allowing a distinction between primary and secondary relationships. Primary relationships are asserted directly by operators while secondary relationships are deduced from the primary ones as needed. While this serves the same purpose as BAGGER's intrasituational rules, multiple intersituational rules for an operator are not allowed [Waldinger77].

Sequential rules, like their simple intersituational counterparts, have an antecedent and a consequent. Also, like the simple versions, if the antecedent is satisfied, the consequent specifies properties of the resulting situation. Unlike the simple rules, the resulting situation can be separated from the initial situation by many operator applications and intermediate situations. For example, to build a tower, many block-moving operations must be performed. It is an important feature of sequential rules that no planning need be done in applying the intermediate operators. That is, if the antecedent of a sequential rule is satisfied, its entire sequence of operators can be applied without the need for individually testing or planning for the preconditions. The preconditions of each operator are guaranteed to be true by the construction of the sequential rule itself. Thus, the consequent of a sequential rule can immediately assert properties which must be true in the final situation. A sequential rule behaves much as a STRIPS-like macro-operator. It is termed a *sequential rule* and not a *macro-operator* because it is, in fact, a situational calculus rule and not an operator. It has a situation variable, does not specify *ADD* and *DELETE* lists, etc.

Sequential rules can be much more efficient than simply chaining together simple constituents. This improved efficiency is largely derived from three sources: 1) collecting together antecedents so that redundant and subsumed operator preconditions are eliminated, 2) heuristically ordering the antecedents, and, especially, 3) eliminating antecedents that test operator preconditions which, due to the structure of the rule, are known to be satisfied.

3.1.4   Representing Sequential Knowledge

A representational shift is crucial to BAGGER's solution to the generalization to N problem. While objects in a world are represented within simple inference rules directly as predicate calculus variables, this is not possible for BAGGER's sequential rules. A standard operator interacts with a known number of objects; usually this number is small. The rule representing the operator that moves blocks, for example, might take as arguments the block to be moved and the new location where it is to be placed. A simple intersituational rule for this operator might specify that in the resulting situation, the block represented by the first argument is at the location specified by the second. This rule represents exactly one application of the move operator. There are always two arguments. They can be conveniently represented by predicate calculus variables. That is, each of the world objects with which a simple operator interacts can be uniquely named with a predicate calculus variable.

Sequential rules cannot uniquely name each of the important world objects. A rule for building towers must be capable of including an arbitrary number of blocks. The uninstantiated rule cannot "know" whether it is to be applied next to build a tower of five, seven, or 24 blocks. Since the individual blocks can no longer be named by unique variables within the rule, a shift is necessary to a scheme that can represent aggregations of world objects. Such a representational shift, similar to [Weld86], makes explicit attributes that are only implicitly present in the example. Thus, it shares many characteristics of constructive induction [Michalski83, Rendell85, Watanabe87].

A new object called an *RIS* (for Rule Instantiation Sequence) is introduced to represent arbitrarily large aggregations of world objects. A sequential rule works directly with one of these generalized structures so that it need not individually name every world object with which it interacts. A sequential rule's *RIS* (essentially a vector of world objects) is constructed in the course of satisfying its antecedent. Once this is done, the *RIS* embodies all of the constraints required for the successive application of the sequence of operators that make up the plan.

3.2 Generalizing

This section presents the BAGGER generalization algorithm. This algorithm analyzes explanation structures and detects when a fixed number of applications of some rule can be generalized. It then forms a new sequential rule that supports an arbitrary number of applications of the original rule. For reasons of efficiency, the preconditions of the sequential rule are expressed in terms of the initial state only and do not depend on the results of intermediate applications of the original rule. A problem solver that applies BAGGER's sequential rules is also described.

3.2.1 The BAGGER Generalization Algorithm

Figure 3.7 schematically presents how BAGGER generalizes the structure of explanations. On the left is the explanation of a solution to some specific problem. In it, some inference rule is repeatedly applied a fixed number of times. In the generalized explanation, the number of applications of the rule is unconstrained. In addition, the properties that must hold in order to satisfy each application's preconditions, and to meet the antecedents in the goal, are expressed in terms of the initial situation. This means that portions of the explanation not directly involved in the chain of rule applications must also be expressed in terms of the initial state. When the initial situation has the necessary properties, the results of the new rule

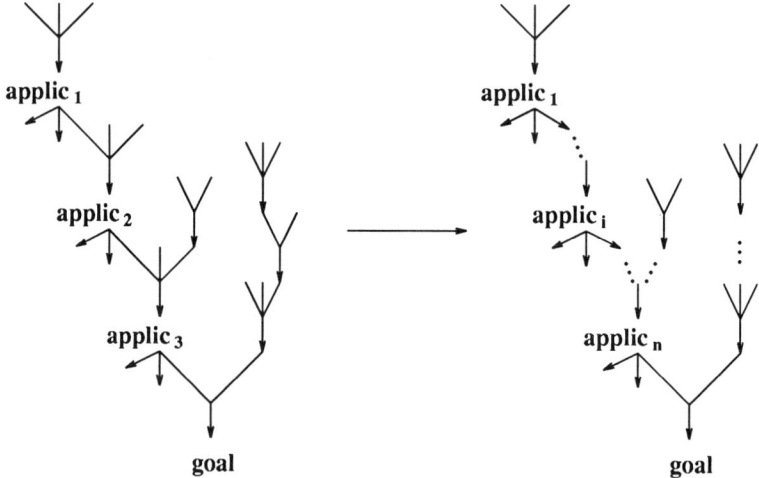

Figure 3.7   Generalizing the Structure of an Explanation

can be immediately determined, without reasoning about any of the intermediate situations.

The generalization algorithm appears in Table 3.1. This algorithm is expressed in a pseudo-code, while the actual implementation is written in INTERLISP. The remainder of this section elaborates the pseudo-code. In the algorithm back arrows ($\leftarrow$) indicate value assignment. The construct

for each *element* **in** *set* **do** *statement*

means that *element* is successively bound to each member of *set*, following which *statement* is evaluated. The functions *AddDisjunct* and *AddConjunct* each alter their first argument. If either of *AddConjunct*'s arguments is *fail*, its answer is *fail*. *AddRule* places the new rule in the database of acquired rules.

The algorithm begins its analysis of a specific solution at the goal node. It then traces backward, looking for repeated rule applications. To be a candidate, some consequent of one instantiation of a rule must support the satisfaction of an antecedent of another instantiation. These repeated applications need not directly connect — there can be intervening inference rules. Once a candidate is found, the method collects all the interconnected instantiations of the underlying general rule.

The general rule repeatedly applied is called a *focus rule*. After a focus rule is found, BAGGER ascertains how an *arbitrary* number of instantiations of this rule and any intervening rules can be concatenated together. It conceptually merges this indefinite-length collection of rules into the explanation, replacing the specific-length collection, and produces a new rule from the augmented explanation.

A specific solution contains several instantiations of the general rule chosen as the focus rule. Each of these applications of the rule addresses the need to satisfy the rule's antecedents, possibly in different ways. For example, when clearing an object, the blocks being moved can be placed in several qualitatively different types of locations. The moved block can be placed on a table (assuming the domain model specifies that tables always have room), a block moved in a previous step, or a block that was originally clear.

BAGGER analyzes all applications of the general focus rule that appear in the specific example. When several instantiations of the focus rule provide sufficient information for different generalizations, it collects the preconditions for satisfying the antecedents of each in a disjunction of conjunctions (one disjunct for each acceptable instantiation). Common terms are factored out of the disjunction. If none of the instantiations of the focus rule provide sufficient information for generalizing the structure of the explanation, BAGGER does not learn a new rule.

The generalizer must collect three classes of terms in order to construct the antecedents of a new rule. First, it must collect the preconditions that specify how to satisfy the antecedents of the initial rule application in the arbitrary length sequence of rule applications. To do this, BAGGER uses the antecedents of the focus rule. Second, it must collect the preconditions imposed by chaining together an arbitrary number of rule applications. These the system derives by analyzing each interconnected instantiation of the focus rule in the sample proof. Those applications that provide enough information to be viewed as the arbitrary *i*th application produce this second class of preconditions. Third, the algorithm collects the preconditions from the rest of the explanation. This determines the constraints on the final

Table 3.1 The BAGGER Generalization Algorithm

procedure BuildNewBAGGERrule (goalNode)

    focusNodes ← CollectFocusRuleApplications(goalNode)

    antecedentsInitial ← BuildInitialAntecedents(Earliest(focusNodes))

    antecedentsIntermediate ← ϕ

    for each focusNode **in** focusNodes **do**

        answer ← ViewAsArbitraryApplic(focusNode, focusNodes)

        if answer ≠ *fail* **then** AddDisjunct(antecedentsIntermediate, answer)

    antecedentsFinal ← ViewAsArbitraryApplic(goalNode, focusNodes))

    consequents ← CollectGoalTerms(goalNode)

    if antecedentsIntermediate ≠ ϕ ∧ antecedentsFinal ≠ *fail*

        then AddRule(antecedentsInitial, antecedentsIntermediate, antecedentsFinal, consequents)

procedure ViewAsArbitraryApplic (node, focusNodes)

    result ← ϕ

    for each antecedent **in** Antecedents(node) **do**

        if Axiom?(antecedent) **then** *true*

        else if SupportedByEarlierNode?(antecedent, focusNodes) **then**

            AddConjunct(result, CollectNecessaryEqualities(antecedent, Supporter(antecedent)))

        else if SituationIndependent?(antecedent) **then** AddConjunct(result, antecedent)

        else if SupportedByPartiallyUnwindableRule?(antecedent) **then**

            AddConjunct(result, CollectResultsOfPartiallyUnwinding(antecedent))

            AddConjunct(result, ViewAsArbitraryApplic(PartiallyUnwind(antecedent), focusNodes))

        else if SupportedByUnwindableRule?(antecedent) **then**

            AddConjunct(result, CollectResultsOfUnwinding(antecedent))

        else if SupportedByRuleConsequent?(antecedent) **then**

            AddConjunct(result, CollectNecessaryEqualities(antecedent, Supporter(antecedent)))

            AddConjunct(result, ViewAsArbitraryApplic(SupportingRule(antecedent), focusNodes))

        else return *fail*

    return result

applications of the focus rule.

Analyzing the Instantiations of the Focus Rule

To package a sequence of rule applications into a single sequential rule, BAGGER collects and combines the preconditions that must be satisfied at each of the N rule applications. The preconditions for applying the resulting extended rule must be specifiable in terms of the initial state, and *not* in terms of intermediate states. This insures, given that the necessary conditions are satisfied in the initial state, a plan represented in a sequential rule will run to completion without further problem solving, regardless of the number of intervening states necessary. For example, there is no possibility that a plan will lead to moving N-2 blocks and then get stuck. If the preconditions for the *i*th rule application were expressed in terms of the result of the *(i-1)*th application, each of the N rule applications would have to be considered in turn to see if the preconditions of the next are satisfied. This is not acceptable. In the approach taken, extra work during generalization and a possible loss of generality are traded off for a rule whose preconditions are easier to check.

When a focus rule is concatenated an arbitrary number of times, BAGGER's problem solver needs to choose variables for each rule application. The *RIS*, a sequence of p-dimensional *vectors*, represents this information. The general form of the *RIS* is:

$$<v_{1,1}, \ldots, v_{1,p}>, <v_{2,1}, \ldots, v_{2,p}>, \ldots, <v_{n,1}, \ldots, v_{n,p}> \qquad (3.1)$$

In the tower-building example of Figure 3.1, initially $p = 3$: the current situation, the object to be moved, and the object upon which the moved object will be placed.

Depending on the rule used, the choice of elements for this sequence may be constrained. For example, certain elements may have to possess various properties, specific relations may have to hold among various elements, some elements may be constrained to be equal to or unequal to other elements, and some elements may be functions of other elements. Often choosing the values of the components of one vector determines the values of components of subsequent vectors. For instance, when building a tower, choosing the block to be moved in step i also determines the location to place the block to be moved in step $i+1$.

To determine the preconditions in terms of the initial state, the generalizer views each of the focus rule instantiations appearing in the specific proof as an arbitrary (or *i*th) application of the underlying rule. It analyzes the antecedents of this rule to see what must be true of the initial state in order to guarantee that the *i*th collection of antecedents will be satisfied when needed. This involves analyzing the proof tree, considering how each antecedent is proved. The EGGS generalization method [Mooney86] is used to determine which variables in the subtree of interest are constrained in terms of other variables in the subtree.

The portion of the proof BAGGER analyzes for a given rule instantiation is that subtree determined by traversing backwards from the given instantiation, collecting nodes until reaching either a leaf node, a situation-independent node, or a node directly supported by a consequent of another focus rule instantiation. Figure 3.8 illustrates this on a section of a hypothetical proof tree. The circles represent focus rule instantiations. The subtree of interest is represented by thicker lines and the given instantiation of the focus rule is represented by a bold circle.

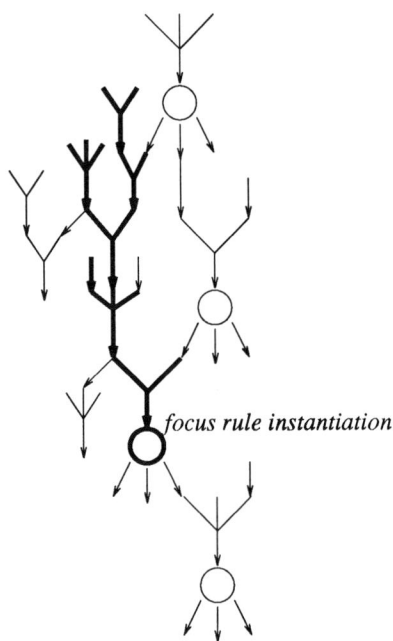

Figure 3.8   Analyzing a Portion of a Proof Tree

The constrained generalized variables in the subtree of interest are expressed, whenever possible, as components of the p-dimensional vectors described above. The algorithm next ascertains what must be true so that each antecedent is satisfied when necessary. All antecedents of the chosen instantiation of the focus rule must be of one of the types in Table 3.2 for generalizing to N to be possible.

Notice that antecedents are considered satisfied when they can be expressed in terms of the initial state, and *not* when a leaf of the proof tree is reached. Conceivably, to satisfy these antecedents in the initial state could require a large number of inference rules. If that is the case, it may be better to trace backwards through these rules until more *operational*[2] terms are encountered. Appendix B contains a sequential rule resulting from a more restricted definition of operationality and compares it to the standard sequential rule learned by BAGGER. Usually the cost of increased operationality is more limited applicability. An empirical analysis of the effect of this trade-off in the BAGGER system appears in Chapter 4.

A second point to notice is that not all proof subtrees will terminate in one of the above ways. When this is the case, this application of the focus rule cannot be viewed as an

---

[2] See Section 1.3.3 for a definition.

Table 3.2 Types of Acceptable Antecedents for BAGGER

(1) The antecedent may be an *axiom*. Since an axiom always holds, it need not appear as a precondition in the final rule.

(2) The antecedent may be supported by a consequent of an earlier application of the focus rule. Terms of this type place inter-vector constraints on the sequence of p-dimensional vectors. These constraints are computed by unifying the general versions of the two terms.

(3) The antecedent may be *situation-independent*. Terms of this type are unaffected by actions. (These differ from axioms as they are not necessarily true.)

(4) The antecedent may be supported by an "unwindable" or partially "unwindable" rule. When this happens, the antecedent is unwound to an arbitrary earlier state and all of the preconditions necessary to insure that the antecedent holds when needed are collected. A *partially unwindable* rule goes back an indefinite number of situations, from which the algorithm continues recursively. If no other inference rules are in the support of the unwindable rule, then it is unwound all the way to the initial state. The processing of unwindable rules is further elaborated later. It, too, may place inter-vector constraints on the sequence of p-dimensional vectors.

(5) The antecedent is supported by other terms that are satisfied in one of the above ways. When traversing backwards across a supported antecedent, the system collects any inter-vector constraints produced by unifying the general version of the antecedent with the general version of the consequent that supports it.

---

arbitrary ith application.[3]

The possibility that a specific solution does not provide enough information to generalize to N is an important point in explanation-based approaches to generalizing number. A concept involving an arbitrary number of substructures may involve an arbitrary number of substantially different subproblems. Any specific solution will only have addressed a finite number of these subproblems. Due to fortuitous circumstances in the example, some of the potential problems may not have arisen. To generalize to N, a system must recognize all the problems that exist in the *general* concept and, by analyzing the specific solution, surmount

---

[3] An alternative approach to this would be to have the system search through its collection of unwindable rules and incorporate a relevant one into the proof structure. To study the limits of this approach to generalizing to N, it is required that *all* necessary information be present in the explanation; no problem-solving search is performed during generalization. Another approach would be to assume the problem solver could overcome this problem at rule application time. This second technique, however, would eliminate the property that a learned plan will always run to completion whenever its preconditions are satisfied in the initial state.

them. Inference rules of a certain form (described later) elegantly support this task in the BAGGER system. They allow the system to reason backwards through an arbitrary number of actions.

The antecedents resulting from analyzing an application of the focus rule may be satisfied an indefinite number of times when a sequential rule is used. Hence, any non-*RIS* variables in the antecedents produced by the generalization algorithm are added to the *RIS*. These extra vector components can be viewed as "local" variables used when, in the sequential rule, a problem solver constructs each instantiation of the original focus.

Figure 3.9 illustrates how consequents of an earlier application of a focus rule can satisfy some antecedents of a later instantiation. This figure contains a portion of the proof for the tower-building example. (The full proof tree is presented and discussed in Section 3.2.4.) Portions of two consecutive transfers are shown. All variables are universally quantified, and arrows run from the antecedents of a rule to its consequents. Triple parallel lines represent terms that are equated in the specific explanation. The generalization algorithm enforces the unification of these paired terms, leading to the collection of equality constraints.

There are four antecedents of a transfer. To define a transfer, one must specify the block moved (x), the object on which it is placed (y), and the current state (s), and must satisfy the constraints among these variables. One antecedent, the one requiring a block not be placed on top of itself, is Type 3 — it is *situation-independent*. The next two antecedents are Type 2. Two of the consequents of the $(i{-}1)th$ transfer are used to satisfy these antecedents of

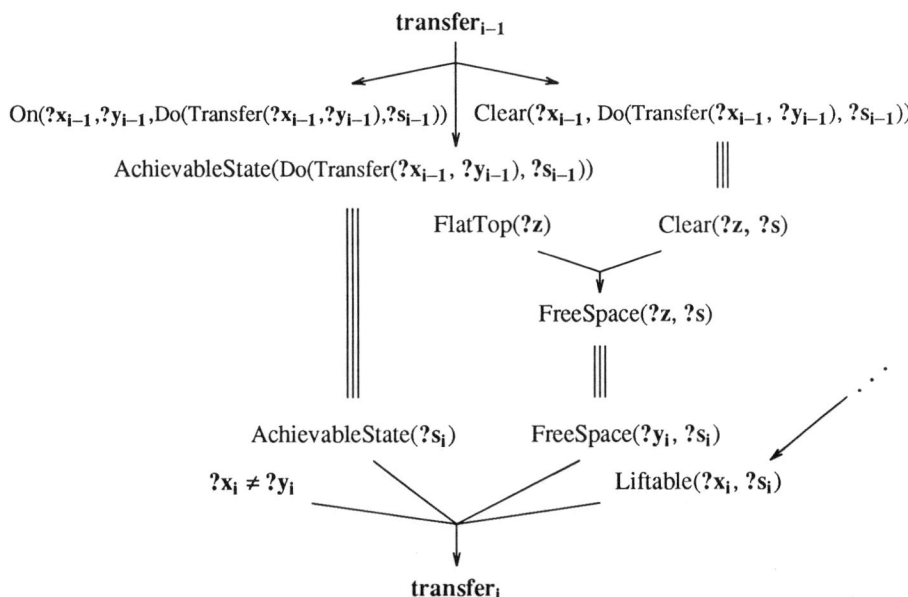

Figure 3.9   Satisfying Antecedents by Previous Consequents

the ith transfer. During $transfer_{i-1}$, in state s_{i-1} object x_{i-1} is moved on to object y_{i-1}. The consequents of this transfer are that a new state is produced, the object moved is clear in the new state, and x_{i-1} is on y_{i-1} in the resulting state.

The state that results from $transfer_{i-1}$ satisfies the second antecedent of $transfer_i$. Unifying these terms defines s_i in terms of the previous variables in the *RIS*.

Another antecedent requires that, in state s_i, there be space on object y_i to put block x_i. This antecedent is Type 5, and, hence, the algorithm traverses backwards through the rule that supports it. An inference rule specifies that a clear object with a flat top has free space. The clearness of x_{i-1} after $transfer_{i-1}$ is used. Unifying this collection of terms leads, in addition to the redundant definition of s_i, to the equating of y_i with z and x_{i-1}. This means that the previously moved block always provides a clear spot to place the current block, which leads to the construction of a tower.

The fourth antecedent, that x_i be liftable, is also Type 5. A rule (not shown) states that an object is liftable if it is a clear block. BAGGER determines Block x_i is clear because it is clear in the initial state and nothing has been placed upon it. Tracing backwards from the liftable term leads to several situation-independent terms and the term $Supports(?x_i, \phi, ?s_i)$. Although this term contains a situation variable, it is satisfied by an "unwindable rule," and is Type 4.

Expression 3.2 presents the form required for a rule to be unwindable. The consequent must match one of the antecedents of the rule. Hence, the rule can be applied recursively. This feature is used to "unwind" the term from the ith state to an earlier state, often the initial state. Occasionally there can be several unwindable rules in a support path. For example, a block might support another block during some number of transfers, be cleared, remain clear during another sequence of transfers, and finally be added to a tower. An example of a multiple unwinding appears in Appendix B. The variables in the rule are divided into four groups. First, there are the x variables. These appear unchanged in both the consequent's term P and the antecedent's term P. Second, there are the y variables which differ in the two P's. Third, there are the z variables that only appear in the antecedents. Finally, there is the state variable (s). There can be additional requirements of the x, y, and z variables (via

$$P(x_{i,1}, \ldots, x_{i,\mu}, y_{i-1,1}, \ldots, y_{i-1,v}, s_{i-1})$$
$$\text{and}$$
$$Q(x_{i,1}, \ldots, x_{i,\mu}, y_{i-1,1}, \ldots, y_{i-1,v}, y_{i,1}, \ldots, y_{i,v}, \ldots, z_{i,1}, \ldots, z_{i,\omega})$$
$$\text{and}$$
$$s_i = Do(x_{i,1}, \ldots, x_{i,\mu}, y_{i-1,1}, \ldots, y_{i-1,v}, \ldots, z_{i,1}, \ldots, z_{i,\omega}, s_{i-1})$$
$$\rightarrow$$
$$P(x_{i,1}, \ldots, x_{i,\mu}, y_{i,1}, \ldots, y_{i,v}, s_i) \tag{3.2}$$

predicate Q), however, these requirements cannot depend on a state variable.

Applying Expression 3.2 recursively produces Expression 3.3. This rule determines the requirements on the earlier state so that the desired term can be guaranteed in state i. Except for the definition of the next state, none of the antecedents depends on the intermediate states. Notice that a collection of y and z variables must be specified. Any of these variables not already contained in the *RIS* are added to it. Hence, the *RIS* is also used to store the results of intermediate computations. Since the predicate Q does not depend on the situation, it can be evaluated in the initial state.

The requirements on the predicate Q are actually somewhat less restrictive. Rather than requiring this predicate to be situation-independent, all that is necessary is that any term containing a situation argument be supported (possibly indirectly) by an application of a focus rule. The important characteristic is that the satisfaction of the predicate Q can be specified in terms of the initial situation only. Separately unwinding a predicate Q while in the midst of unwinding a predicate P is not possible with the current algorithm, and how to accomplish this is an open research issue.

Frame axioms often satisfy the form of Expression 3.2. Figure 3.10 shows one way to satisfy the need to have a clear object at the ith step. Assume the left-hand side of Figure 3.10 is a portion of some proof. This explanation says Block x_i is clear in state s_i because it is clear in state s_{i-1} and the block moved in $transfer_{i-1}$ is not placed upon x_i. Unwinding this rule leads to the result that Block x_i will be clear in state s_i if it is clear in state s_1 and x_i is never used as the new support block in any of the intervening transfers.

To classify an instantiation of a rule as being unwindable, the rule must be applied at least *twice* successively. This heuristic prevents generalizations that are likely to be spurious. The intent of this is to increase the likelihood that a generalization is being made that will prove useful in the future. For example, imagine some rule represents withdrawing some money from a bank and also imagine this rule is of the form of Expression 3.2. Assume that in state 5, John withdraws \$500 to buy a television, while in states 1-4, the amount of money he has in the bank is unaffected. While it is correct to generalize this plan to include any number

---

$P\ (x_{i,\,1}, \ldots, x_{i,\mu}, y_{j,\,1}, \ldots, y_{j,v}, s_1)$ and $0 < j < i$
    and
$\forall\ k \in j+1, \ldots, i$

    $Q\ (x_{i,\,1}, \ldots, x_{i,\mu}, y_{k-j,\,1}, \ldots, y_{k-j,v}, y_{k,\,1}, \ldots, y_{k,v}, \ldots, z_{k,\,1}, \ldots, z_{k,\omega})$
       and
    $s_k = Do\ (x_{i,\,1}, \ldots, x_{i,\mu}, y_{k-j,\,1}, \ldots, y_{k-j,v}, \ldots, z_{k-j,\,1}, \ldots, z_{k-j,\omega}, s_{k-1})$

$\rightarrow$

$P\ (x_{i,\,1}, \ldots, x_{i,\mu}, y_{i,\,1}, \ldots, y_{i,v}, s_i)$ (3.3)

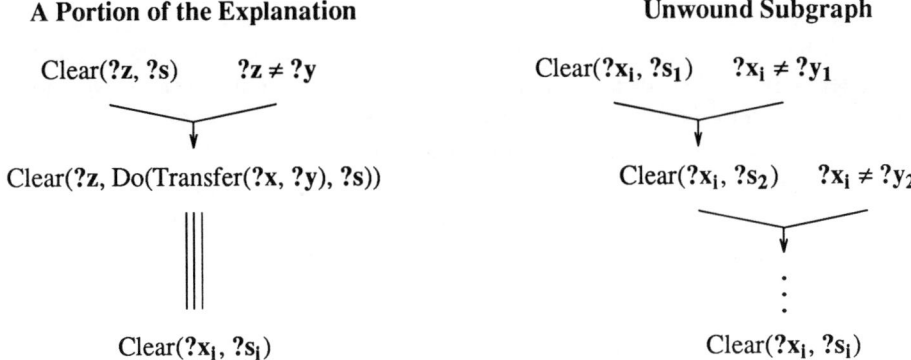

A Portion of the Explanation	Unwound Subgraph

Figure 3.10 Unwinding a Rule

of trips to the bank in order to get sufficient money for a purchase, it does not seem proper to do so. Rather, the generalization should be to a single trip to the bank at *any* time. Frame axioms are exceptions to this constraint — they only need to be applied once to be considered unwindable. Since frame axioms only specify what remains unchanged, there is no risk in assuming an arbitrary number of successive applications.

Incorporating the Rest of the Explanation

Once the repeated rule portion of the extended rule is determined, the generalizer incorporates the rest of the explanation into the final result. It accomplishes this in the same manner it uses to satisfy antecedents in the repeated rule portion. The only difference is that it now views the focus rule as the *Nth* rule application. As before, antecedents must be of one of the five specified types. If all the terms in the goal cannot be satisfied in the arbitrary *Nth* state, BAGGER learns nothing; rather than undergeneralizing, it waits for a better training example.

Determining the Consequents of the New Rule

The consequents of the final rule are constructed by collecting those generalized final consequents of the explanation that directly support the goal.

3.2.2 Problem Solving in BAGGER

A problem solver that applies sequential rules has been implemented. BAGGER's problem solver, in order to construct the *RIS*, is a slightly extended version of a standard backward-chaining problem solver. First, it checks the constraints on $?v_1$ — the initial vector in the *RIS*[4] — against the initial state, using the standard backward-chaining algorithm. This leads to the binding of other components of the first vector in the sequence. Next, the problem

---

[4] Sometimes, as explained below, the problem solver starts with $?v_n$ and works backwards to $?v_1$.

solver checks if the last vector in the sequence (at this point, $?v_1$) satisfies the preconditions for $?v_n$. If so, a satisfactory sequence has been found and back-chaining terminates successfully. Otherwise, it views the last vector in the sequence as $?v_{i-1}$ and attempts to satisfy the intermediate antecedent. This may lead to it incorporating vector $?v_i$ into the sequence. If a new vector is added, it checks the final constraints on the sequence again. If they are not satisfied, it views the new head of the sequence as $?v_{i-1}$ and repeats the process. This cycle continues until either the current sequence satisfies the rule's antecedents or the initial state cannot support the insertion of another vector into the sequence. When the current sequence cannot be further extended, the solver performs chronological back-tracking, moving back to the last point where there are choices as how to lengthen the sequence.

Several additional points about BAGGER's problem solver must be made. First, as is standard, arithmetic functions and predicates (e.g., *addition, less-than*) are procedurally defined. As discussed in the next section, the generalizer rearranges terms of this type so that their arguments are bound when the solver evaluates them. Second, the antecedents in a rule may involve vectors in addition to $?v_1$, $?v_{i-1}$, $?v_i$, and $?v_n$. Third, a sequential rule may contain universal and existential terms, where the quantified variable ranges over the vectors in the *RIS*.

In the implementation, the procedure described two paragraphs above is extended so that, when satisfying the initial antecedents, all the vectors of the form $?v_k$, for fixed k, are instantiated. Similarly, the solver checks all the vectors of the form $?v_{n-k}$, again for fixed k, to determine termination. In addition, the intermediate antecedents may involve vectors of the form $?v_{i-k}$, for fixed k.

When the quantified variable is a vector in the *RIS*, universal and existential terms can be handled in a brute force manner, due to the finiteness of the *RIS*. If an existential term appears as an antecedent, the problem solver successively binds the quantified variable to vectors in the current *RIS* and attempts to satisfy the body of the term. For universally quantified terms, the quantified variable is set to each vector in the current *RIS*, and the body must be satisfied for each binding. The implemented problem solver does not handle existential terms when the *RIS* is constructed from vector N backwards. (One inefficient way to implement this would be to first ignore the existential terms and construct an otherwise successful *RIS*, then to check the existential terms in the manner described above, producing a new *RIS* if checking fails.) In the reverse-construction case, the solver satisfies universal terms by binding the quantified variable to the earliest vector (the new vector being incorporated) and then viewing every vector as the *ith* vector.

3.2.3   Simplifying the Antecedents in Sequential Rules

Even though the solver evaluates all the antecedents of a sequential BAGGER rule in the initial state, substantial time can be spent finding satisfactory bindings for the variables in the rule. Simplifying the antecedents of a rule acquired using EBL can increase the efficiency of the rule [Minton87, Prieditis87]. After a rule is constructed by the BAGGER generalization algorithm, the generalizer removes duplicate antecedents and heuristically rearranges the remainder in an attempt to speedup the process of satisfying the rule.

Simplification in BAGGER involves several processes. Heuristics are used to estimate whether is better to construct the *RIS* from the first vector forward or from the last vector backward. The generalizer moves terms not effected by the intermediate antecedent so that they are tested as soon as possible. It simplifies intermediate antecedents that are redundantly evaluated and relocates terms involving arithmetic so that all their arguments are bound when they are evaluated. Finally, within each grouping, it rearranges antecedents so that terms involving the same variable are grouped near one another.

Determining the Order in which to Expand the RIS

Since all the antecedents of a sequential rule are specified in terms of the initial state, and not in terms of the results of intermediate states, the *RIS* can be instantiated either from vector 1 to vector N or from vector N to vector 1. However, the order in which new vectors are added to the *RIS* can greatly effect the efficiency of a sequential rule. BAGGER contains two heuristics for determining which appears to be the best way to instantiate the *RIS*, given the characteristics of its problem solver.

To see the effect order can have on efficiency, assume that the *RIS* records the height of a tower being planned and that the goal specifies the minimum acceptable tower height. Figure 3.11 shows how the tower would be planned, depending on the order the planner expands the *RIS*. If it constructs the *RIS* by first instantiating the last vector and then proceeding to instantiate the preceding vectors, the final tower height may be chosen first. Next, it would select blocks to be placed in the tower, in reverse order, each time recording how much of the bottom of the tower remains. At the last step, there may not a suitably-sized block.[5] If no collection of movable blocks achieves the chosen final tower height, it must select a new final tower height and repeat the process. Conversely, if it instantiates the *RIS* from vector 1 forward, much efficiency can be gained. In this approach, it would select blocks for insertion in the tower and at each step record the current tower height. Once this height exceeds the goal height, it would have constructed a successful *RIS*.

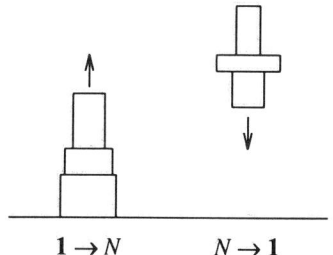

$$1 \to N \qquad N \to 1$$

Figure 3.11   Two Ways of Extending an RIS

---

[5] Termination is discussed later. Assume here that once the remaining tower height is negative, the problem solver backtracks. However, BAGGER's problem solver does not operate this cleverly.

For an example of when the *RIS* should be constructed from vector *N* backwards, consider unstacking a tower of blocks in order to clear the block at the bottom of the tower. In this case, which is detailed in Appendix B, the intermediate antecedents in the sequential rule require that the *i-1th* block to be moved support, in the initial state, the *ith* block to be moved. A final antecedent requires that the last block moved be directly on top of the block to be cleared, while an initial antecedent requires the first block to be moved be clear. If the *RIS* is expanded from vector 1 forward, any clear block will be chosen as the first one to be moved. Next, the blocks underneath it will be successively chosen, each cycle checking to see that the *ith* block to be moved is directly on the block being cleared. If so, a successful *RIS* has been constructed. Otherwise, the expansion continues until no more vectors can be added to the *RIS* and then another initial vector is constructed.

If the sequential rule can be used to clear the desired block, sooner or later a successful *RIS* will be constructed. However, this process can be much more directed if the *RIS* is produced in the reverse direction. The *nth* vector will contain the block directly on the block to be cleared. The preceding vector will then contain the block directly on the block in the *nth* vector. This chain will continue until a clear block is incorporated into the *RIS*, satisfying the initial antecedents.

A more sophisticated problem solver than BAGGER's could avoid some of these problems. Possibly it could expand an *RIS* both ways from the middle or, if working backwards, leave some of the terms in the final antecedents unsatisfied until it satisfies the initial antecedents. Domain-specific knowledge could also provide additional guidance. However, it is desired in this research on learning to minimize the complexity of the problem solver.

BAGGER produces a sequential rule from vector *N* to vector 1 *unless* one of the following occurs:

(1)   The intermediate antecedents contain a *structure-reducing* term whose *decreasing* argument involves a component of vector *i* and whose *increasing* argument involves the same component of an earlier vector. An example of a structure-reducing term is *RemoveFromBag* $(?x, ?y, ?z)$. The variable $?z$ is the collection that results from removing object $?x$ from the collection $?y$. The decreasing argument is $?z$, while $?y$ is the increasing argument. The requirements to be a structure-reducing term are that the values of its decreasing argument always be ordered with respect to those of its increasing argument and that there be a smallest possible value of the decreasing argument.

(2)   A term in the final antecedents contains a *threshold* function involving a vector of the form $?v_{n-k}$, for some fixed k. A threshold function is one where: if the values of all but one of its arguments are set, there are still an infinite number of acceptable values for the final argument. Sample threshold functions are *less−than* and *greater−than*.

Successfully applying these heuristics means that the properties of some of its predicates must be supplied to BAGGER.

Additional and more sophisticated techniques for determining the most efficient way to construct an *RIS* are needed. The section on open research issues in the conclusion further addresses this topic.

Guaranteeing Termination of RIS Expansion

There is the possibility that a problem solver using one of BAGGER's sequential rules can go wandering off along an infinite search tree, as can happen, for example, with depth-first search. Although BAGGER's rules have termination constraints for expanding an *RIS* in either direction (the initial and final antecedents), termination[6] can be a problem.

For example, if a tower is being built, the *RIS* may be representing the height of the current tower planned. If there is a narrow range of acceptable tower heights, during the construction of the *RIS* the problem solver may "jump" over the acceptable region. Since blocks can only be in a tower once, assuming a finite collection of blocks means the problem solver will terminate, however there is a serious problem looming here. Assume, for instance, that new blocks can always be created. One partial solution may involve reasoning about functions and predicates that deal with ordered arguments (e.g., numbers). For example, if a termination precondition involves the predicate *less—than* and blocks (which must have positive height) are being added, the problem solver can stop before placing all the blocks in a tower. Once the tower height recorded in the *RIS* exceeds the goal, there is no reason to continue extending the *RIS*.

Appendix B presents an example where reasoning about the predicates in a sequential rule leads to the insertion of another term that reduces the likelihood of time being wasted needlessly expanding an *RIS*. The technique presented there is only preliminary, and the problem of inserting new terms to guarantee termination or increase efficiency is an open research issue. Fortunately, the issue of termination has been addressed substantially in program verification research (see [Manna74]). Approaches developed there should prove applicable in restricted situations (the general problem of proving termination — the *halting problem* — is undecidable). The idea of a structure-reducing term discussed above comes from the concept of *well-founded sets*, used in proofs of program termination [Floyd67, Manna70].

Relocating Intermediate Antecedents

Occasionally the intermediate terms may specify redundant constraints on the *RIS*. In addition to removing exact duplicates, the following simplifications are made:

(1) The intermediate terms may contain $P(?v_{i-1})$ and $P(?v_i)$. This is changed to $P(?v_1)$ and $P(?v_i)$, if the *RIS* is expanded forward, and $P(?v_{i-1})$ and $P(?v_n)$ otherwise.

(2) The intermediate terms may contain $?v_{i-1,c} = ?v_{i,c}$. In this case, the simplifier eliminates this term and replaces all occurrences of $?v_{i-1,c}$ and $?v_{i,c}$ by $?v_{1,c}$ or $?v_{n,c}$, depending on the direction the *RIS* is constructed. Since BAGGER's generalization algorithm produces many equality constraints, this simplification often proves useful.

---

[6] That is, termination of the expansion of the *RIS*. The problem solver must also terminate when satisfying each term in the antecedents if it is to successfully instantiate an *RIS*.

Once the direction in which BAGGER's problem solver will extend a rule's *RIS* is determined, the simplifier can move some terms from one antecedent group to another. If a rule's *RIS* is to be constructed from vector 1 forward, it moves to the initial antecedent group all the terms in the intermediate and final antecedent groups that involve neither vector *I* nor vector *N*. The analogous relocations occur when an *RIS* is constructed from vector *N* backward. This insures that the solver satisfies terms not effected by other portions of the *RIS* as early as possible.

Grouping Antecedents

The last attempt to increase efficiency involves rearranging the antecedents within an antecedent group. The algorithm for doing this attempts to locate terms involving the same variables near one another. This algorithm proceeds by first collecting all the variables in the given antecedent group. It next takes the variables from this collection one at a time and places them in a second collection. After each step, all of the terms containing only those variables in the second collection at that point are placed in the new antecedent group. Since some predicates are procedurally defined (e.g., +), a final processing step is needed. All procedurally defined terms are moved to the end of their antecedent groups, in order to increase the likelihood that their variables are bound by the time they are evaluated.

3.2.4   Two Examples

Two example applications of the BAGGER generalization algorithm conclude this section. The first example involves learning a general version of DeMorgan's law for Boolean Algebra (Figure 3.6), while the second involves the acquisition of a plan for building towers of arbitrary height (Figure 3.5).

The proof trees presented here and in Appendix B are produced by the BAGGER system. Arrows run from the antecedent of a rule to its consequent. When a rule has multiple antecedents or consequents, an ampersand (&) is used. Descriptions of all the rules used in this structure appears in Appendix C.

A General Version of DeMorgan's Law

As an example, consider the application of BAGGER in the domain of circuit implementation. Replication of structure is an important operation in the circuit domain. Examples in this simple domain, commonly used to illustrate EBL techniques, clearly show the weaknesses of standard EBL methods and demonstrate how BAGGER overcomes them. Also, the first example illustrates the application of BAGGER to problems where situation calculus is not used. In these cases, all terms are situation-independent and there is no need to unwind any rule applications to the initial state. Hence, in building the new sequential rule, terms are either omitted because they are axioms, dropped because they are satisfied by an earlier consequent, or included because they are situation-independent.

The rules in Table 3.3 determine how to implement a circuit using OR's and NOT's. Leading question marks indicate variables. The term *Implements(?x, ?y)* means that circuit *?x* can be used to implement design *?y*.

Table 3.3 Circuit Implementation Rules	
Rule	Description
Wire(?wire) → Implements(?wire,?wire)	Wires are easily implemented.
Implements(?x,?y) → Implements(¬¬?x,?y)	Double negations have no effect.
Implements((¬?x ∧ ¬?y),?a) → Implements(¬(?x ∨ ?y),?a)	DeMorgan's law for two-input gates.
Implements(?x,?a) ∧ Implements(?y,?b) → Implements((?x ∧ ?y),(?a ∧ ?b))	An implementation of a circuit headed by a two-input *AND* can be found by finding implementations of the two subcircuits.

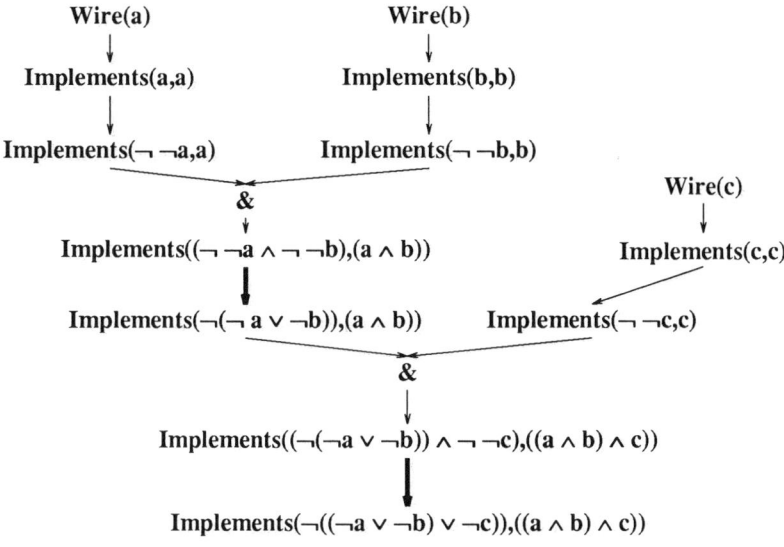

Figure 3.12   Implementing Two AND Gates with OR and NOT Gates

The proof of the construction on the left side of Figure 3.6 appears in Figure 3.12. This proof shows that a circuit design involving two connected *AND* gates can be implemented using *OR* and *NOT* gates. DeMorgan's Law (for two-input gates) is used twice to prove this equivalence. This becomes BAGGER's focus rule and is marked by thick bold arrows. However, before presenting BAGGER's result, consider the rule produced by EGGS.

When applied to this example, the EGGS algorithm produces the rule below.

$$Wire\,(?x) \wedge Wire\,(?y) \wedge Wire\,(?z) \rightarrow Implements\,(((\neg ?x \vee \neg ?y) \vee \neg ?z), ((?x \wedge ?y) \wedge ?z)$$

This rule implements a three-input *AND* by negating three inputs and using two *OR*s and a *NOT* gate. This is the variablized version of the goal node. The inputs are all required to be wires. These preconditions result from collecting the leaf nodes. Note that this rule only works for three-input *AND* designs.

The sequential rule BAGGER produces appears in Table 3.5. The sequential rule it acquires represents a general version of DeMorgan's Law. Table 3.4 demonstrates how BAGGER's problem solver would instantiate this rule's *RIS* on a sample problem, one where the implementation of a four-input *AND* is requested. That is, the query posed is *Implements(?circuit, (((f ∧ g) ∧ h) ∧ i))*. The *RIS* is instantiated from N to 1; at each step, the solver strips off one input to the *AND* gate, until only two inputs remain. While this is happening, it combines the inverted inputs into a cascaded collection of *OR* gates.

Table 3.4 Instantiating the RIS for the General DeMorgan's Law

Vector	$?v_{i,1}$	$?v_{i,2}$	$?v_{i,3}$	$?v_{i,4}$
3	$((\neg f \vee \neg g) \vee \neg h)$	$\neg i$	$(((f \wedge g) \wedge h) \wedge i)$	i
2	$(\neg f \vee \neg g)$	$\neg h$	$((f \wedge g) \wedge h)$	h
1	$\neg f$	$\neg g$	$(f \wedge g)$	g

Table 3.5 A General Version of DeMorgan's Law

Antecedents$_{initial}$

/* Requirements on the *initial* vector in a successful RIS. */

(1)   InitialVector($?v_1$, ?seq) $\wedge$ $?v_{1,\,1} = \neg?a$ $\wedge$ Wire(?a) $\wedge$ $?v_{1,\,3} = (?a \wedge ?v_{1,\,4})$ $\wedge$

(2) $?v_{1,\,2} = \neg?v_{1,\,4}$ $\wedge$ Wire($?v_{1,\,4}$)

Antecedent$_{intermediate}$

/* Requirements on vectors, other than the first one, in a successful RIS.
Requirements specified in terms of the *previous* vector. */

(3)   [Member($?v_i$,?seq) $\wedge$ $?v_i \neq ?v_1$ $\wedge$ Member($?v_{i-1}$,?seq) $\wedge$ Predecessor($?v_{i-1}$,$?v_i$,?seq)

$\rightarrow$

(4) $?v_{i,\,2} = \neg?v_{i,\,4}$ $\wedge$ Wire($?v_{i,\,4}$) $\wedge$ $?v_{i,\,3}=(?v_{i-1,\,3}\wedge?v_{i,\,4})$ $\wedge$ $?v_{i,\,1}=(?v_{i-1,\,1}\vee?v_{i-1,\,2})]$

Antecedents$_{final}$

/* Requirements on the *final* vector in a successful RIS. */

(5)   Sequence(?seq) $\wedge$ FinalVector($?v_n$,?seq) $\wedge$?circuit $= \neg(?v_{n,\,1} \vee ?v_{n,\,2})$ $\wedge$?spec $= ?v_{n,\,3}$

Consequents

(6)   Implements(?circuit, ?spec)

This rule extends sequences N $\rightarrow$ 1.

Building a Tower

The proof that explains the tower-building actions of Figure 3.1, where three blocks are stacked on top of one another, appears in Figure 3.13. The primed ampersands are the instantiations of the focus rule, while the ampersand nearest the bottom of the graph is the conjunctive goal node. Since the situation arguments are quite lengthy, they are abbreviated and a key appears in the figure.

The goal provided to the backward-chaining theorem prover that produced this graph is:

$$\exists\ \text{AchievableState(?state)}\ \wedge$$
$$\text{Xpos(?object, ?px, ?state)}\ \wedge\ ?px \geq 550\ \wedge\ ?px \leq 750\ \wedge$$
$$\text{Ypos(?object, ?py, ?state)}\ \wedge\ ?py \geq 150.$$

This says that the goal is to prove the existence of an achievable state, such that in that state the horizontal position of some object is between 550 and 750 and the vertical position of that same objects is at least 150.

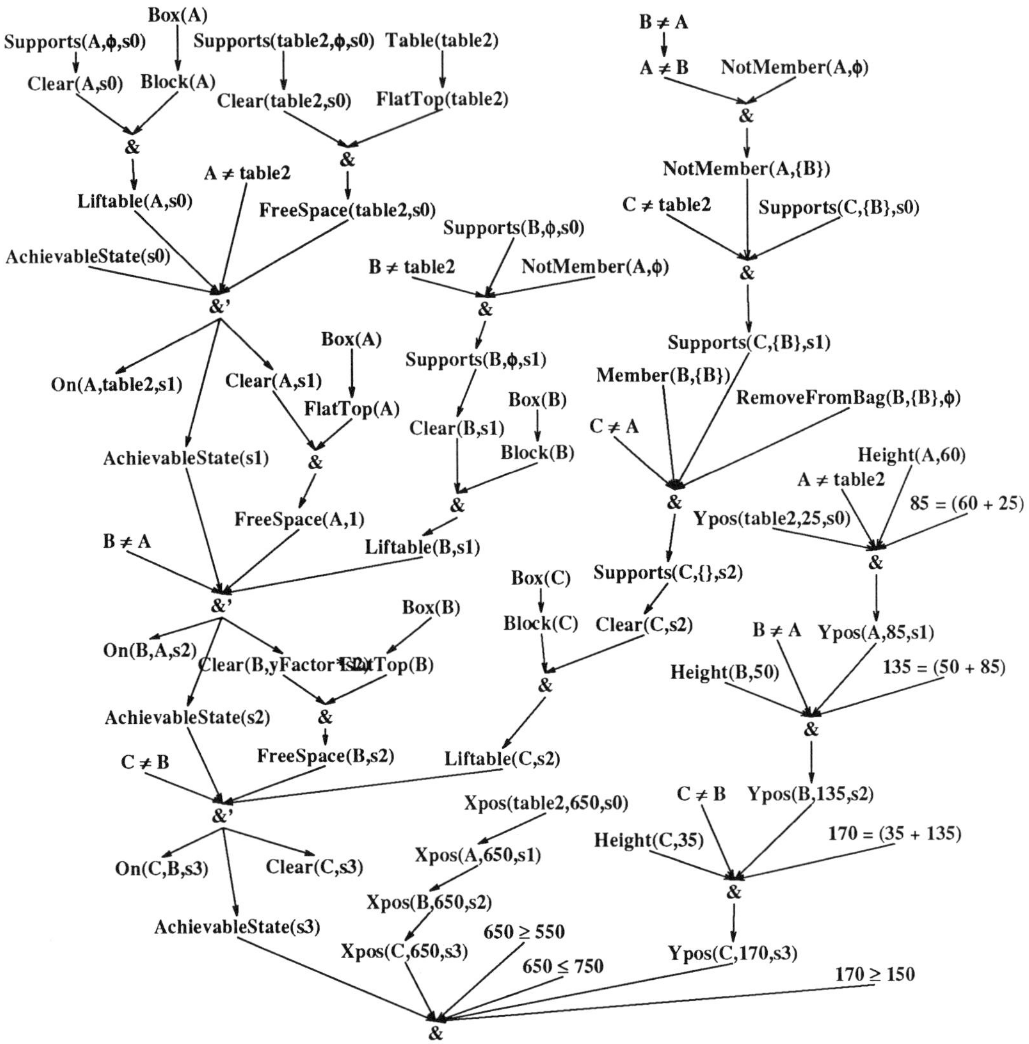

Box(A)

Supports(A,φ,s0)   Supports(table2,φ,s0)   Table(table2)

Clear(A,s0)   Block(A)

Clear(table2,s0)   FlatTop(table2)

B ≠ A

A ≠ B   NotMember(A,φ)

&

&

&

Liftable(A,s0)

A ≠ table2

FreeSpace(table2,s0)

NotMember(A,{B})

AchievableState(s0)

Supports(B,φ,s0)

C ≠ table2   Supports(C,{B},s0)

B ≠ table2   NotMember(A,φ)

&'

&

&

On(A,table2,s1)   Clear(A,s1)

Box(A)

FlatTop(A)

Supports(B,φ,s1)

Supports(C,{B},s1)

Member(B,{B})

RemoveFromBag(B,{B},φ)

AchievableState(s1)

Clear(B,s1)   Box(B)   Block(B)

Height(A,60)

&

FreeSpace(A,1)

C ≠ A

A ≠ table2   85 = (60 + 25)

B ≠ A

Liftable(B,s1)

&   Ypos(table2,25,s0)

&

On(B,A,s2)   Clear(B,yFactor·152)FlatTop(B)

Box(C)   Supports(C,{},s2)

AchievableState(s2)   &

C ≠ B   FreeSpace(B,s2)

Box(C)

Block(C)   Clear(C,s2)   B ≠ A   Ypos(A,85,s1)

Height(B,50)   135 = (50 + 85)

&'

&

On(C,B,s3)   Clear(C,s3)

Liftable(C,s2)

Xpos(table2,650,s0)

C ≠ B   Ypos(B,135,s2)

AchievableState(s3)

Xpos(A,650,s1)

Height(C,35)   170 = (35 + 135)

Xpos(B,650,s2)

&

Xpos(C,650,s3)   650 ≥ 550

650 ≤ 750   Ypos(C,170,s3)

170 ≥ 150

&

Figure 3.13   Situation Calculus Plan for Stacking Three Blocks

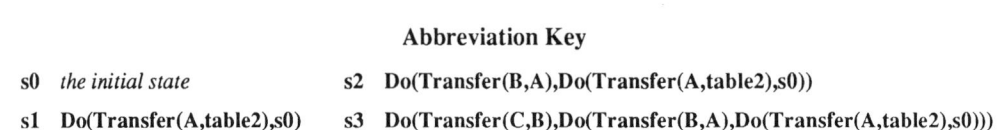

Abbreviation Key

s0 *the initial state*	s2 Do(Transfer(B,A),Do(Transfer(A,table2),s0))
s1 Do(Transfer(A,table2),s0)	s3 Do(Transfer(C,B),Do(Transfer(B,A),Do(Transfer(A,table2),s0)))

96

The sequential-rule BAGGER produces by analyzing this explanation structure appears in Table 3.6. The remainder of this section describes in great detail how the system produces each term in this table. Line numbers have been included for purposes of reference. For readability, the new rule is broken down into components, as shown in Expression 3.4. In this example, the components of the *RIS*'s vector have the following meanings:

<current situation, block to be moved, place to stack block, height of moved block, new tower height>.

Producing the Initial Antecedents

The initial antecedents in the first line of the rule establish a sequence of vectors, the initial state, and the first vector contained in the sequence. Subscripts are used to indicate components of vectors, as a shorthand for functions that perform this task. For example, $?v_{1,3}$ is shorthand for *ThirdComponent* $(?v_1)$. Lines 2 and 3 contain the antecedents of the first application in the chain of applications. These are the same terms that appear in the focus rule (the first rule in Appendix C's Table C.3), except that the components of v_1 are used. The system has knowledge of which arguments are situation variables, and the initial state constant $s0$ is placed in these positions. The other terms in this grouping are produced by the unwinding process (*Height, Xpos, Ypos*, and the addition term) or are moved ($\geq$ and $\leq$) from the final antecedents to the initial antecedents because their variables are not influenced by the intermediate antecedents. The terms produced by unwinding are described further in what follows.

Analyzing the Applications of the Focus Rule

Lines 5-11 contain the preconditions BAGGER derives by analyzing the three instantiations of the focus rule. In this implication, v_i — an arbitrary vector in the sequence (other than the first) — is used, as these constraints must be satisfied for each of the applications that follow the first. Vector v_{i-1} is the vector immediately preceding v_i. It is needed because some of the antecedents of the *ith* application are satisfied by the *i-1th* application. Although some preconditions in the new rule involve v_i and v_{i-1}, these preconditions all refer to conditions in the initial state. They do *not* refer to results in intermediate states.

The final two of the three instantiations of the focus rule produce sufficient information to determine how the antecedents of the rule can be satisfied in the *ith* application. In the first application (upper left of Figure 3.13), neither the support for *Liftable* nor the support for *FreeSpace* provide enough information to determine the constraints on the initial state so that these terms can be satisfied in an arbitrary step. In both cases, the proof only has to address clearness in the current state. No information is provided within the proof as to how clearness can be guaranteed to hold in some later state.

BAGGER discovers two different ways of satisfying the antecedents by analyzing the two other instantiations of the focus rule, and, hence, learns a disjunction. The common terms in these two disjuncts appear in lines 6 and 7, while the remaining terms for the first disjunction are in line 8 and for the second in lines 9-11.

The third term in line 7 is the vector form of the inequality that is one of the antecedents of the focus rule. This, being situation-independent, is a Type 3 antecedent (Table 3.1). In

Table 3.6 The Components of the Learned Rule

Antecedents$_{\text{initial}}$

(1) Sequence(?seq) $\wedge$ InitialVector(?v_1,?seq) $\wedge$ State(s0) $\wedge$?$v_{1,1}$ = s0 $\wedge$

(2) FreeSpace(?$v_{1,3}$, s0) $\wedge$ Liftable(?$v_{1,2}$, s0) $\wedge$ Height(?$v_{1,2}$, ?$v_{1,4}$) $\wedge$

(3) Xpos(?$v_{1,3}$, ?px, s0) $\wedge$ Ypos(?$v_{1,3}$, ?new, s0) $\wedge$?$v_{1,2}$ ≠ ?$v_{1,3}$ $\wedge$

(4) ?$v_{1,5}$ = (?$v_{1,4}$ + ?new) $\wedge$?px ≥ ?xmin $\wedge$?px ≤ ?xmax $\wedge$

Antecedent$_{\text{intermediate}}$

(5) [Member(?v_i,?seq) $\wedge$?v_i ≠ ?v_1 $\wedge$ Member(?v_{i-1},?seq) $\wedge$ Predecessor(?v_{i-1},?v_i,?seq)

   $\rightarrow$

(6) ?$v_{i,3}$ = ?$v_{i-1,2}$ $\wedge$?$v_{i,1}$ = Do(Transfer(?$v_{i-1,2}$,?$v_{i-1,3}$),?$v_{i-1,1}$) $\wedge$ FlatTop(?$v_{i,3}$) $\wedge$

(7) Block(?$v_{i,2}$) $\wedge$ Height(?$v_{i,2}$, ?$v_{i,4}$) $\wedge$?$v_{i,2}$ ≠ ?$v_{i,3}$ $\wedge$?$v_{i,5}$ = (?$v_{i,4}$ + ?$v_{i-1,5}$) $\wedge$

(8) [[[Member(?v_j,?seq) $\wedge$ Earlier(?v_j,?v_i,?seq) $\rightarrow$?$v_{i,2}$ ≠ ?$v_{j,3}$] $\wedge$ Supports(?$v_{i,2}$,ϕ,s0)]

(9) $\vee$ [[Member(?v_j,?seq) $\wedge$ Earlier(?v_j,?v_{i-1},?seq) $\rightarrow$ NotMember(?$v_{j,2}$,{?$v_{i-1,2}$})] $\wedge$

(10) [Member(?v_j, ?seq) $\wedge$ Earlier(?v_j, ?v_{i-1}, ?seq) $\rightarrow$?$v_{i,2}$ ≠ ?$v_{j,3}$] $\wedge$

(11) Supports(?$v_{i,2}$, {?$v_{i-1,2}$}, s0) $\wedge$?$v_{i,2}$ ≠ ?$v_{i-1,3}$]]] $\wedge$

Antecedents$_{\text{final}}$

(12) FinalVector(?v_n,?seq) $\wedge$?py = ?$v_{n,5}$ $\wedge$?state = Do(Transfer(?$v_{n,2}$, ?$v_{n,3}$), ?$v_{n,1}$) $\wedge$

(13) ?object = ?$v_{n,2}$ $\wedge$?py ≥ ?ymin

Consequents

(14) State(?state) $\wedge$ Xpos(?object, ?px, ?state) $\wedge$?px ≤ ?xmax $\wedge$?px ≥ ?xmin $\wedge$

(15) Ypos(?object, ?py, ?state) $\wedge$?py ≥ ?ymin

This rule extends sequences 1 $\rightarrow$ N.

$$Antecedents_{initial} \wedge Antecedent_{intermediate} \wedge Antecedents_{rest} \rightarrow Consequents \quad (3.4)$$

vector form, it becomes $v_{i,2} \neq v_{i,3}$. It constrains possible collections of vectors to those that have different second and third members. This constraint stems from the requirement that a block cannot be stacked on itself.

Both of the successful applications of the focus rule have their *AchievableState* term satisfied by a consequent of a previous application. These terms are Type 2 and require collection of the equalities produced by unifying the general versions of the matching consequents and antecedents. (See Figure 3.10 for the details of these matchings.) The equality that results from these unifications is the second term of line 6. Thus, the next state is always completely determined by the previous one. No searching needs to be done in order to choose the next state. (Actually, no terms are ever evaluated in these intermediate states. The only reason they are recorded is so that the final state can be determined, for use in setting the situation variable in the consequents.)

Both successful applications have their *FreeSpace* term satisfied in the same manner. Traversing backwards across one rule leads to a situation independent term (*FlatTop* - line 6) and the consequent of an earlier application (*Clear*). Unifying the two clear terms (again, see Figure 3.10) produces the first two equalities in line 6. This first equality means that the block to be moved in the *ith* step can always be placed on top of the block to be moved in the "(i-1)th* step. No problem solving need be done to determine the location at which to continue building the tower.

The generalizer produces the *Block* term in line 7 during the process of analyzing the way the *Liftable* term is satisfied. The remaining portion of the analysis of *Liftable* produces the terms in the disjunctions. As in the initial antecedents, the generalizer produces the *Height* and addition terms in line 7 during the analysis of the terms in the goal, which is described later.

In the second application of the focus rule, which produces the first disjunct, a clear block to move is acquired by finding a block that is clear because it supports nothing in the initial state and nothing is placed on it later. The frame axiom supporting this is an unwindable rule. Unwinding it to the initial state produces line 8. The *Supports* term must hold in the initial state and the block to be moved in step *i* can never be used as the place to locate a block to be moved in an earlier step. The general version of the term *NotMember* (A, ϕ) does not appear in the learned rule because it is an axiom that nothing is a member of the empty set, and the generalizer axioms are pruned. (An earlier unification, from the rule involving *Clear*, requires that the second variable in the general version of *NotMember* term be ϕ.)

Notice that this unwinding, which leads to a more operational rule because it produces preconditions entirely expressed in terms of the initial state, restricts the applicability of the acquired rule. The first disjunct requires that if an initially clear block is to be added to the tower, nothing can ever be placed on it, even temporarily. A more general plan would be learned, however, if in the specific example a block is temporarily covered. In that case, in the proof there would be several groupings of unwindable rules; for awhile the block would remain clear, something would then be placed on it and it would remain covered for several steps, and finally it would be cleared and remain that way until moved. Although such clearing and unclearing can occur repeatedly, the BAGGER algorithm is unable to generalize number within unwindable subproofs.

The second disjunct (lines 9-11) results from the different way a liftable block is found in the third application of the focus rule. Here a liftable block is found by using a block that initially supported one other block, which is moved in the previous step, and where nothing else is moved to the lower block during an earlier rule application. Unwinding the subgraph for this application leads to the requirements that initially one block is on the block to be moved in step i, that block be moved in step $(i-1)$, and nothing else is scheduled to be moved to the lower block during an earlier rule application. Again, some terms do not appear in the learned rule (*Member* and *RemoveFromBag*) because, given the necessary unifications, they are axioms. This time *NotMember* is not an axiom, and hence appears. If the specific example were more complicated, the acquired rule would reflect the fact that the block on top can be removed in some *earlier* step, rather than necessarily in the *previous* step. This case is discussed in Appendix B.2.

Analyzing the Rest of the Explanation

Once it analyzes all of the instantiations of the focus rule, the generalizer visits the goal node. This produces lines 12 and 13, plus some of the earlier terms.

The *AchievableState* term of the goal is satisfied by the final application of the focus rule, leading to the third term in line 12.

The final X-position is calculated using an unwindable rule. Tracing backwards from the *Xpos* in the goal to the consequent of the unwindable rule produces the first term in line 13 (as well as reproducing the third term in line 12). When this rule is unwound it produces the first term of line 3 and the second term of line 6. Also, matching the *Xpos* term in the antecedents with the one in the consequents, so that Equation 2 applies, again produces the first term in line 6. Since there are no "Q"-terms (Expression 3.3), the generalizer adds no other preconditions to the intermediate antecedent.

The inequalities involving the tower's horizontal position are state-independent; BAGGER's simplifier moves their general forms to the initial antecedents because their arguments are not affected by satisfying the intermediate antecedent. These terms in the initial antecedents involving $?px$ insure that the tower is started underneath the goal.

Unwindable rules also determine the final Y-position. Here "Q"-terms are present. The connection of two instantiations of the underlying general rule appears in Figure 3.14. This general rule is unwound to the initial state, which creates the second term of line 3 and the second term of line 6. The last three terms of line 7 are also produced, as the "Q"-terms must hold for each application of the unwound rule. This process adds two components to the vectors in the *RIS*. The first $(?v_{i,\ 4})$ comes from the $?hx$ variable, which records the height of the block being added to the tower. The other $(?v_{i,\ 5})$ comes from the variable $?yPos\,2$. It records the vertical position of the block added, and, hence, represents the height of the tower. The $?ypos$ variable does not lead to the creation of another *RIS* entry because it matches the $?yPos\,2$ variable of the previous application. All that is needed is a $?ypos$ variable for the first application. Similarly, matching the *Ypos* term in the antecedents with the one in the consequents produces the first term in line 6.

The last conjunct in the goal produces the second term on line 13. This precondition insures that the final tower is tall enough.

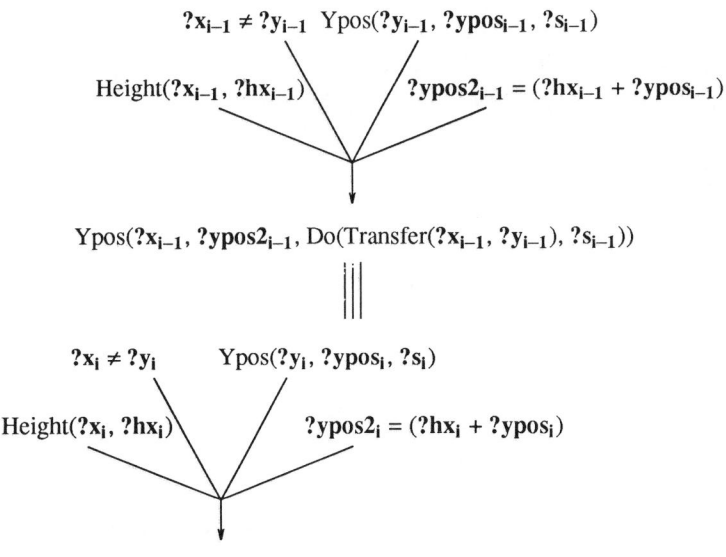

$?x_{i-1} \neq ?y_{i-1}$ $\text{Ypos}(?y_{i-1}, ?\mathbf{ypos}_{i-1}, ?s_{i-1})$

$\text{Height}(?x_{i-1}, ?\mathbf{hx}_{i-1})$ $?\mathbf{ypos2}_{i-1} = (?\mathbf{hx}_{i-1} + ?\mathbf{ypos}_{i-1})$

$\text{Ypos}(?x_{i-1}, ?\mathbf{ypos2}_{i-1}, \text{Do}(\text{Transfer}(?x_{i-1}, ?y_{i-1}), ?s_{i-1}))$

$?x_i \neq ?y_i$ $\text{Ypos}(?y_i, ?\mathbf{ypos}_i, ?s_i)$

$\text{Height}(?x_i, ?\mathbf{hx}_i)$ $?\mathbf{ypos2}_i = (?\mathbf{hx}_i + ?\mathbf{ypos}_i)$

$\text{Ypos}(?x_i, ?\mathbf{ypos2}_i, \text{Do}(\text{Transfer}(?x_i, ?y_i), ?s_i))$

Figure 3.14   Calculating the Vertical Position of the *i*th Stacked Block

Finally, the general version of the goal description is used to construct the consequents of the new rule (lines 14 and 15).

3.3   Extending BAGGER

The BAGGER algorithm is not recursive in the sense that when it operates on an explanation structure it does not apply itself to subparts of the explanation. This limits it to learning number-generalized plans with only linear sequences of rule applications. For example, the number-generalized version of DeMorgan's Law BAGGER learns only applies to cascaded circuits; it cannot handle tree-like designs. This section presents the BAGGER2 algorithm, which is essentially a recursive form of the initial BAGGER method. Unlike its predecessor, BAGGER2 is capable of acquiring recursive concepts involving arbitrary tree-like applications of rules; in addition it can produce multiple generalizations to N from a single example and can integrate the results of multiple examples.

Like BAGGER, BAGGER2 generalizes explanation structures by looking for repeated, inter-dependent substructures in an explanation. Figure 3.15 schematically presents the process BAGGER2 follows. Assume that in explaining how a goal is achieved, the same general subproblem (P) arises several times. The full explanation can be divided into several qualitatively different portions. First, there are the subexplanations in which an instantiation of P is supported by the explanations of other instantiations of the general problem P. In the figure, these are the subexplanations marked 1 and 4. Second, there are the subexplanations in which an instantiation of P is explained without reference to another instantiation of itself.

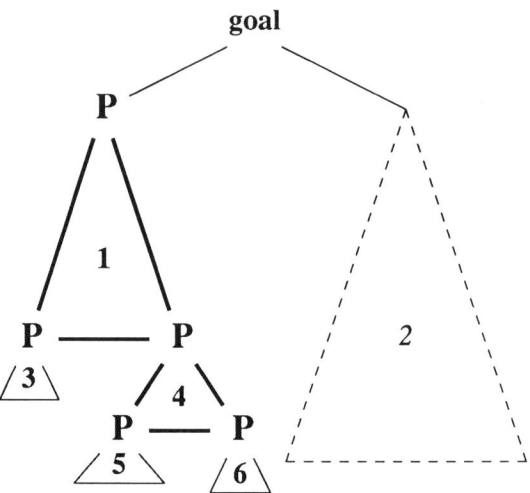

Figure 3.15   Partitioning the Structure of an Explanation

These are the subexplanations labeled 3, 5, and 6. Finally, there are the portions not involving P (subexplanation 2).

The explanation in Figure 3.15 can be viewed as the trace of a recursive process. This is exactly what one must recognize in the explanation of a specific example in order to learn a recursive or iterative concept. The generalizations of Subexplanations 1 and 4 form the recursive portion of the concept, whereas the generalizations of Subexplanations 3, 5, and 6 produce the termination conditions. BAGGER2 partitions explanations into groups, as Figure 3.15 illustrates, from which it produces a new recursive concept.

Roughly speaking, BAGGER2 produces the following two rules from Figure 2's explanation:

$$P \wedge gen_2 \quad \rightarrow \quad goal$$
$$gen_3 \vee gen_5 \vee gen_6 \vee recursive\text{-}gen_1 \vee recursive\text{-}gen_4 \quad \rightarrow \quad P$$

To achieve the goal, a problem solver must satisfy the recursive subgoal P and whatever general preconditions Subexplanation 2 requires. The solver can satisfy P by satisfying the general preconditions of any of the non-recursive or recursive subexplanations; the generalizations of the recursive subexplanations lead to recursive calls to subgoal P.

3.3.1   Algorithmic Details and Correctness Proof

Table 3.7 contains the BAGGER2 generalization algorithm. Although the algorithm appears here in a pseudo-code, the actual implementation is written in COMMON LISP. The remainder of this subsection elaborates the pseudo-code and presents a theorem about its correctness.

The BAGGER2 approach assumes that explanations are derivation *trees*, which are structures that could be produced by a Horn clause theorem prover such as PROLOG. The algorithm starts at the root of the explanation. If the general consequent at the root appears elsewhere in the structure, then the method produces a recursive rule (called a *recurrence*) whose consequent

Table 3.7. The BAGGER2 Generalization Algorithm

Procedure BuildNewBAGGER2Rule(*goal-node*)   /* Generalize the explanation headed by this node. */

Let *consequent* be the consequent of the goal node.

If *consequent* is supported by a term that unifies with it,

Then return *ProduceRecurrence(goal-node)*,

Else let *antecedents* be *CollectGeneralAntecedents(goal-node)*

and return the rule *consequent* ← *antecedents*.

Procedure CollectGeneralAntecedents(*node*) /* Collect the generalized version of *node's* antecedents.*/

Let *result* be the empty set.

For each direct *antecedent* of *node*,

If it is operational or a call to a recurrence,

Then conjunctively add it to *result*,

Else if it is supported by a term that unifies with it,   /* Found a potential recurrence. */

Then conjunctively add *ProduceRecurrence(antecedent)* to *result*,

Else if it is directly supported by the consequent of a rule,

Then:Let *consequent* be the rule's consequent.

Conjunctively add to *result* the equalities that must

hold to unify *antecedent* and *consequent*.

Conjunctively add *CollectGeneralAntecedents(consequent)*.

Else return *false*.   /* Reached a non-operational leaf node. */

Return *result*.

Procedure ProduceRecurrence(*node*) /* Produce a recurrence from the subexplanation headed by *node*. */

Let *consequent* be the root of *node*.

Let *antecedents* be the empty set.

For each terminal and recursive *subproof* supporting *node*: /* Look at ways of satisfying *node*. */

Let *subconsequent* be the root of *subproof*.

Let *disjunct* contain the equalities that must hold to unify *subconsequent* and *node*.

Conjunctively add *CollectGeneralAntecedents(subconsequent)* to *disjunct*.

Disjunctively add *disjunct* to *antecedents*.

Construct the recurrence *consequent* ← *antecedents* and return a call to it.

is the root node. Otherwise, it collects the general version of the root node's antecedents and produces a new rule. Since a recurrence can also arise within an explanation structure, this discussion will assume that the root node does not directly lead to a recurrence.

As shown in Table 3.7, *CollectGeneralAntecedents* produces sufficient requirements for the consequent of a rule to hold. Ignoring for a moment the possibility of recurrences being constructed, *CollectGeneralAntecedents* traverses through the explanation structure and stops at operational nodes. (Recall that operational nodes are antecedents somehow judged to be easily satisfied, for example because they are satisfied by a problem-specific fact.) Along the way, the function collects all the unifications necessary to connect the rules in the explanation structure, thus eliminating the need to check these when the acquired rule is later applied. This portion of the algorithm is merely a rehash of EGGS. Hence, when BAGGER2 detects no potential generalizations to N, it produces the same result as EGGS.

More interesting events occur when BAGGER2 detects a potential recurrence. This is done by seeing if a unifiable version of the general antecedent appears in its own derivation (e.g., the P's in Figure 3.15). If so, *ProduceRecurrence* partitions the explanation structure headed by the general antecedent into two types of subexplanations: *terminal proofs* where a unifiable version of the antecedent does not appear in its proof, and *recursive proofs* where at least one does. In the recursive proofs, the function replaces the recursive subexplanations by a call to the recurrence being constructed. These calls contain the term that must be unified with the consequent of the recurrence. Hence, when cutting out Figure 3.15's Subexplanation 1, the function removes Subexplanations 3 and 4 and replaces them by a call to the recurrence whose consequent is P. Notice that the subexplanations are non-overlapping.

Once *ProduceRecurrence* produces the subexplanations, it generalizes each by calling BAGGER2. This means that another recurrence may be found within a subexplanation, allowing multiple generalizations to N in a single example. When generalizing the subexplanations, the function collects the necessary unifications between the root of the subexplanation and the consequent of the recurrence under construction. Satisfying these unifications insures that the general solution in the subexplanation applies to the recurrence's consequent. The function disjunctively combines the generalizations of the subexplanations and produces a recurrence.

Notice that rather than only learning a single rule from an explanation, BAGGER2 also produces several useful subrules (the recurrences). The detection of recurrences provides a useful decomposition of explanations. Because recurrences are separate entities from the rule produced for the full explanation, they support transfer of the results learned during one task to the performance of another, provided the two tasks involve common subtasks. This separation also supports learning from multiple examples. If the system encounters a new method for satisfying the consequent of a recurrence, it can merge the new method with the previous disjuncts[7], as discussed further in Section 3.3.3.

Before BAGGER2 produces a new rule, it removes redundant antecedents and reorders the others to increase the efficiency of future retrievals. In recurrences, if an antecedent appears in every terminal disjunct, it can be removed from the recursive disjuncts provided it is independent of the variables in the recurrence's consequent. Dropping them from the recursive disjuncts is valid because these antecedents will be checked when retrieval reaches a terminal disjunct.

Assuming that explanations are logical proofs, the BAGGER2 algorithm can be proved correct, as shown in the following theorem.

Theorem 1. The basic BAGGER2 algorithm is *sound*, in that the rules it learns will never derive anything that cannot be derived by the initial domain theory.

Proof. Consider the explanation in Figure 3.15. Basically, one must show that the algorithm properly generalizes the subexplanations and that the method for combining subexplanations preserves soundness. Assume for the moment that there are no potential recurrences other than P within Figure 3.15's explanation. Since the EGGS algorithm has been proven sound [Mooney89c], BAGGER2 will correctly generalize each of the numbered subexplanations. The result from Subexplanation 2 is handled in the same fashion by BAGGER2 and EGGS; it will not be considered further. Next, consider the recursive portion of the explanation. To derive the generalized goal, the uppermost P must be satisfied using the generalization of either a terminal or a recursive subproof. The soundness of a derivation using only a terminal proof follows directly from the proof for EGGS and the fact that the algorithm maintains the unifications necessary to insure that the generalized consequent of a subexplanation matches P. A derivation using a recursive proof must terminate by using the results of terminal proofs. Since these final derivation steps are sound, and soundness between steps is maintained by checking the necessary inter-step unifications, the soundness of recursive derivations follows inductively.

The case for embedded recurrences also follows inductively. After partitioning an explanation there are no embedded P's in the subexplanations, since those at the leaves are converted to a recurrence call. Hence, each subdivision of the explanation reduces the number of potential recurrences. The deepest subexplanation contains only one recurrence, and BAGGER2 correctly generalizes it according to the argument in the previous paragraph. Encapsulating subexplanations are also correctly generalized, by induction. To see this, assume correctness for i levels of embedded recurrences. The argument in the previous paragraph can now be applied to demonstrate correctness for the level $i+1$, thereby completing the proof.

---

[7] This may lead to poor performance if too many disjuncts are learned. The user can decide when a concept is sufficiently learned and tell the system to "freeze" all of its recurrences. After that, new recurrences will be constructed even if they have the same consequent as an existing one.

3.3.2 The Circuit Implementation Domain Revisited

An example in Section 3.2.4 demonstrates how BAGGER learns a general version of DeMorgan's Law. However, the acquired rule only applies to circuits containing a linear chain of gates; the rule essentially iterates down this chain, applying DeMorgan's Law repeatedly. Figure 3.16 shows a circuit whose implementation requires repeated application of DeMorgan's Law, but in such a way that the rule BAGGER learns in Section 3.2.4 is not applicable. This subsection applies BAGGER2 to this implementation problem.

The rules in Table 3.3 can be used to provide an explanation of how to implement the design in Figure 3.16. It is instructive to compare the behavior of EGGS and BAGGER2 on this problem. If EGGS is applied to the resulting explanation, the rule in Table 3.8 results. Notice that this rule not only requires a fixed number of inputs, but also a fixed topology, that of Figure 3.16. Clearly the explanation structure needs to be generalized. The result produced by BAGGER2 appears in Table 3.9. In this problem, the full explanation leads to a single recurrence, which involves four disjuncts. The first applies when only a single application of DeMorgan's Law is necessary. The remaining three disjuncts are recursive. The second and third disjuncts apply when one input is a wire, in which case the rule recurs on the other input. In the final disjunct, recursion is needed for both inputs.

The notation in Tables 3.8 and 3.9 merits some discussion. For instance, the capitalized *Or*'s, *And*'s, and *Nots*'s refer to gates in the circuit domain; they are not part of the rule description language. The *matches* operator unifies its two arguments. As an extension to PROLOG, direct calls to recurrences are permitted in order to satisfy a goal. Finally, BAGGER2 renames the variables in recurrences; variables starting with *v* appear in the consequent,

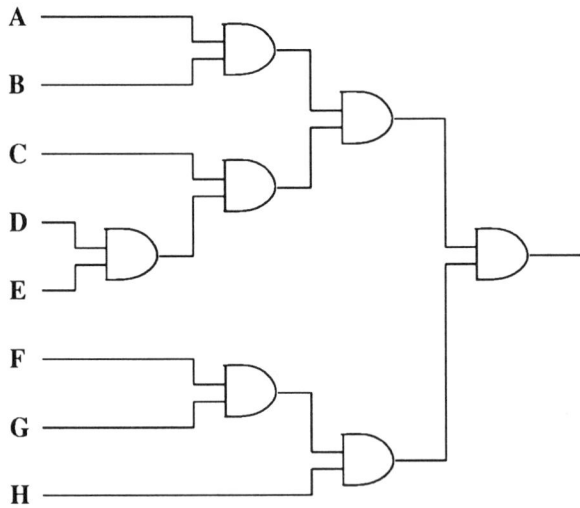

Figure 3.16   A Sample Circuit Design to be Implemented

Table 3.8. The Rule Acquired by EGGS for the Circuit Problem in Figure 3.16

```
Wire(?G43) ∧   Wire(?G6)   ∧   Wire(?G9)   ∧   Wire(?G16) ∧
Wire(?G37) ∧   Wire(?G40) ∧   Wire(?G23) ∧   Wire(?G26)
    →
Implements(Not(Or(Or(Or(Not(?G6),    Not(?G9)),
                  Or(Not(?G16), Or(Not(?G23), Not(?G26)))),
              Or(Or(Not(?G37), Not(?G40)),
                  Not(?G43)))),
          And(And(And(?G6,   ?G9),
                  And(?G16, And(?G23, ?G26))),
              And(And(?G37, ?G40),
                  ?G43)))
```

Table 3.9. The Recursive Rule Acquired by BAGGER2 for the Circuit Problem

To satisfy: Implements(Not(Or(?v1, ?v2)), ?v3)

One of the following must hold:

?v1 matches Not(?e1) ∧ ?v2 matches Not(?e2) ∧   /* no more gates */
?v3 matches And(?e1, ?e2) ∧ Wire(?v3) ∧ Wire(?v4)

        or

?v1 matches Or(?e1, ?e2) ∧ ?v2 matches Not(?e3) ∧   /* no gates on right */
?v3 matches And(?e3, ?e4) ∧ Wire(?e3) ∧
recursively satisfy Implements(Not(Or(?e1, ?e2)), ?e4)

        or

?v1 matches Not(?e1) ∧ ?v2 matches Or(?e2, ?e3) ∧   /* no gates on left */
?v3 matches And(?e1, ?e4) ∧ Wire(?e1) ∧
recursively satisfy Implements(Not(Or(?e2, ?e3)), ?e4)

        or

?v1 matches Or(?e1, ?e2) ∧ ?v2 matches Or(?e3, ?e4) ∧   /* gates on both sides */
?v3 matches And(?e5, ?e6) ∧ ?v4 matches And(?e7, ?e8) ∧
recursively satisfy Implements(Not(Or(?e1, ?e2)), ?e5) ∧
recursively satisfy Implements(Not(Or(?e3, ?e4)), ?e6)

whereas those starting with E are local variables.

The rule BAGGER2 learns is truly a general version of DeMorgan's Law; it converts an N-input AND gate into a negated N-input OR gate. It applies to a much larger class of problems than do the rule learned by EGGS and the rule the original BAGGER learned in Section 3.2.4. Notice that BAGGER2's acquired recurrence does not refer to any of the initial rules. Thus, it is self-contained and is topologically similar to a recursive LISP function. The consequent specifies the parameters, and the antecedents form something like a LISP conditional statement. This "function" is produced from a collection of simple declarative PROLOG-like rules, which are called explicitly rather than by determining which rules in a large rule base unify with the current consequent. Hence, BAGGER2 provides a way to transform a simple, but inefficient, logic program into another program stated in a more efficient language. An investigation of the application of this approach to the problem of acquiring programs appears in [Shavlik88].

3.3.3 Learning from Multiple Examples

Unlike BAGGER, BAGGER2 can combine the results learned in separate examples. Recurrences are disjunctive subrules and, hence, are prime candidates for enhancement during additional learning. When generalization of a new explanation produces a basic recurrence that has the same consequent as a previous recurrence, the generalizer merges the disjuncts in the new recurrence with those in the existing one. As an illustration, assume that the training example in Figure 3.17 was simpler, and the second recursive case in Table 3.7 was not encountered. A future training example involving the missing case would be needed in order to completely learn Table 3.7's general version of DeMorgan's Law.

Commonly in explanation-based learning, additional examples lead to disjuncts in acquired rules (e.g., [Cohen88, Kedar-Cabelli85, Minton88a]). There are two important aspects of BAGGER2's approach to learning from multiple examples. First, the system need not learn disjuncts during the achievement of the same goal. For instance, a technique learned during the building of an arch can improve what was previously learned about building towers. Second, BAGGER2 does not require the explanation from which the existing recurrence arose, so there is no need to save old explanations. Hence, learning can proceed incrementally without requiring full memory of all past experiences.

Learning from multiple examples produces much the same effect as initially learning from a more complicated example. Since BAGGER2 breaks up explanations and merges together similar generalizations (see Figure 3.16), in terms of the results of generalization it does not matter if the subexplanations come from one example or many. However, there is an advantage of learning from multiple examples in explanation-based learning. A complicated concept can be acquired by observing several simple versions of the concept. This can greatly reduce the load on the agent that produces the training examples and also simplifies the explanation process. Looking at this a different way, if a rule is initially incompletely learned because a training example is too simplistic, later experiences can refine the rule.

3.3.4 Problem Solving with Rules Acquired by BAGGER2

Applying BAGGER2's recurrences requires a slight extension to PROLOG,[8] namely the ability to explicitly call a specific rule. When it calls a particular rule to satisfy a given subgoal, the problem solver applies no other rules to that subgoal upon backtracking. To avoid wasted effort, when first calling a recurrence the solver checks those terms in the recurrence's terminal disjuncts that are independent of the variables in the recurrence's consequent. Such antecedents are unaffected by calls to the recurrence, and if they cannot be satisfied the problem solver does not call the recurrence.

3.3.5 Improving the Efficiency of the Rules BAGGER2 Learns

The basic BAGGER2 algorithm produces valid generalizations of specific solutions, but, as illustrated later in this section, it does not produce rules that can be applied as efficiently as the essentially iterative rules the original BAGGER acquires. This section presents three techniques for improving the efficiency of rules learned by the basic approach. These extensions to the basic method are particularly useful for generalizing actions in situation calculus plans.

Consider again the tower-building task illustrated in Figure 3.1. BAGGER2 is incapable of generalizing non-tree structured explanations, hence it cannot generalize Figure 3.14's explanation. Instead, a slightly different formalization of the blocks world is used; it appears in Appendix C's Table C.5. By generalizing the resulting explanation of Figure 3.1's actions, the basic BAGGER2 algorithm produces the rules in Table 3.10.[9]

Notice that, unlike the rule that EGGS would produce, BAGGER2's rule is not limited to cases in which *three* blocks need be moved. Also notice that the recurrences only test predicates that are either situation-independent or that refer to the initial situation, *s0*. The main rule says that to build a tower, one should first find an achievable situation, then see if the final block moved is at the goal location. This *generate-and-test* approach leads to wasted work, as demonstrated later; it would be better if the problem solver started the tower at an acceptable horizontal position and checked the tower's height *while* producing a valid final state. The remainder of this section describes how one can produce a rule that embodies this strategy.

The extended BAGGER2 algorithm carries out three additional processing steps; each of these can improve the efficiency of the acquired rule, as demonstrated later. Table 3.11 contains the results of applying the extensions of BAGGER2 to the rules in Table 3.10. The next several paragraphs describe the extensions and explain how they produce the rules in Table 3.11.

The first extension applies when multiple calls to recurrences appear in the antecedents of a rule (as in the first rule of Table 3.8). If these recurrences can be ascertained to occur

---

[8] Recall that this specific implementation uses a COMMON LISP version of PROLOG, but the use of COMMON LISP is not, of course, necessary.

[9] The recurrence *On-1* is analogous to *Clear-1* and, hence, is not shown.

Table 3.10. Rules Learned by the Basic BAGGER2 Algorithm in the Blocks World

Rule Tower-2:   /* Build a tower of arbitrary height. */
call recurrence AchievableState-1 to satisfy AchievableState(Do(Transfer(?v1, ?v6), ?v7)) ∧
call recurrence Xpos-1 to satisfy Xpos(?v1, ?v8, Do(Transfer(?v1, ?v6), ?v7)) ∧
?v8 ≥ ?v4 ∧ ?v8 ≤ ?v5 ∧
call recurrence Ypos-1 to satisfy Ypos(?v1, ?v9, Do(Transfer(?v1, ?v6), ?v7)) ∧
?v9 ≥ ?v2 ∧ ?v9 ≤ ?v3
    →
Tower(?v1, ?v2, ?v3, ?v4, ?v5, Do(Transfer(?v1, ?v6), ?v7))

Recurrence AchievableState-1:   /* Reach legal states by moving clear blocks. */
To satisfy: AchievableState(Do(Transfer(?v1, ?v2), ?v3))

One of the following must hold:

   ?v3 matches s0 ∧ Liftable(?v1, s0) ∧ FreeSpace(?v2, s0) ∧ ?v1 ≠ ?v2.
                              or
   ?v3 matches Do(Transfer(?v2, ?e1), ?e2) ∧ recursively satisfy AchievableState(?v3) ∧
   [call recurrence Clear-1 to satisfy Clear(?v1, ?v3) ∨
     call recurrence On-1 to satisfy On(?v2, ?v1, ?e2) ∧ ?v1 ≠ ?e1] ∧
   Block(?v1) ∧ FlatTop(?v2) ∧ ?v1 ≠ ?v2

Recurrence Xpos-1: /* Determine the *x-pos* of the last block moved by finding the first supporting object. */
To satisfy: Xpos(?v1, ?v2, Do(Transfer(?v1, ?v3), ?v4))

One of the following must hold:

   ?v4 matches s0 ∧ Xpos(?v3, ?v2, s0).
                              or
   ?v4 matches Do(Transfer(?v3, ?e1), ?e2) ∧ recursively satisfy Xpos(?v3, ?v2, ?v4)

Recurrence Ypos-1:   /* Determine the *y*-position of a block by summing heights. */
To satisfy: Ypos(?v1, ?v2, Do(Transfer(?v1, ?v3), ?v4))

One of the following must hold:

   ?v4 matches s0 ∧ Ypos(?v3, ?e2, s0) ∧ Height(?v1, ?e1) ∧ ?v1 ≠ ?v3 ∧ ?v2 = ?e1 + ?e2
                              or
   ?v4 matches Do(Transfer(?v3, ?e1), ?e2) ∧ recursively satisfy Ypos(?v3, ?e4, ?v4) ∧
   Height(?v1, ?e3) ∧ ?v1 ≠ ?v3 ∧ ?v2 = ?e3 + ?e4

Recurrence Clear-1:   /* See if a block is clear due to nothing being placed on it. */
To satisfy: Clear(?v1, Do(Transfer(?v2, ?v3), ?v4))

One of the following must hold:

   ?v4 matches s0 ∧ Clear(?v1, s0) ∧ ?v1 ≠ ?v3
                              or
   ?v4 matches Do(Transfer(?e1, ?e2), ?e3) ∧ recursively satisfy Clear(?v1, ?v4) ∧ ?v1 ≠ ?v3

Table 3.11.   Rules Learned by the Extended Bagger2 Algorithm in the Blocks World

Rule Tower-3:   /* Build a tower of arbitrary height. */
  call recurrence AchievableState-Xpos-Ypos-1 to satisfy
        AND(AchievableState(Do(Transfer(?v1, ?v6), ?v7)),
               Xpos(?v1, ?g1, Do(Transfer(?v1, ?v6), ?v7)),
               Ypos(?v1, ?v9, Do(Transfer(?v1, ?v6), ?v7)),
               ?g1 ≥ ?v4, ?g1 ≤ ?v5) ∧
?v9 ≥ ?v2 ∧ ?v9 ≤ ?v3
     →
Tower(?v1, ?v2, ?v3, ?v4, ?v5, Do(Transfer(?v1, ?v6), ?v7))

Forward Recurrence AchievableState-Xpos-Ypos-1: /* Legally stack blocks and record positions. */
  To satisfy: AND(AchievableState(Do(Transfer(?v1, ?v3), ?v4)),
                  Xpos(?v1, ?g1, Do(Transfer(?v1, ?v3), ?v4)),
                  Ypos(?v1, ?v2, Do(Transfer(?v1, ?v3), ?v4)),
                  ?g1 ≥ ?g2, ?g1 ≤ ?g3)

One of the following must hold:

   ?v4 matches s0 ∧ Liftable(?v1, s0) ∧ Height(?v1, ?e1) ∧ FreeSpace(?v3, s0) ∧ ?v1≠ ?v3 ∧
   Xpos(?v3, ?g1, s0) ∧ ?g1 ≥ ?g2 ∧ ?g1 ≤ ?g3 ∧ Ypos(?v3, ?e2, s0) ∧ ?v2 = ?e1 + ?e2
                    or
   ?v4 matches Do(Transfer(?v3, ?e1), ?e2) ∧
   recursively satisfy AND(AchievableState(Do(Transfer(?v3, ?e1), ?e2)),
                       Xpos(?v1, ?g1, Do(Transfer(?v3, ?e1), ?e2)),
                       Ypos(?v1, ?e4, Do(Transfer(?v3, ?e1), ?e2)),
                       ?g1 ≥ ?g2, ?g1 ≤ ?g3) ∧
   [call recurrence Clear-1 to satisfy Clear(?v1, ?v4) ∨
     call recurrence On-1 to satisfy On(?v3, ?v1, ?e2) ∧ ?v1 ≠ ?e1] ∧
   Block(?v1) ∧ FlatTop(?v3) ∧ ?v1 ≠ ?v3 ∧ Height(?v1, ?e3) ∧ ?v2 = ?e3 + ?e4

Forward Recurrence Clear-1:   /* See if a block is clear due to nothing being placed on it. */
  To satisfy: Clear(?g1, Do(Transfer(?v2, ?v3), ?v4))

One of the following must hold:

   ?v4 matches s0 ∧ Clear(?g1, s0) ∧ ?g1 ≠ ?v3.
                    or
   ?v4 matches Do(Transfer(?e1, ?e2), ?e3) ∧ recursively satisfy Clear(?g1, ?v4) ∧ ?v1 ≠ ?v3

together in a compatible way, they can be merged, and BAGGER2's generalizer can replace the multiple calls by a single call to the merged recurrence. One class of compatible recurrences contains those that traverse through the same sequence of situations; each individual recurrence places constraints on an acceptable traversal. Rather than satisfying these constraints successively for each recurrence, the problem solver can satisfy them simultaneously. When this extension merges several recurrences together, it names the new recurrence by concatenating the names of the individual recurrences, and basically produces the union of the individual recurrences. In a sense, this extension further restructures an explanation; it merges independent portions of an explanation structure. A specific solution may involve several independent recursive tasks, while the acquired rule may address these tasks concurrently.

In Table 3.8's acquired rule for tower building, the calls to *AchievableState-1*, *Xpos-1*, and *Ypos-1* all involve the same final state. Since in situation calculus the final state is defined in terms of a path starting at the initial state, all three recurrences must traverse the same sequence of states and, hence, they can be merged together. Merging requires making copies of the recurrences involved, using the fact that all of the recurrences traverse the same sequence of situations to properly rename variables, and then producing all possible combinations of recursive disjuncts and terminating disjuncts. In the table, each of the recurrences involved only have one recursive and one terminating disjunct, so there is only one way to combine them. However, in general combination can be explosive. For example, if two recurrences each have three terminating disjuncts, the combined recurrence will have up to nine distinct terminating disjuncts.

The second step determines "unchanging" variables; its value primarily arises in combination with the third step, as will be seen momentarily. Determining the variables that remain unchanged is easy; a variable in a recurrence's consequent is unchanged if, in all possible recursive calls, it appears in the same position. For readability, variables that remain unchanged are renamed to start with g, indicating they are "global" variables.

The final step determines if a linear recurrence should be satisfied forward or backward. If a recurrence only involves a linear chain of recursive calls, it may be more efficient to satisfy the recurrence by starting at the initial state and working forward until reaching the desired final state. BAGGER2 heuristically chooses the direction to satisfy recurrences. It selects working forward from the initial state only when any unchanging variables are present, since these variables specify constraints on the initial action to be performed.

When the problem solver is to satisfy a recurrence from the initial state forward, some other terms in the conjunct that calls the recurrence may be moved into the recurrence's terminating disjuncts, as these extra terms further constrain the initial action. The terms moved are those that only involve variables that are unchanging or independent of the recurrence. This is done for the inequalities involving *?v8* in Table 3.8's tower-building rule. It is preferable to satisfy these constraints early, rather than after the recurrence produces a candidate tower. The *x*-location of the first block moved determines the *x*-location of the tower, so the inequalities eliminate time wasted investigating improperly placed towers. Here an extension also restructures an explanation; it moves preconditions from the end of a linear chain of rule applications down to the first step in the sequence.

112

The result in Table 3.11 is essentially an iterative plan. It is a notational variant on the result produced by the original BAGGER (Table 3.4). Blocks are stacked until a tower of the desired height is produced; at each step in the iteration the problem solver must choose a block to move. The plan does not require the use of any other inter-situational rule in the rule base. There may be many ways to build towers or to verify that a block is clear, but the solver expends no resources trying out these portions of the search space. Attention during problem solving is tightly focused; any testing done outside of the acquired plan only involves checking properties of the initial state.

(There are two technical points concerning the interaction of learning from multiple examples and the three extensions to the basic BAGGER2 method. One, the extensions can alter the consequent of the recurrence, which complicates the task of determining that a new recurrence's disjuncts support the same conclusion as that of an old one. Two, the addition of a disjunct can invalidate the applicability of an extension. For these reasons, modified recurrences maintain records of the basic recurrences from which they were produced. The generalizer only adds new disjuncts to pre-existing basic recurrences; it then reconstructs all of the modified recurrences that depend on the basic recurrences.)

The remainder of this section investigates the hypothesis that the extensions improve BAGGER2's performance. Using the blocks world domain, it compares the basic and extended approaches, as well as the three partial extensions that result from dropping one technique. These partial extensions provide information about the individual contributions of the three refinements. Each configuration generalizes the explanation of Figure 3.1. The problem generator then produces 100 random configurations of five blocks on one table, and the goal is to build a five-block tower on a second table. Finally, each configuration solves these 100 test problems, and its mean solution time is recorded. Table 3.12 contains the results, which demonstrate the value of the three extensions.

In this experiment the three extensions provide a speedup of more than ten over the basic approach. The bottom rows in Table 3.12 indicate the individual contributions of the three extensions. Deciding that the problem solver should satisfy recurrences from the initial state

Table 3.12 Evaluation of the Extensions to the Basic BAGGER2 Algorithm	
System	*Mean Solution Time*
Basic BAGGER2	53.7 sec.
Extended BAGGER2	3.8 sec.
without merging related recurrences	7.9 sec.
without marking unchanging variables	5.9 sec.
without selecting problem-solving direction	14.8 sec.

forward provides the largest contribution. Tower building is a task for which planning naturally proceeds from the first action forward; select the starting position, then choose movable blocks and stack them. When it starts by choosing the last block to stack, the problem solver may perform substantial work before realizing that, given the bound on the number of actions, no plan exists where this block is moved last. Conversely, some plans more naturally proceed from the last action backward. The task of clearing a block is one example; move the block on top after first clearing it. The second largest contribution to efficiency is produced by merging recurrences that traverse through the same situations; while producing legal states, it is worthwhile to also record the positions of the blocks moved. Finally, marking variables that remain constant throughout a recurrence produces additional speedup. In the stacking problem, this allows BAGGER2 to move the requirements on the starting x-position into the recurrence. This insures that the problem solver only considers properly located bases for the tower. While the relative contributions of the three extensions heavily depend on the task of tower building, this study indicates the value of reorganizing a collection of basic recurrences.

3.3.6 Learning about Wagons

Chapter 1 presents an example where number should not be generalized; a toy wagon is constructed by attaching two axles to a wooden platform (see Figure 1.1). This section presents a formulization of that problem and shows what BAGGER2 learns from it.

Table 3.13 contains a highly simplified domain theory for this task. The first rule defines a wagon as something that supports weight and is easily moved. The second and third rules provide one way to determine that something can support weight. The fourth states that an object is easily moved if if is supported by two balanced axle assemblies, while the final rule defines an axle assembly as an axle with two wheels attached. Predicates not defined by an inference rule are assumed to be operational. Table 3.14 contains the result of explaining the construction of a wagon, and then generalizing the result using the BAGGER2 algorithm. Notice that neither the number of axles nor the number of wheels is generalized. Neither is generalized because no repeated goal/subgoal structure appears in the explanation.

It may seem that number is not generalized because the domain theory is specially crafted and overly naive. However, the point is that because an EBL system possesses a domain theory, it is able to recognize when generalizing number is warranted. An empirical learning theory would not have this knowledge, and for this reason would lack a justified reason for *not* generalizing the number of axles and wheels.

3.3.7 Comparing BAGGER and BAGGER2

BAGGER2 essentially is the result of making the original BAGGER recursive. The original BAGGER partitions explanation structures into subparts, then applies EGGS to these subparts. BAGGER2 differs in that it applies itself recursively to the subparts it produces; the major result of this is that recursive, rather than only iterative, concepts can now be learned. Another difference is that BAGGER looks for repeated applications of the same *rule* in order to decide where to partition an explanation structure, while BAGGER2 looks for repeated satisfaction of

Table 3.13. Initial Domain Theory for Wagons

supports-weight(?x) ∧ moves-easily(?x)	→	wagon(?x)
made-of-strong-material(?x)	→	supports-weight(?x)
made-of-wood(?x)	→	made-of-strong-material(?x)
supported-by(?x, ?assem1,? assem2) ∧ axle-assembly(?assem1) ∧ axle-assembly(?assem2) ∧ balanced(?x, ?assem1, ?assem2)	→	moves-easily(?x)
components(?x, ?axle, ?wheel1, ?wheel2) ∧ axle(?axle) ∧ wheel(?wheel1) ∧ wheel(?wheel2) ∧ attached(?wheel1, ?axle) ∧ attached(?wheel2, ?axle)	→	axle-assembly(?x)

Table 3.14. The Acquired (Operational) Definition of Wagon

made-of-wood(?x) ∧ supported-by(?x, ?assem1,? assem2) ∧
components(?assem1, ?axle1, ?wheel1, ?wheel2) ∧ axle(?axle1) ∧
wheel(?wheel1) ∧ wheel(?wheel2) ∧
attached(?wheel1, ?axle1) ∧ attached(?wheel2, ?axle1) ∧
components(?assem2, ?axle2, ?wheel3, ?wheel4) ∧ axle(?axle2) ∧
wheel(?wheel3) ∧ wheel(?wheel4) ∧ attached(?wheel4, ?axle2) ∧
attached(?wheel4, ?axle2) ∧ balanced(?x, ?assem1,? assem2) → wagon(?x)

the same *subgoal* (actually, unifiable subgoals). However, BAGGER2 does not currently possess all of BAGGER's strengths. For instance, BAGGER2 only applies to tree-structured explanations (see Section 5.3.4), while BAGGER can handle directed acyclic graphs. Among other things, using directed acyclic graphs means that the consequent of one action can support several future actions. Also, BAGGER's *RIS* (rule instantiation sequence) provides a powerful data structure that a sophisticated problem solver can exploit to gain efficiency. Reformulating multiply-recursive rules in BAGGER2 as simple iterative ones by merging recurrences addresses some, but not all, of the advantages of the *RIS*. For example, BAGGER can express inter-step constraints involving, say, the first five steps in a sequence, while BAGGER2 currently cannot. However, without too much additional work, BAGGER2 should be extendible so that it completely subsumes the original BAGGER while still maintaining all of the original method's strengths.

3.4 Summary

Most research in explanation-based learning involves relaxing constraints on the variables in an explanation, rather than generalizing the number of inference rules used. This chapter presents two (closely related) domain-independent approaches to the task of generalizing the structure of explanations.

The fully-implemented BAGGER system analyzes explanation structures (in this case, predicate calculus proofs) and detects repeated, inter-dependent applications of rules. Once a rule on which to focus attention is found, the system determines how an *arbitrary* number of instantiations of this rule can be concatenated together. In a representational shift, it then conceptually merges this indefinite-length collection of rules into the explanation, replacing the specific-length collection of rules, and an extension of a standard explanation-based algorithm produces a new rule from the augmented explanation.

BAGGER uses a data structure called an *RIS* to record the bindings of variables in the learned rule. The *RIS* accommodates an indefinite number of applications of the focus rule. It also stores intermediate results needed when instantiating the new sequential rule.

Rules produced by BAGGER have the important property that their preconditions are expressed in terms of the initial state — they do not depend on the situations produced by intermediate applications of the focus rule. This means that the results of multiple applications of the rule are determined by reasoning only about the current situation. There is no need to apply the focus rule successively, each time checking if the preconditions for the next application are satisfied.

The specific example guides the extension of the focus rule into a structure representing an arbitrary number of repeated applications. Information not contained in the focus rule, but appearing in the example, is often incorporated into the extended rule. In particular, *unwindable* rules provide the guidance as to how preconditions of the *i*th application can be specified in terms of the current state.

BAGGER2 is a successor to BAGGER; it essentially is the result of making the original BAGGER recursive. Unlike its predecessor, BAGGER2 acquires recursive concepts involving arbitrary tree-like applications of rules, can produce multiple generalizations to N from a single example, and is able to integrate the results of multiple examples into a single rule. When learning a recursive rule is not appropriate, this approach produces the same result as Mooney's EGGS algorithm, a standard EBL technique. Applying the rules BAGGER2 learns only requires a minor extension to a PROLOG-like problem solver, namely, the ability to explicitly call a specific rule. This lets the problem solver focus its attention on a small subset of a large rule base.

A final point to notice is that neither BAGGER nor BAGGER2 learn iterative rules of the form:

for i from 1 to N do <something>.

Instead, they essentially learn iterative rules of the form:

repeat <something> until <success>.

They are incapable of determining N before completely instantiating the iterative rule or plan. Rather, N is implicitly determined (e.g., the length of BAGGER's *RIS* equals N). More sophisticated reasoning systems, possibly augmented with additional domain-specific knowledge, may be able to produce rules where the number of iterations can be determined as explicit functions of the current problem state; however this is an area for future research.

4 An Empirical Analysis of Explanation-Based Learning

4.1 Introduction

One may question the desirability of generalizing explanation structures. Such learning leads to more general rules, but because the resulting rules are more complicated, applying them entails more work. Experiments reported in this chapter investigate whether it is better to learn a number-generalized rule or to individually learn the subsumed fixed-number rules as they are needed. A secondary question focuses on whether explanation-based learning is worthwhile at all. As more is learned, the process might slow down a problem solver that uses the learned concepts [Fikes72, Markovitch89, Minton88b, Mooney89a]. This chapter presents an empirical study of the performance of the BAGGER system. It is compared to an implementation of a standard explanation-based generalization algorithm and to a problem-solving system that performs no learning. The results demonstrate the efficacy of generalizing to N in particular, and of explanation-based learning in general.

Two different training strategies are analyzed, along with several variants of the basic experiments. The two basic experiments compare systems that learn from their own problem solving to systems that learn by observing the actions of external agents. The external agent merely solves problems, there need not be any thought given to properly ordering the examples to facilitate learning. Hence, in this mode the learning systems can be viewed as *learning apprentices* [Mitchell85, (also see Section 1.3.3)], analyzing the normal actions of their users in order to absorb new knowledge. The experimental results indicate that substantially better performance can be achieved by observing the behavior of external agents. As will be seen, this occurs because the time spent internally solving complicated problems from first principles can dissipate much of the savings made by learning.

4.2 Experimental Methodology

Experiments are run using the blocks-world inference rules appearing in Appendix C. The problem generator creates an initial situation by generating ten blocks, each with a randomly-chosen width and height. One at a time, it drops them from an arbitrary horizontal position over a table; if one falls in an unstable location, it picks up the block and re-releases it over a new location. Once it places the ten blocks[1], it randomly selects a goal height, centered above a second table. The target tower height is chosen by adding from one to four average block heights. In addition, the goal specifies a maximum height of towers. The

---

[1] After the ten blocks are dropped to construct an initial situation, the database of assertions describing the initial state is constructed. The entries in this database are randomly ordered before each experiment begins.

difference between the minimum and maximum acceptable tower heights is equal to the maximum possible height of a block. The reason for this upper bound is explained later. A sample problem situation appears in Figure 4.1. Some experiments involving the acquisition of plans for clearing objects are also described in this chapter. In these experiments the scene is set up the same as done for tower-building, then some block that is not clear is randomly chosen as the one to be cleared.

Once the generator constructs a scene, three different problem solvers attempt to satisfy the goal. The first is called NO-LEARN, as it acquires no new rules during problem solving. The second, called STD-EBL, is an implementation of EGGS [Mooney86]. BAGGER is the third system.

All three systems use a backward-chaining problem solver (basically a COMMON LISP implementation of PROLOG [Clocksin84]) to satisfy the preconditions of rules. The problem solver is extended to handle BAGGER's rules, as previously described in Section 3.2.2. When the two learning systems attack a new problem, they first try to apply the rules they have acquired, possibly also using existing intrasituational rules. No intersituational rules are used in combination with acquired rules, in order to limit searching, which would quickly become intractable [Mooney89a]. Hence, to be successful, an acquired rule must directly lead to a solution without using other intersituational rules.

The problem solver used is rather simplistic. A more sophisticated one could take advantage of sophisticated matching algorithms (such as RETE [Forgy82]), complicated conflict resolution strategies, meta-level control strategies, etc. However using these enhancements would require that more parameters be set for the experiments and that the experiments also evaluate the enhancements. Fortunately, the same problem-solving strategy is used by all three systems, so that improved problem solving would help each of them. However, the amount each would be helped by improvements may differ. Investigating the overall impact of problem-solving enhancements is an area for future research. However, it is important not to overlook the possibility that the gains from learning reduce the need to have a complicated problem solver.

STD-EBL, during generalization, prunes explanation structures at terms that are either situation-independent or describe the initial state. It groups antecedents of new rules so that terms involving the same variables are located near each other, using the algorithm described for BAGGER in Section 3.2.3. A sample rule STD-EBL acquires appears in Appendix B.2.1.

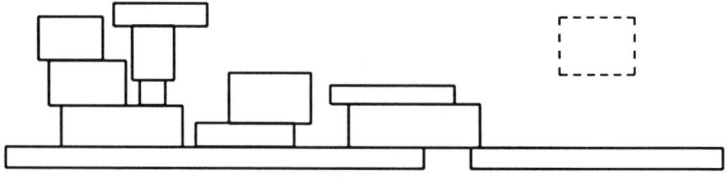

Figure 4.1   A Sample Problem for BAGGER

This chapter's experiments consider two different strategies for training the learning systems. In the first, called *autonomous mode*, the two learning systems resort to solving a problem from "first principles" when none of their acquired rules can solve it.[2] This means that the original intersituational rules can be used, but learned rules are not used. When they construct the proof of the solution to a problem in this manner, the learners apply their generalization algorithm and store any general rule that is produced. In the other strategy, called *training mode*, some number of solved problems (the *training set*) are initially presented to the systems, and the rules acquired from generalizing these solutions are applied to additional problems (the *test set*). Under this second strategy, if none of a system's acquired rules solves the problem at hand, the system is considered to have failed. No problem solving from first principles is ever performed by the learning systems in this mode. Later, this chapter discusses hybrids between these two approaches.

The two learners always generalize the expert's solutions in the training mode, even if a previously acquired rule suffices to solve the current problem. (If the resulting rule is the same as a previous one, it is discarded.) Although an existing rule may solve the current problem, the expert may be presenting an approach that works in a wider range of future problems.

Problem solving in the two modes is illustrated by Figures 4.2 and 4.3, respectively. Notice that the acquired rules are not used when constructing new explanations. Partly this is a limitation due to computational resource restrictions, as explained in the next paragraph. However, it is also in the spirit of schema-based problem solving, where the idea is to rapidly select and apply schemata, rather than spending large amounts of time connecting together many disjoint pieces of knowledge. While it might be reasonable to consider combining a handful of schemata (rules), unrestricted combination can be too computationally expensive. These experiments follow the limiting case of only allowing one rule to be applied.

Unfortunately, constructing towers containing more than two blocks from first principles exceeds the limits of the computers used in the experiments. For this reason, the performance of the NO-LEARN system is estimated by fitting an exponential curve to the data obtained from constructing towers of size one and two. This curve is used by all three systems to estimate the time needed to construct towers from first principles when required, and a specialized procedure is used to generate a solution. The estimated performance curve and the specialized algorithm are presented in Section 4.3.7.

Data collection in these experiments is accomplished as follows. Initially, the two learning systems possess no acquired rules. They are then exposed to a number of sample situations, building up their rule collections according to the learning strategy applied. (At each point, all three systems address the same randomly-generated problem. For each problem, the order the three problem solvers address it is randomly chosen, to eliminate ordering effects.) Statistics are collected as the systems solve problems and learn. This continues for a fixed number of problems, constituting an experimental run. However, a

---

[2] "First principles" problem solving is the only kind NO-LEARN performs.

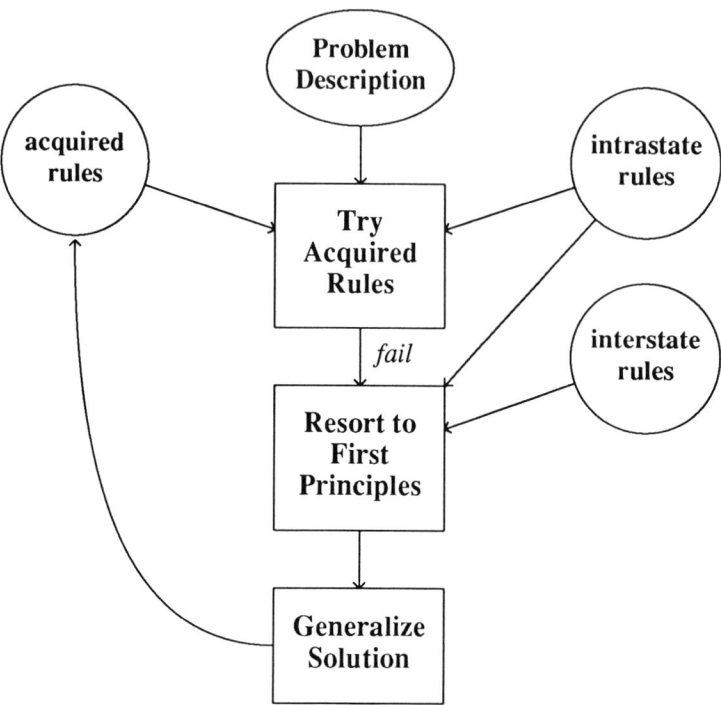

Figure 4.2   Problem Solving in the Autonomous Mode

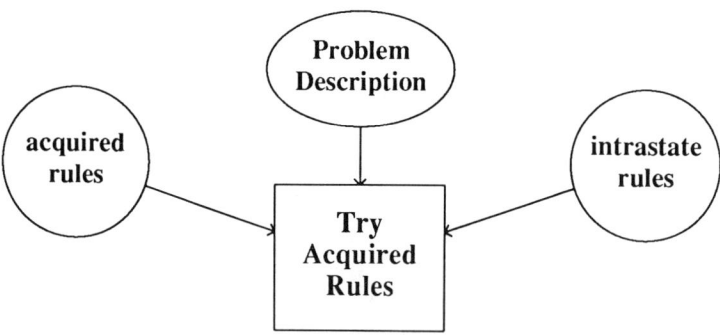

Figure 4.3   Problem Solving in the Training Mode

single run can be greatly effected by the ordering of the sample problems. To provide better estimates of performance, multiple experimental runs are performed. At the start of each run, the rules acquired in the previous run are discarded. When completed, the results of all the runs are averaged together. The curves presented in this chapter are the result of averaging 25 experimental runs.

Each learning system stores its acquired rules in a linear list. During problem solving, they try their rules in order, using the first successful one. When a rule is successful, it is moved to the front of the list. This way, less useful rules will migrate toward the back of the list. Testing indicated this dynamic reordering can substantially improve performance, as further discussed in Section 4.3.6.

The reordering strategy is the reason that, in the goal, tower heights are limited. The STD-EBL system would sooner or later encounter a goal requiring four blocks, and a rule for this would migrate to the front of its rule list. From that time on, regardless of the goal height, it would construct a four-block tower. With a limit on tower heights, the rules for more efficiently building towers of lower heights have an opportunity to be tried. This issue would be exacerbated if the goal was not limited to small towers due to simulation time restrictions.

These experiments, except those described in Section 4.3.8, were run at the University of Illinois on six identically configured Xerox Dandelion 1108's. Each machine had 3.5 megabytes of memory and ran the Kyoto release of INTERLISP. Section 4.3.8's experiments were run at the University of Wisconsin in Lucid COMMON LISP on a Sun 4/110 with 8 megabytes of memory. Random numbers for the experiments were generated using the algorithm *RAN2* described on page 197 of [Press86]. The built-in LISP function for random numbers was used to generate the seed. Timing on the Dandelions was performed using the INTERLISP function *(CLOCK 2)*, which does not include garbage collection time. For efficiency reasons, the backward-chaining problem solver uses streams and generators [Charniak80].

Block dimensions are generated using a uniform probability distribution; the average block width is 75, while the average height is 35. The location at which blocks are dropped is uniformly distributed over a table 450 units wide. A decaying exponential distribution is used to generate tower heights. Scaling is such that the likelihood of a one-block tower is about twice that of a four-block tower.

Unfortunately these experiments measure some quantities that grow exponentially with problem size, which leads to large variances in the results. These large variances should be taken into consideration when interpreting the results presented in this chapter. Appendix D presents tables containing the numbers, along with their standard deviations, used to plot most of the curves and histograms appearing in this chapter.

4.3   Experiments

4.3.1   Comparison of the Two Training Strategies

The first experiment presents the performance of the three systems in the two basic modes of operation — autonomous and training. The autonomous mode is considered first. In this mode, whenever a system's current collection of acquired rules fails to solve a problem, it constructs and generalizes a solution from first principles.

Figure 4.4 shows the probability that the learning systems will need to resort to first principles as a function of the number of sample problems experienced. As more problems are experienced, this probability decreases. (On the first problem the probability is always 1.) BAGGER is less likely to need to resort to first principles than is STD-EBL because, as a result of generalizing explanation structure, BAGGER produces a more general plan by analyzing the solution to the first problem.

On average, BAGGER learns 1.7 rules in each experimental run, while STD-EBL learns 4.3 rules. It takes BAGGER about 50 seconds and STD-EBL about 45 seconds to generalize a specific problem's solution. Averaging over problems 26–50 in each run (to estimate the asymptotic behavior), produces a mean solution time of 3720 seconds for BAGGER, 8100 seconds for STD-EBL, and 79,300 seconds for NO-LEARN. For BAGGER, this is a speedup of 2.2 over STD-EBL and 21.3 over NO-LEARN, where speedup is defined as follows:

$$speedup\ of\ A\ over\ B\ =\ \frac{mean\ solution\ time\ for\ B}{mean\ solution\ time\ for\ A}$$

Figure 4.5 presents the performance during a single experimental run of the two learning systems in the autonomous mode. The average time to solve a problem is plotted, on a logarithmic scale, against the number of sample problems experienced. Notice that the time taken to produce a solution from first principles dominates the time taken to apply the acquired rules, accounting for the peaks in the curves. One of the reasons BAGGER performs better than STD-EBL is that it needs to resort to first principles less frequently.

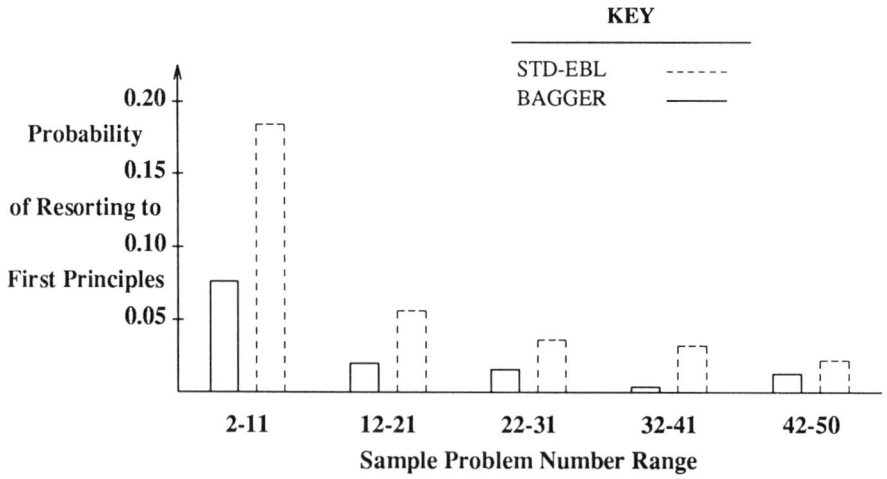

Figure 4.4   Probability of Resorting to First Principles in Autonomous Mode

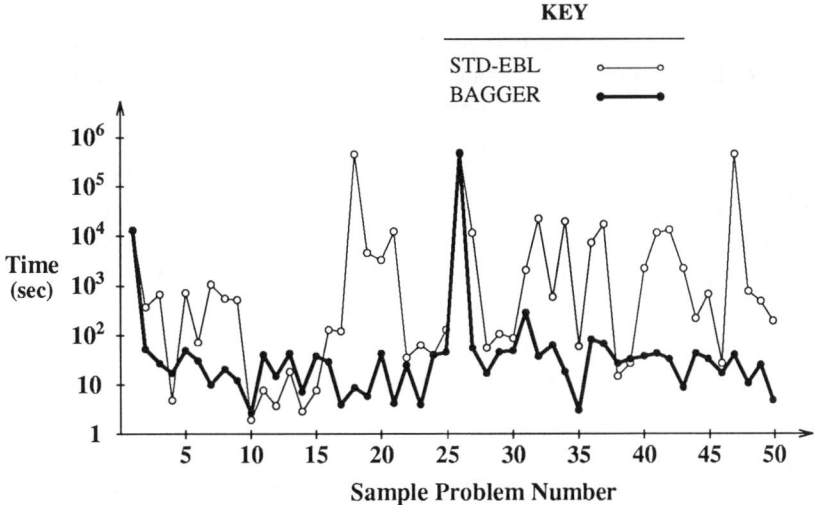

Figure 4.5   Performance Comparison of the Autonomous Problem Solvers
(on a single experimental run)

Because the cost of solving a big problem from first principles greatly dominates the cost of applying acquired rules, the autonomous mode may not be an acceptable strategy. Although learning in this mode means many problems will be solved quicker than without learning, the time occasionally taken to construct a solution when a system's acquired rules fail can dominate the gains made by learning. The peaks in the right-side of Figure 4.5 illustrate this. A system may be working nicely, using its learned composite rules to produce solutions in minutes, then all of a sudden spend days producing one novel solution. A long period may be required before a learning system acquires enough rules to cover all future problem-solving episodes without resorting to first principles.

The second learning mode provides an alternative. If an expert is available to provide solutions to sample problems and an occasional failure to solve a problem is acceptable, this mode is attractive. Here, a number of sample solutions are provided and the learning systems generalize these solutions, discarding new rules that are variants of others already acquired. After training, the systems use their acquired rules to solve new problems. Because of its high cost, they never perform problem solving from first principles. Occasional failure to solve a problem is assumed to be more acceptable than long times spent solving from first principles. This methodology means that BAGGER and STD-EBL are compared independent of the issue of how much time each spends reasoning from first principles; only the amount of search among their acquired rules is considered.

The performance results in the training mode appear in Figure 4.6. After ten training problems, the systems solve 20 additional problems. In these 20 test problems, the two learning systems never resort to using first principles. BAGGER takes, on average, 36.6 seconds on the test problems (versus 3720 seconds in the autonomous mode), STD-EBL requires an average of 827 seconds (versus 8100 seconds), and NO-LEARN averages 68,400 seconds (versus 79,300 seconds — a difference due to statistical fluctuations).

The substantial savings for the two learning systems (99% for BAGGER and 90% for STD-EBL) are due to the fact that in this mode these systems spend no time generating solutions from first principles. In this experiment, BAGGER has a speedup of 22.6 over STD-EBL (versus 2.2 in the other experiment) and 1870 over NO-LEARN (versus 23).

One of the costs of using the training mode is that occasionally the learning systems will not be able to solve a problem. Figure 4.7 plots the number of failures as a function of the size of the training set. In each experimental run used to construct this figure, 20 test problems are solved after the training examples are presented. With ten training solutions, both of the systems solve over 98.5% of the test problems.

The next figure in this section, Figure 4.8, summarizes the performance of the three systems in the two training modes; note that a logarithmic scale is used. This figure illustrates the value of generalizing explanation structures and demonstrates the value of having an external agent present EBL systems with sample solutions.

The two modes of operation investigated — autonomous and training — are at opposite ends of a spectrum. In one, the learning systems are completely independent of external guidance. In this mode, learning occurs whenever none of the acquired rules suffice to solve the current problem, while in the other all of the learning occurs during an initial training phase, where sample solutions are provided by an external agent. The cost of producing explanations from first principles in the autonomous mode can be prohibitive. Conversely, the training set of problems may not be fully representative of future problems, which means

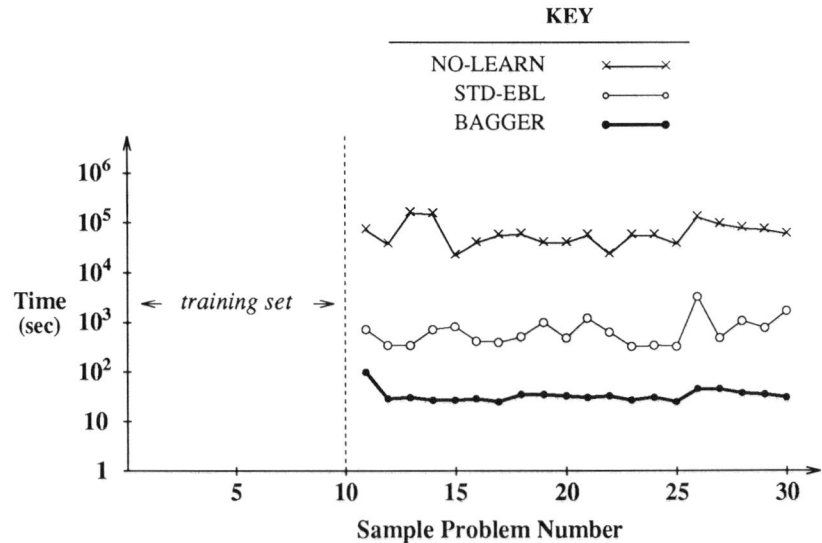

Figure 4.6   Performance Comparison of the Trained Problem Solvers

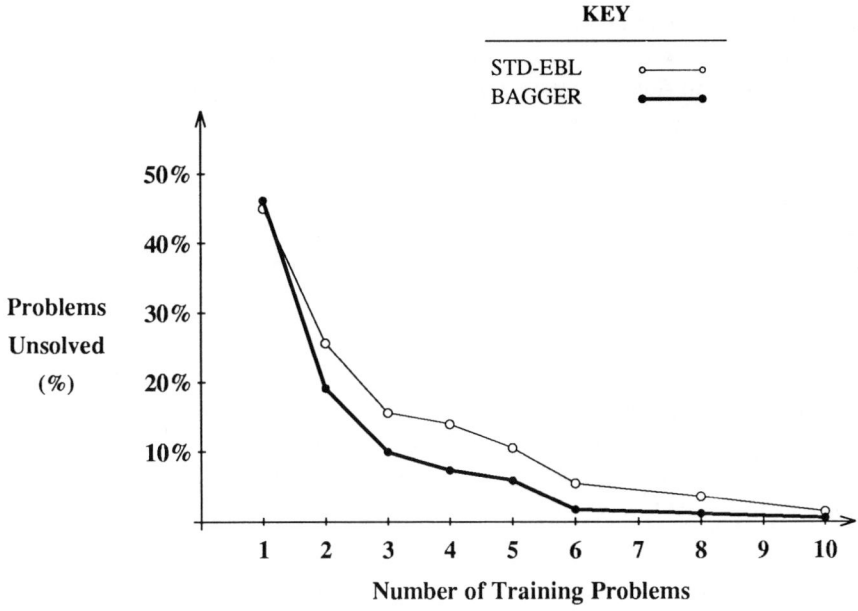

Figure 4.7   Failure Comparison of the Trained Problem Solvers

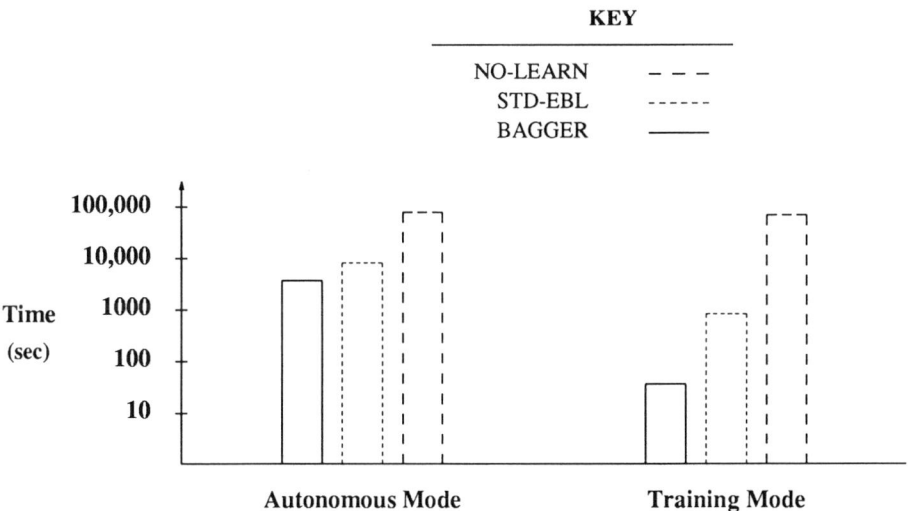

Figure 4.8   Performance Summary of the Three Systems in the Two Modes

that some future problems may not be soluble.

The remainder of this section considers some ways of combining the strengths of the two approaches. The results are especially relevant to the design of learning systems that dynamically acquire new rules by observing expert behavior. Consider the following two ways to utilize external expertise which are alternatives to the training mode.

(1) The expert can be continually on call. When one of the learning systems cannot solve a problem using its collection of acquired rules, the expert produces a solution. The learner then explains this solution and adds any new rule that results to its collection of acquired rules. As it learns more rules, the mean time between its requests for the expert will increase.

(2) Again an expert is always available, except here he or she is not called until a time threshold is exceeded by one of the three systems. Time can be spent both checking acquired rules and building solutions from first principles. With this method, the systems can solve relatively simple problems from first principles, thereby decreasing the load on the expert, especially during the early stages of learning. However if the threshold is set too low, the expert will be unnecessarily called on problems that are soluble by the acquired rules.

These techniques mitigate the expense of solving from first principles. If the failure to solve a problem is unacceptable, combinations of the above techniques with the training mode are also possible. For example, the expert can provide solutions to an initial set of problems, then provide additional solutions during the test phase whenever the rules learned during the training phase prove insufficient.

Table 4.1 Comparison of Operation Modes			
Mode of Operation	NO-LEARN	STD-EBL	BAGGER
Autonomous	2,140	219	101
Autonomous (external solutions provided after 10,000 sec)		35	4
Autonomous (external solutions provided if all acquired rules fail)		40	1
Trained	1,870	23	1

Table 4.1 compares the results of these approaches with the standard autonomous and training modes. All of the times are normalized to that for BAGGER in the training mode. The averages under the autonomous mode are for problems 26–50. An interesting point is that the two hybrid approaches perform about equally well for STD-EBL. This occurs because it is possible for STD-EBL to spend more than 10,000 seconds checking its acquired rules. These results indicate that these hybrid approaches significantly exceed the performance of the fully autonomous approach, while still guaranteeing solutions to all problems. The cost, however, is that an expert must be available at any time, although as time progresses he or she should be needed less frequently.

4.3.2 Effect of Increased Problem Complexity

The results in the previous section describe the behavior of the three systems for a class of problems, namely, the construction of towers containing from one to four blocks. An interesting question is how the relative performance of the three systems depends on the variability of the problems addressed. The ability to scale well is an important trait of any learning system. This section investigates performance as a function of problem complexity. Experiments are run on successively more complicated problem spaces, where complexity is varied by increasing the range of possible goal heights. The problem generator selects goal heights by randomly summing the average height of one to N blocks. The computational resources available restrict the maximum N to be five. Since in each case the lower bound on possible tower heights is one block, successive problem spaces subsume earlier ones.

The figures in this section show how the performance of the three problem solvers depends on the magnitude of the range of possible goal heights. Figure 4.9 plots mean solution time, under both training modes, as a function of problem complexity. Since BAGGER learns no rules when the goal only involves moving one block, points are not plotted for the case when the maximum number of blocks in a tower is one. In all cases, the learning systems outperform the problem solver that does not learn. There is no evidence that, on average, learning degrades performance.

Table 4.2 reports the various speedups produced by comparing the problem solvers for this collection of experimental runs. This data demonstrates that the performance difference among the various system configurations generally widens as the complexity of the problem space increases. The trend is not monotonic in the autonomous mode, possibly due to the disproportionate effect of the infrequent need to construct a solution from first principles. Since resorting to first principles occurs infrequently, statistical fluctuations strongly effect the speedup ratios. The advantage of the training mode over the autonomous mode becomes more pronounced as problem complexity increases because, as larger towers are called for, the cost of building a solution from first principles becomes more dominant.

The experiments reported in this section demonstrates that the gains of explanation-based learning increase as the range of potential problems increases. They provide no evidence for the conjecture that learning can impede overall problem-solving performance. Rather, they indicate that as the range of problems increases, learning is increasingly beneficial. In addition, the relative performance of BAGGER over STD-EBL grows as this range increases.

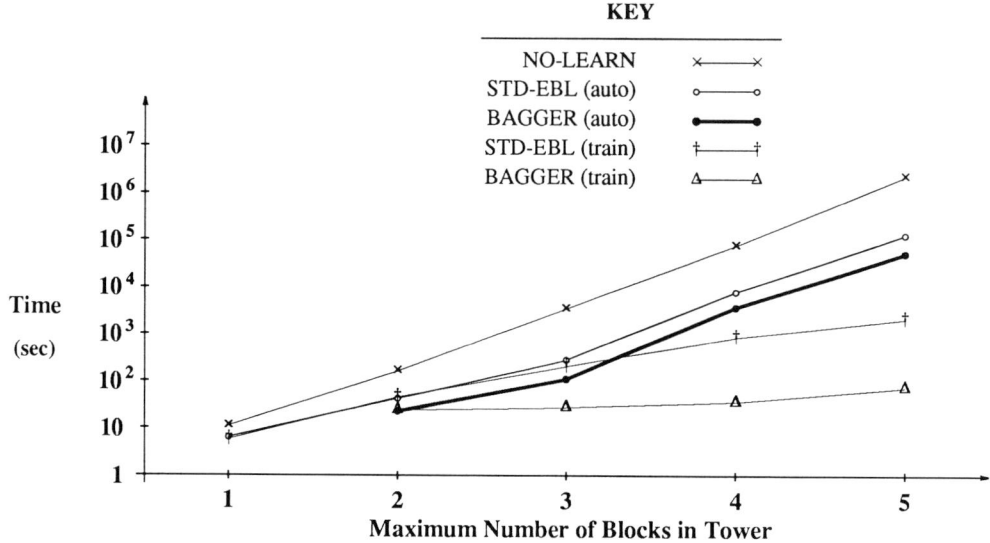

Figure 4.9 Mean Solution Time as a Function of Problem Complexity

Table 4.2 Speedup as a Function of Problem Complexity			
Tower Size Range	*BAGGER over STD-EBL*	*BAGGER over NO-LEARN*	*STD-EBL over NO-LEARN*
autonomous mode			
1-1	–	–	1.73
1-2	1.81	7.01	3.87
1-3	2.75	30.20	11.00
1-4	2.18	21.30	9.79
1-5	2.25	39.00	17.30
training mode			
1-1	–	–	1.97
1-2	1.92	6.35	3.32
1-3	6.69	110.00	16.40
1-4	22.60	1,870.00	82.60
1-5	27.10	24,100.00	889.00

128

Finally, these experiments strengthen the argument that the training mode is preferable to the autonomous mode of operation.

4.3.3 Operationality versus Generality

As discussed in the introduction, the relationship between the operationality and generality of learned rules is an important issue in explanation-based learning. One way of increasing the generality of an explanation is to prune away some of the nodes. However this decreases operationality because now a problem solver must expend effort satisfying the new, non-operational leaf nodes. In this chapter's experiments, the default is to prune away intrasituational inference rules. It is assumed that intrasituational reasoning is operational, while intersituational is not. This section's experiment investigates the effect on both BAGGER and STD-EBL of not pruning nodes. A sample operational rule is presented in Appendix B.2.2.

Performance in the autonomous mode with and without pruning appears in Figures 4.10 and 4.11. When constructing more operational rules, the learning systems more frequently resort to solving problems from first principles. This occurs because the more operational rules, being less general, are more likely to fail.

Table 4.3 summarizes the major differences between the operational and general versions. Results from the two cases are presented for various statistics, along with the ratio of the two results. The results indicate that, although more rules are learned and used in the more operational version, the fact that they are evaluated faster leads to quicker overall solutions. The one exception to this is BAGGER in autonomous mode. Here the need for more solutions from first principles eliminates the gain from the more rapid evaluation of the operational rules.

The average number of rules tried when solving a problem is inversely proportional to the probability of a successful rule application. This probability is defined by:

$$Probability\ (success) = \frac{\sum\limits_{rules} successful\ applications}{\sum\limits_{rules} attempted\ applications}$$

The data in the table shows that, as expected, more rules are evaluated on average when solving problems with the operational rules.

The final point in this section is that, in training mode, the probability that the test problem is not solved (i.e., the failure rate) is higher in the operational version. This occurs because more operational rules are needed to cover the same number of future problems. Thus, for the operational version to be attractive, the training set must contain a highly representative sample of future problems.

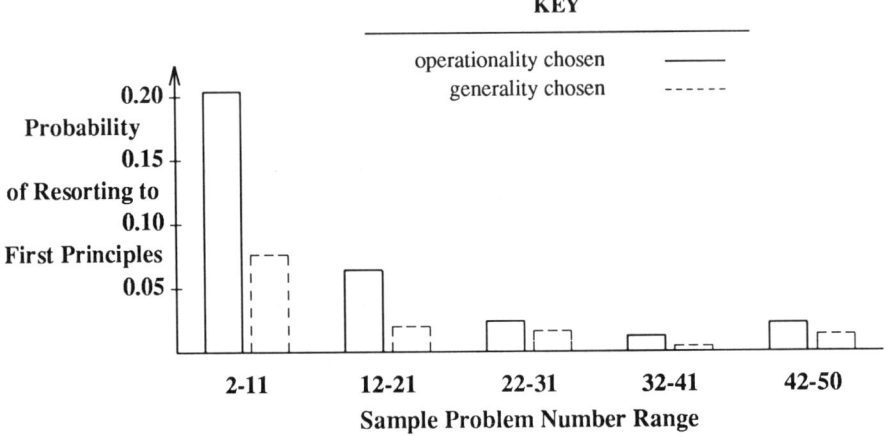

Figure 4.10   Operationality Results in Autonomous Mode for BAGGER

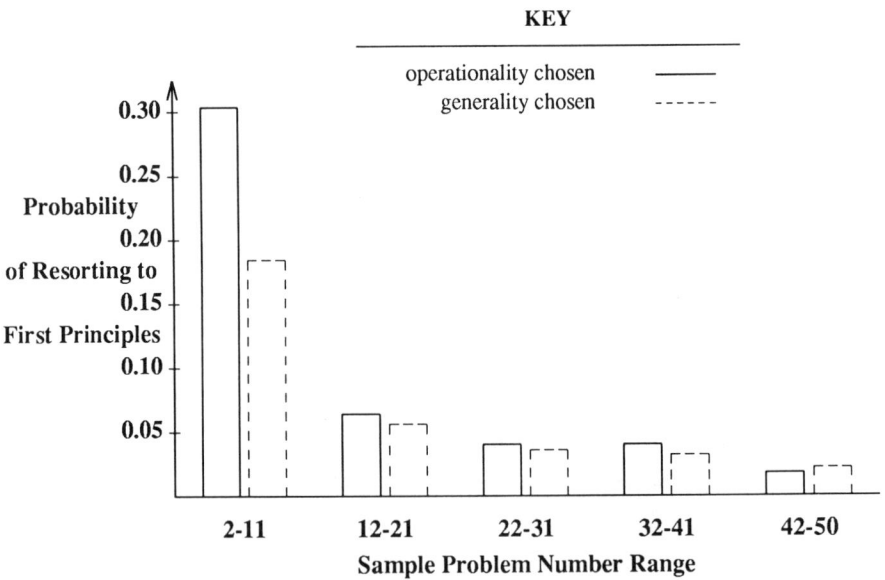

Figure 4.11   Operationality Results in Autonomous Mode for Standard EBL

Table 4.3. Operationality vs. Generality Results

Description	Operationality Chosen	Generality Chosen	Ratio (Op/Gen)
Mean Solution Time			
autonomous mode			
STD-EBL	6790 sec	8100	0.83
BAGGER	6660	3720	1.79
training mode			
STD-EBL	155(174)	779(828)	0.20
BAGGER	27(29)	36(37)	0.75
Rules Learned			
autonomous mode			
STD-EBL	5.52	4.28	1.29
BAGGER	2.60	1.72	1.51
training mode			
STD-EBL	6.88	5.96	1.15
BAGGER	3.24	2.01	1.61
Probability of Successful Application			
autonomous mode			
STD-EBL	0.50	0.56	0.89
BAGGER	0.90	0.99	0.91
training mode			
STD-EBL	0.41	0.59	0.69
BAGGER	0.79	0.99	0.79
Percentage Solved			
training mode			
STD-EBL	91.4%	98.5	0.93
BAGGER	94.0	99.4	0.95

Numbers in parentheses indicate mean solution time for *all* problems, including problems *not* solved.

4.3.4 Time Spent Learning

This section reports how much time is spent within the generalization algorithms. The time required to generalize an explanation is reported as a function of the size of the explanation.

The time spent learning in the training mode can be divided into three components.

$$
\begin{aligned}
\textit{total time spent learning} \quad = \quad &\textit{time to build explanation from user's actions} \;\; + \\
&\textit{time to generalize explanation} \;\; + \\
&\textit{time to reorganize and save new rule}
\end{aligned}
$$

The learning time curves in Figure 4.12 reflect this decomposition. The time to reorganize and save a new rule includes looking to see if it is a variant of an old rule. In the training mode, the externally-provided solutions only indicate which blocks are moved and where they are placed. The systems must validate these steps and ascertain whether or not they achieve the desired goal. Notice that the BAGGER generalization algorithm is only slightly slower than the EGGS algorithm.

This curve also provides further support for the value of learning by observing an external agent. A theoretical analysis of the problem-solving speedup that can be achieved by providing steps within a proof appears in [Mooney89c]. His results indicate an exponential speedup is possible (although problem solving is still exponential). Comparing Figure 4.12's times for explaining expert solutions to the estimated performance of NO-LEARN (Section 4.3.7) produces a speedup of 19^{N-1}, where N is the number of blocks moved.

4.3.5 Clearing Blocks

This experiment investigates the performance of the three systems on a different task. In this case, initial situations are constructed in the same manner as for tower-building, but the goal this time specifies a block to be cleared. After the ten blocks are randomly dropped, one of the covered blocks is randomly chosen as the goal block to be cleared. To keep the two experiments comparable, if the goal block supports, directly or indirectly, more than four other blocks the problem generator chooses a new goal block.

Table 4.4 presents a comparison of the three problem solvers on the two types of problems. The learning systems outperform NO-LEARN by 4-5 orders of magnitude, several orders of magnitude better than in the tower-building experiments. One interpretation of this is that clearing is a much more "local" operation than is tower building. Clearing a block involves moving nearby blocks, blocks coupled to the goal block by relations such as *On* and *Supports*. However, when building a tower, blocks located anywhere in a scene can be used.

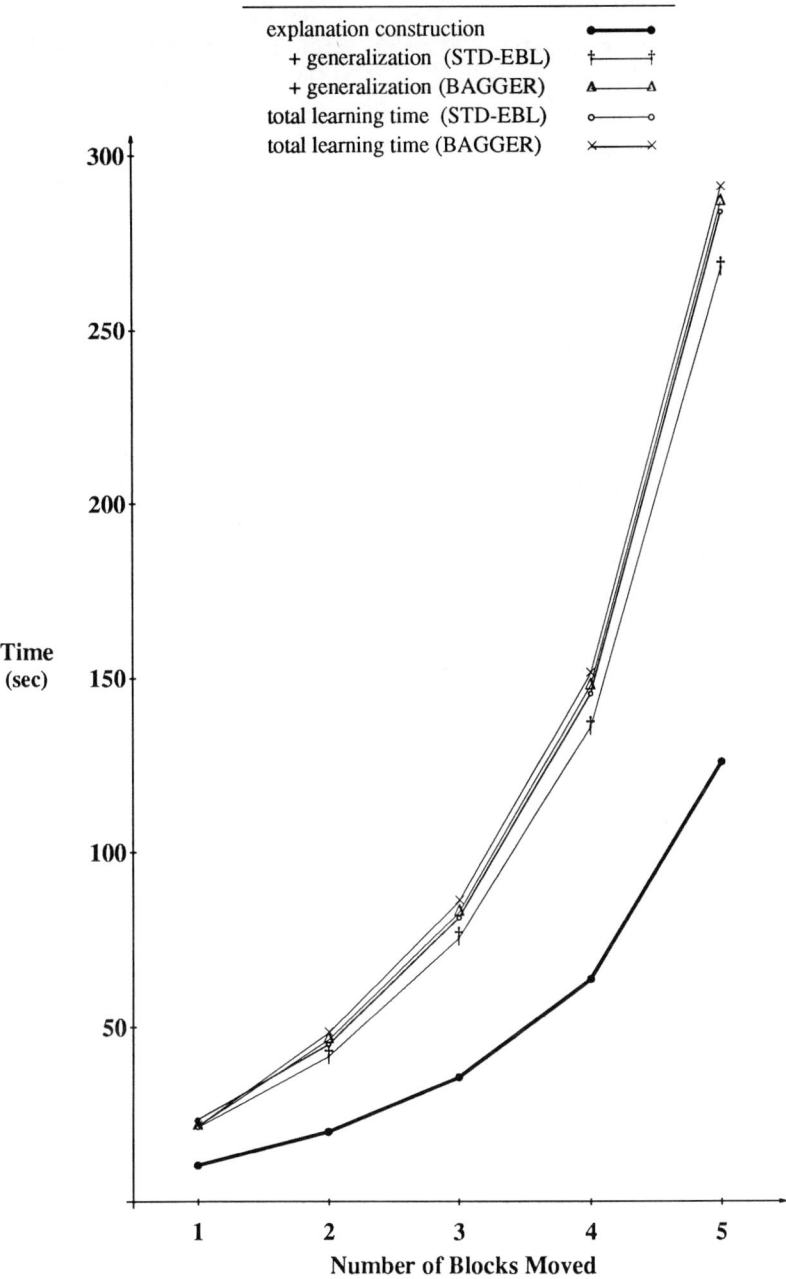

Figure 4.12   Time Spent Learning as a Function of Blocks Stacked

In general there is less to constrain the choice of a block to move when building a tower.[3] For these reasons, the advantages of explanation-based learning, which collects the essential constraints in an example, become more pronounced in the clearing task.

The speedup of BAGGER over STD-EBL is about one-fifth for clearing as it is for building towers. This may be due to the fact that, on average, less blocks are moved in the clearing problems. As reported in Section 4.3.2, the speedup of BAGGER over STD-EBL increases as the complexity of the problem space increases.

Table 4.4 also contains the results from an experiment that generates *both* clearing and tower-building goals. The type of goal is chosen randomly and the training set contains twenty problems, rather than the usual ten, so that on average ten of each type are experienced. The results are largely the average of those from the two types of experiments, except that more rules are learned and the probability of a successful rule application is decreased. The extra rules do not significantly hinder the problem solvers because the consequents of the two rule types are different enough that a rule for the wrong goal can be quickly disregarded.

These experiments involving clearing provide further support for the claims that explanation-based learning is beneficial and that BAGGER outperforms STD-EBL.

4.3.6 Rule Access Strategies

The vast majority of machine learning research has focussed on how a new concept can be learned. The question of how acquired concepts should be organized (and possibly later reorganized) has been largely neglected. However, the order acquired concepts are accessed can greatly affect problem-solving performance. The issue of organizing learned concepts will become a central one when machine learning systems begin to learn large numbers of concepts. This section investigates eight strategies for organizing newly-acquired concepts and reports empirical studies of their performance. Some of the strategies only address where a newly-acquired concept should be placed in relation to previously-acquired ones, while others also involve dynamically reorganizing acquired concepts as problem-solving experience is accumulated. Hence, the strategies in the second category address another aspect of machine learning — learning how to better organize a collection of acquired concepts. These strategies that involve dynamic reordering of rules are also relevant to non-learning systems in which all rules are externally produced.

This experiment investigates a question of combining learning and problem solving, rather than one of learning alone. The question is "how should the results of learning best be organized to increase the efficiency of future problem solving?" The strategies investigated have no effect on the number of concepts learned[4], nor on the probability of a successful solution. All that differs is the organization of the acquired concepts. Whenever necessary,

---

[3] This would be less true if the acquired rules were complicated enough to explicitly represent how much of the tower height remained after each move.

Table 4.4 Comparison of Tower Building and Clearing in Training Mode

Description	NO-LEARN	STD-EBL	BAGGER
Mean Solution Time			
Clearing	4,200,000 *sec*	58(86)	15(20)
Tower-Building	68,400	779(828)	36(37)
Both	1,790,000	601(607)	31(33)
Speed-Up Over			
NO-LEARN			
Clearing	–	72,400	280,000
Tower-Building	–	88	1,900
Both	–	2,980	57,700
Percentage Solved			
Clearing	100.0%	84.6	85.2
Tower-Building	100.0	98.5	99.4
Both	100.0	93.4	94.8
Rules Learned			
Clearing	0.00	3.96	1.36
Tower-Building	0.00	5.96	2.00
Both	0.00	9.09	3.59
Probability of			
Successful Application			
Clearing	–	0.37	0.81
Tower-Building	–	0.59	0.99
Both	–	0.25	0.60

Numbers in parentheses indicate mean solution time for *all* problems, including problems *not* solved.

the problem solver will try all of them.

The eight proposed strategies for accessing acquired rules are described below and are presented roughly in order of complexity. These access strategies can be divided into two qualitative groups. The first four strategies are independent of problem-solving performance. With these, the problem solver need not maintain statistics about rules. The second four strategies dynamically depend on the examples in the test set. That is, the results of problem solving continually effect the order in which rules are accessed.

In all eight of the strategies, acquired rules are organized in a linear list. During problem solving, the rules are tried in order. After describing the eight strategies for determining the

---

[4] If learned rules were used to learn additional new rules, the strategy chosen could affect what is learned.

organization and reorganization of rules, their performance is compared. Data structures more complicated than linear lists, such as discrimination networks [Charniak80], can also improve problem-solving performance. However, all of the rules acquired in the experiments satisfy the same goal, namely, the construction of a tower. Since they all contain the same predicates in their consequent, it is reasonable to assume that they are all grouped at the same node in a discrimination net. Hence, the results of these experiments are relevant to more complicated data structures, and even to parallel architectures, provided at some point a group of candidates are serially visited.

Strategy Descriptions

Most Recently Learned (MRL)

The first strategy is to access rules in *reverse* order from the order they are learned. This is easily implemented by pushing, during the training phase, new rules onto the front of the list of acquired rules. Unless otherwise stated, the other strategies use this method to initially insert new rules into the list of previously acquired rules during the training phase.

Least Recently Learned (LRL)

The second strategy is to access rules in the same order as they are learned. This is implemented by placing new rules at the *end* of the list of acquired rules.

Sorted by Situations Traversed (SORT)

This strategy applies when using situation calculus and is only relevant to rules learned by standard explanation-based learning (i.e., non number-generalized rules). By looking at the consequent of a new rule, the number of situations traversed by applying the rule can be determined. Once the training phase completes, the rules are sorted so that those that traverse the fewest number of states are in the front of the list of acquired rules. This list is not altered during the test phase. (This strategy shares many of the characteristics of iterative-deepening [Korf85].)

Randomly Selected (RAND)

This strategy is to access rules in a random order. This is implemented by randomizing the list of acquired rules before *each* test problem, then trying to apply them in their randomized order.

Most Recently Used (MRU)

In the *MRU* strategy, the order that rules are accessed depends on the last time they were successfully applied. This is implemented by moving a rule to the front of the list of rules whenever it is successfully applied. The hypothesis of this strategy is that the more useful a rule is, the more likely it will be tried earlier.

This and the next three strategies can be viewed as if each rule is somehow scored and these scores are used to sort the rules so that highest scoring rules are at the front of the list. The implementations of the following three strategies use such a sorting strategy, although, as described in the above paragraph, *MRU* does not. For *MRU*, no statistics need be associated with each rule. The expression used by each strategy to predict a rule's future value is listed after each strategy is described.

$$Value_{MRU} = time\ of\ last\ successful\ application$$

Most Frequently Used (MFU)

In this strategy, the order that rules are accessed depends on how often they have been successfully applied. Unlike *MRU*, this strategy, as do the following two, requires additional information be recorded. In this case, each rule records the number of time it is used to solve a problem. *MFU* is implemented by sorting, after each successful solution, the list of acquired rules so that the one with the highest number of successful applications is tried first.

$$Value_{MFU} = number\ of\ successful\ applications$$

Most Successfully Used (MSU)

This strategy orders rules according to the *a posteriori* probability they are useful. This probability is calculated by dividing the number of successful applications of the rule by the number of times the rule is tried. Rules not yet tried are ordered after rules successfully applied and before rules tried without success. This strategy requires two statistics be kept for each rule.

$$Value_{MSU} = \frac{number\ of\ successful\ applications}{number\ of\ attempts\ to\ apply\ rule}$$

Most Efficiently Used (MEU)

This strategy involves another way to get previously useful rules near the front of the list of acquired rules. Here the measure of a rule is determined by recording the total amount of time spent trying to satisfy the rule's preconditions and then dividing this time by the number of successful applications of the rule. This measures the time spent per successful application, and the lower this number the more promising the rule. Hence, this measurement is inversely proportional to the value of the rule. Rules not yet tried are ordered as in *MSU*. Again, two statistics must be kept.

$$Value^{-1}_{MEU} = \frac{total\ time\ spent\ trying\ this\ rule}{number\ of\ successful\ applications}$$

Results

Figure 4.13 presents the performance of each strategy for accessing rules on 20 randomly generated test problems. In each run, there are 10 randomly generated training problems. In this figure, the strategies are presented so that the most efficient one (for STD-EBL) is on the left and the least efficient one is on the right. There is about an 8-fold difference between the best and the worst. The speedup of BAGGER over STD-EBL ranges from 5 to 40.

To give a better perspective on the results in Figure 4.13, in the next histogram (Figure 4.14), the performances of the strategies are compared with respect to the performance of *MFU*. (The strategy involving sorting rules by the number of situations traversed — *SORT* — is not included in this figure because it is not relevant for BAGGER.)

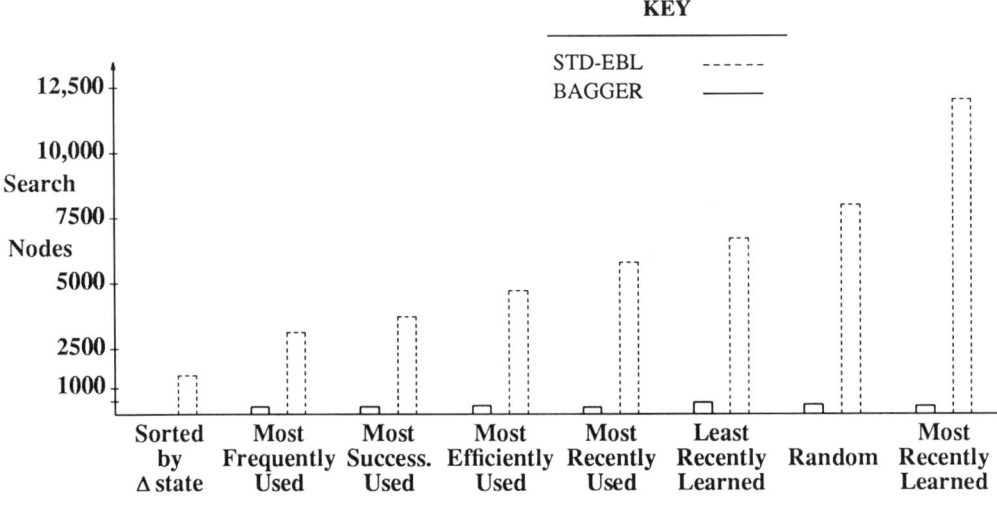

Figure 4.13   Performance of the Access Strategies

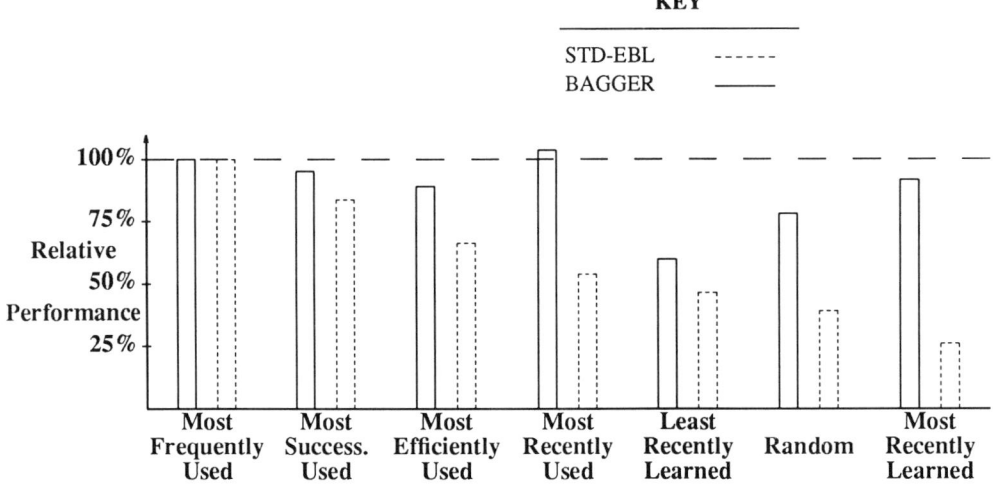

Figure 4.14   Performance of the Access Strategies Normalized Relative to MFU

Relative performance is determined by:

$$Relative\ Performance\,(strategy) \ = \ \frac{search\ nodes\ _{MFU}}{search\ nodes\ _{strategy}}$$

Of the access strategies, the best performer for STD-EBL is *SORT*. This occurs because the time to check the preconditions of a rule can increase exponentially with the number of situations traversed.

An interesting question is which access strategies organize rules so that performance improves as more and more problems are solved. The next histogram contains data relevant to this issue. Each strategy's performance on the first ten test problems is compared to its performance on the second ten; Figure 4.15 presents the results. The ratio of performance on the two groups of test problems is theoretically unity for NO-LEARN, since it only depends on the random draw of desired tower heights. The ratio should also be unity for *SORT, LRL, RAND,* and *MRL,* because the order they try to apply rules is not effected by the results of previous test problems. The heights of these bars provide an indication of the variability due to statistical fluctuations. This figure demonstrates that the strategies in which rules are continually reorganized during problem solving improve performance, especially in STD-EBL, which learns more rules on average.

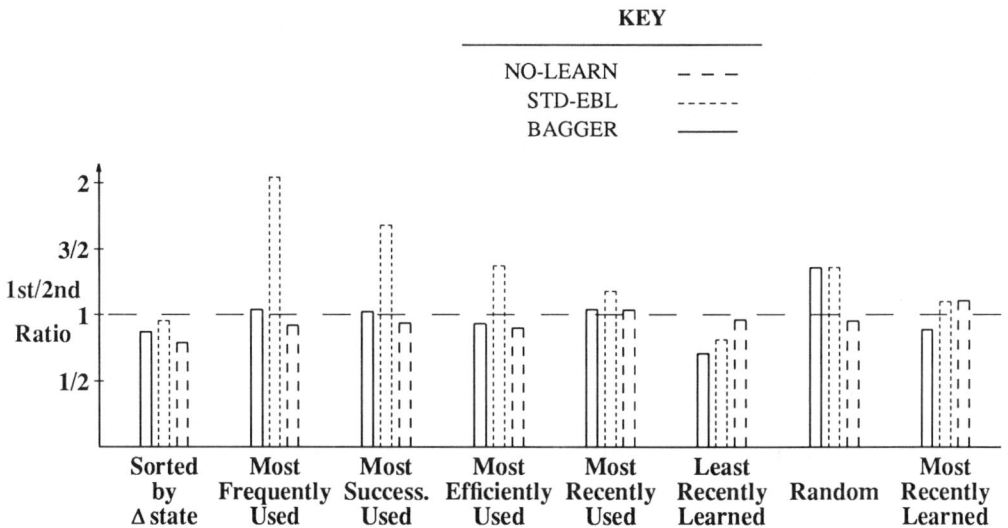

Figure 4.15 Temporal Improvement under Each Access Strategy

Discussion of Access Strategies

Eight strategies for organizing acquired rules have been proposed and are empirically investigated. Some of the strategies only depend on the order in which rules are learned, while others also depend on future problem-solving performance.

The most successful access strategy for STD-EBL is to sort rules according to the number of states traversed, a technique applicable if situation calculus is being used. If this type of sorting is not possible, the order of rule access should depend on the examples experienced. Trying the most frequently successful rule first substantially improves performance. For STD-EBL (and other systems that learn "standard" rules) new rules should be added to the *end* of the list of previously-acquired rules, while for BAGGER (and other systems that learn "number-generalized" rules) they should be added to the *front.* The reason for this is discussed in the paragraphs below.

The strategies that depend on previous problem solving, dynamically altering the order rules are accessed, prove beneficial. Simply keeping a count of the number of times a rule is successfully used works well, while the method of trying the most recently used rule first works less well. This can be explained as follows. If the occurrence of a intricate, rare example requires the use of a complicated rule, moving it to the front of the queue may be a bad idea. On the next problem, substantial time may be spent discovering it is not applicable. It is better to have rules work their way forward by successfully solving several problems. However, as evidenced by *SORT*, it can be advantageous to first try rules whose preconditions can be rapidly checked, even if they are likely to solve fewer problems [Shavlik87c, (also see Section 2.4.3)]. More complicated access strategies that incorporate both of these advantages should be developed.

Somewhat surprisingly, while first trying the least-recently learned rule works better for STD-EBL than trying the most-recently learned one, the opposite is true for BAGGER. (See Figure 4.14.) The reason for this is that earlier rules result from more typical examples, while later rules result from examples that are probabilistically less likely to occur again soon. In STD-EBL it is best to first try the rules that result from the most probable situations. However, BAGGER often learns more from the more complicated examples and the acquired number-generalized rule usually covers the simpler, and more likely, examples. Hence, rules acquired later are more likely to be broadly applicable and should be considered earlier.

4.3.7 Estimating the Performance of the Non-Learning System

Due to computational resource limits, the performance of NO-LEARN is estimated. The equations used to estimate the performance of NO-LEARN appear in Table 4.5; N is the number of blocks to be moved. These equations are constructed by measuring the system's performance on 250 problems where N equals one or two, then using the curve fitting algorithm of Section 14.2 in [Press86]. Problems where N equals three occasionally exhaust the available memory. The successful cases with $N=3$ are consistent with the estimations.

These equations are used when first-principles solutions are generated. Special-purpose code generates solutions (sequences of block movements) and uses these equations to calculate the estimated solution time. For tower-building, the specialized solution procedure selects blocks to add to the tower in reverse order of the way they are dropped (e.g., Block 10 is chosen first, then Block 9, etc.). Blocks are chosen until the sum of their heights satisfies the goal. This method insures that a block is always clear when it is chosen to be moved. However, it does not necessarily produce the shortest possible solution. For clearing, solutions are found by finding all supported blocks and then moving them in reverse numerical order (i.e., in the reverse order from which they were dropped).

4.3.8 Empirical Study of BAGGER2

The experiments presented so far have investigated the value of explanation-based learning using two tasks: tower-building and block-clearing. This final experimental section considers a third task — circuit implementation — and reports two studies. They again involve NO-LEARN and STD-EBL, but this time BAGGER2[5] is used to generalize number, because, as

Table 4.5 Estimated Performance of No-Learn

$$time_{tower}(N) = 0.32 \times 10^{1.54 \times N} \; seconds$$

$$time_{clear}(N) = 0.25 \times 10^{2.08 \times N} \; seconds$$

$$nodes_{tower}(N) = 5.45 \times 10^{1.35 \times N}$$

$$nodes_{clear}(N) = 2.68 \times 10^{1.95 \times N}$$

discussed in Section 3.3, circuit design involves recursive concepts.

The experimental hypothesis of the first experiment is that BAGGER2 requires less training than STD-EBL to acquire a concept; for a given amount of training it will be more likely to solve a new problem. In this study, problems consist of randomly generated designs of eight-input AND gates using binary AND's; Figure 3.16 contains a sample design. The task is to implement this design using only NOT and binary OR gates. An experimental run proceeds as follows. First, ten randomly-generated test problems are produced and saved. Next, 250 randomly-generated circuit designs are produced, and the two learners implement them. If they use more than one rule to do so, they generalize the resulting explanation and save the result. Periodically their performance is measured on the ten test problems, during which learning is turned off. There are ten experimental runs, each with a different initial random number; hence each point in this study is the mean of 100 measurements.

Figure 4.16 presents the number of test problems solvable using only each system's acquired rules. Clearly, BAGGER2 needs significantly fewer training examples to learn the concept than does STD-EBL. The reason is that BAGGER2 learns a rule that encodes a general strategy for repeatedly applying DeMorgan's Law to implement any network of binary AND gates (see Table 3.9), while STD-EBL learns separate rules for each possible layout (see Table 3.8 for a sample). STD-EBL can only apply its learned rules to new problems that have the same topology as a previously seen one. This again illustrates one of the strengths of a system that restructures explanations; since it recognizes repeated portions of explanations and generalizes the number of repetitions, it can require less training to acquire a concept.

Being able to apply learned rules to solve new problems is of little use if doing so requires a substantial amount of effort. The second experiment investigates the speedup achieved by using the explanation-based systems. The primary hypothesis is that performing explanation-based learning is better than solving all problems by only resorting to the initial

---

[5] Unfortunately due to their different implementation languages and supporting hardware, BAGGER and BAGGER2 cannot be directly compared.

domain rules. The secondary hypothesis is that BAGGER2's learned rules produce solutions faster than STD-EBL's rules. It is possible that the added complexity of recursive rules leads to longer solution times. Although STD-EBL must learn more rules than BAGGER2 to cover a concept involving recursion, a problem solver may be able to more efficiently search through these non-recursive rules for a solution.

To examine the hypothesis, each learning system is trained on AND circuit problems of various sizes (from five to ten inputs).[6] For each problem size, 1000 random circuits constitute the training set. Following training, all three systems attempt to solve the same ten test problems, with learning turned off.[7] This is repeated ten times, each time with different test problems, so again the plotted points represent the means of 100 measurements. STD-EBL organizes its rules according to the number of inputs involved (i.e., in six groups) and only checks possibly relevant rules during problem solving. For STD-EBL, only the time spent on problems solved by a learned rule is recorded. Both this and the assumption about rule organization favor STD-EBL over BAGGER2. Figure 4.17 contains the mean solution time on the test problems. Learning recursive rules is always better than not learning at all. However, there are several places where STD-EBL's performance curve crosses another system's curve. When there are a small number of possible problems, STD-EBL does better than BAGGER2, however it soon becomes worthwhile to learn recursive rules. The ability to scale to larger problems is an important property of any learning system; as the space of possible problems grows, BAGGER2's edge over STD-EBL increases. Note that after awhile, it would be better to not learn at all than to use STD-EBL. The locations in Figure 4.17 where curves cross merit discussion.

As discussed in the introduction, explanation-based generalizers produce composite rules that capture useful combinations of other rules. Using the resulting generalization, a problem solver can solve many problems more quickly than without it; the solver need not spend time rediscovering the successful combination. However, as a system acquires more new rules, its problem-solving performance can *decrease*, because it may spend substantial time trying to apply learned rules that appear promising, but ultimately fail [Minton88a, Minton88b, Mooney89c]. This explains why STD-EBL performs worse than NO-LEARN when the space of possible circuit designs is large; the solver must try too many promising but unfruitful rules before succeeding. Because BAGGER2 can capture a concept in a single rule, a solver need not

---

[6] The number of different ways to implement an N-input AND gate with binary gates is $\dfrac{(2N-2)!}{N!\,(N-1)!}$ (page 18 of [Jacobson51]).

[7] The rules in Table 3.3 constitute the initial domain theory. To prevent infinite regression, the problem solver performs a subsumption check. If the current query subsumes at least *three* queries currently on the stack, backtracking occurs. The performance of NO-LEARN could be improved by disallowing any subsumptions or by reordering the rules in the domain theory. However, the setup used reflects the fact that EBL reduces the time spent following "blind alleys" during problem solving. A more realistic domain theory would have hundreds of circuit implementation rules. With such a theory, NO-LEARN's performance would be significantly worse, while the performance of the learners would not change much, because they incorporate only a subset of the domain theory into the rules they learn. See [Shavlik90a] for a study of a different formalization of the circuit implementation task; the results are qualitatively the same.

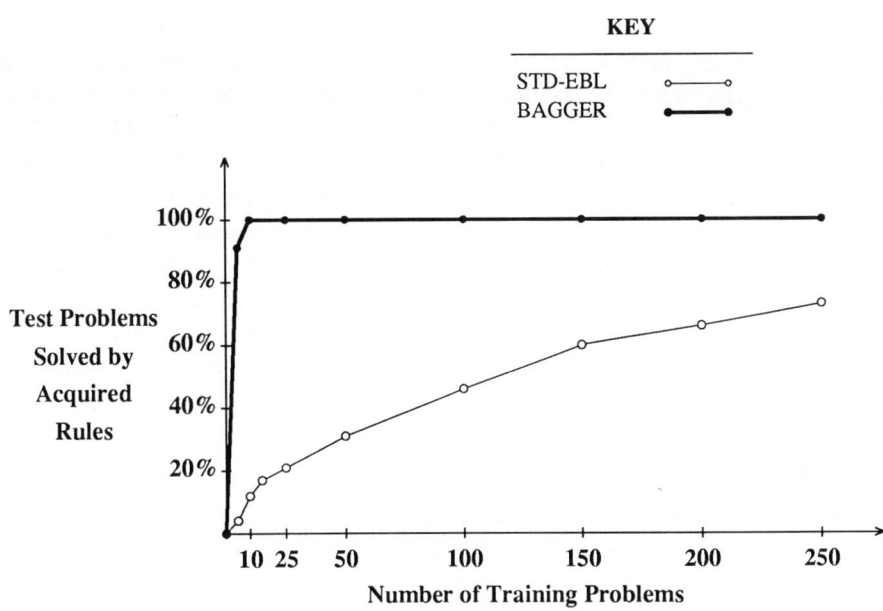

Figure 4.16   New Circuit Problems Solved with Acquired Rules as a Function of Training

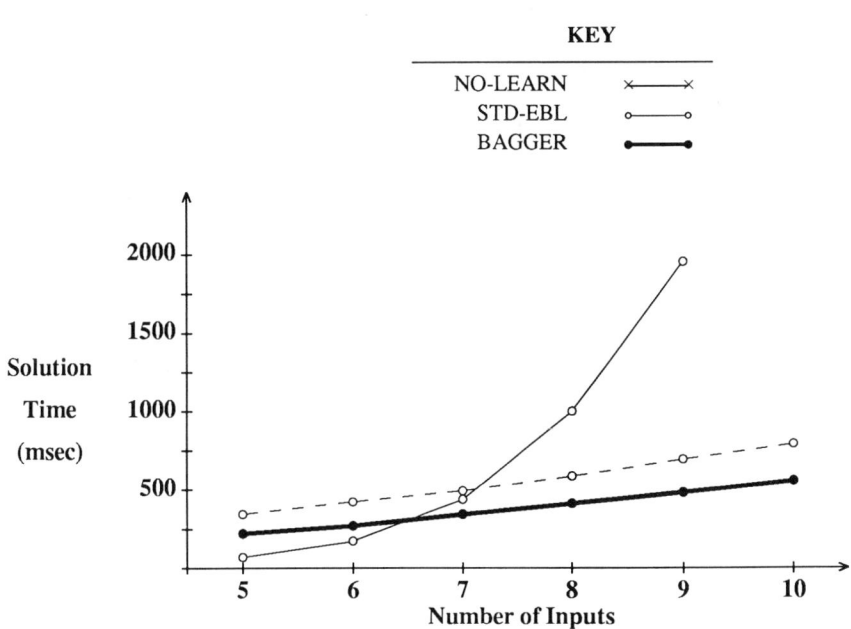

Figure 4.17   Mean Solution Time as a Function of Problem Size

waste time searching through a collection of closely related rules looking for an appropriate one; for this reason BAGGER2 helps avoid the negative effects of learning recently reported.

The results in Figure 4.17 can be better understood by considering the difference between the rules STD-EBL learns and those BAGGER2 learns. One can view the rules STD-EBL learns as fixed-sized templates, each of which contains a fixed number of variables to bind. Problem solving with these rules involves matching their preconditions to the current task; if the problem is similar to a previous one, the solver can apply the generalized version of the previous solution. It does not produce new solutions, but only determines if it can reuse an old one. Conversely, BAGGER2 learns a technique for *generating* new solutions (as does the original BAGGER), in which an arbitrary number of variables can be bound. By analyzing an explanation, it extracts an algorithm reflected in a specific problem's solution. This generative capability means it can express an unbounded number of templates, while still maintaining the efficiencies obtained by performing explanation-based learning.

4.4   Discussion

The empirical results presented in this chapter demonstrate the value of generalizing the structure of explanations in particular, and explanation-based learning in general. Three different systems are compared. Two of them learn: BAGGER and STD-EBL (an implementation of the EGGS [Mooney86] explanation-based generalization algorithm). The other, called NO-LEARN, performs no learning. In the experiments investigated, BAGGER and STD-EBL perform substantially better than the system that performs no learning, by up to five orders of magnitude. BAGGER also outperforms the standard EBL system, as does its successor BAGGER2.

Investigation of two training modes demonstrates the importance of external guidance to learning systems. In the autonomous mode, the systems must solve all problems on their own. The high cost of doing this when no learned rule applies dissipates much of the gains from learning. Substantial gains can be achieved by initially providing solutions to a collection of sample problems, and having the learners acquire their rules by generalizing these solutions [Shavlik89a]. The usefulness of this depends on how representative the training samples are of future problems and how acceptable occasional failures are. Since BAGGER requires fewer training examples and produces more general rules, it addresses these issues better than does standard explanation-based learning.

The BAGGER algorithm leads to the acquisition of fewer rules, because one of its rules may subsume many related rules learned using standard explanation-based learning. In this chapter, experiments demonstrate that acquiring fewer rules decreases the likelihood that time will be wasted on rules that appear to be applicable. The probability that, in the training mode, a retrieved rule successfully solves a tower-building problem is about 0.60 for STD-EBL and 0.99 for BAGGER.

A number of additional statistics are also reported. One is that the time BAGGER takes to generalize an explanation is comparable to that for STD-EBL. A second set of statistics involves several strategies for determining the order to access acquired rules are analyzed. Dynamically organizing rules so that the most recently or frequently used ones are tried first

144

proves beneficial. If situation calculus is used, STD-EBL benefits most by ordering rules according to the number of situations they traverse. For BAGGER, new rules should be added to the front of its collection of rules, while for STD-EBL they should be added to the back. A third statistic is that rules that are more operational perform better when the training mode is used. A four statistic indicates fewer training examples are needed by BAGGER and BAGGER2 than STD-EBL to acquire a sufficient set of new rules. A fifth result is that the advantages of BAGGER and BAGGER2 over standard explanation-based learning can magnify as the range of potential problems increases.

It may seem that primarily investigating tower-building problems unfairly favors explanation-based learning. An alternative would be to investigate a more diverse collection of problem types. However, the negative effects of learning are manifested most strongly when the acquired concepts are closely related. If the effects of some rule support the satisfaction of a goal, substantial time can be spent trying to satisfy the preconditions of the rule. If this cannot be done, much time is wasted. To the STD-EBL system, a rule for stacking two blocks is quite different from one that moves four blocks. Frequently a rule that appears relevant fails. For example, often STD-EBL tries to satisfy a rule that specifies moving four blocks to meet the goal of having a block at a given height, only to fail after much effort because all combinations of four blocks exceed the limitations on the tower height. On average, STD-EBL tries about 1½ rules before solving a problem. When the effects of a rule are unrelated to the current goal, much less time will be wasted, especially if a complicated data structure is used to organize rules according to the goals they support.

It may also seem that tower-building and block-clearing favor systems that generalize number. While these are problems that do require number generalization, recall that BAGGER2 operates identically to EGGS when generalizing number is inappropriate. BAGGER can easily be extended to call EGGS when it can find no focus rule to repeatedly apply. Hence, these number-generalizing systems can improve performance on those tasks requiring number generalization, while operating identically to EGGS on the remainder.

Other researchers have also reported on the performance improvement of standard explanation-based learning systems over problem solvers that do not learn [Fikes72, Minton85, Minton88b, Mooney89a, O'Rorke87a, Prieditis87, Steier87, Tambe88]. One major issue is that, as more new concepts are learned, problem-solving performance can *decrease*. This usually occurs because substantial problem-solving time can be spent trying to apply rules that appear promising, but ultimately fail [Markovitch89, Minton85, Mooney89a]. This occurs when a problem solver checks the preconditions of a new rule but cannot find a successful binding of the rule's variables. The experiments in this chapter address this issue, because all of the acquired rules build towers but often no binding of a rule's preconditions can construct a tower of a given height. For example, there may be no way to bind the variables in an STD-EBL rule for building four-block towers such that the resulting tower is as tall as one average block. However, substantial time can be wasted discovering this. This negative effect also occurs for BAGGER rules. If BAGGER only learns that originally clear blocks can be moved to construct a tower, substantial time may be wasted before it finds out that there are not enough clear blocks in the initial state to achieve the specified height. However, in the experiments reported in this chapter the general overall effect is that learning is beneficial. Significantly, as the complexity of the problem space increases, so does the improvement achieved by explanation-based learning.

In the circuit domain, however, for large problem spaces STD-EBL did worse than not learning at all. The negative effects of learning depend on the relationship between the basic problem-solving complexity of a set of domain rules and the number of qualitatively different composite rules required in that domain. Explanation-based learning may prove particularly beneficial in domains where the number of composite rules a problem solver needs is small compared to the number of possible combinations of the basic domain rules. Analytic studies of explanation-based learning may provide important insight into this issue.

A second potential performance degradation can occur when a new broadly-applicable rule, which can require substantial time to instantiate, blocks access to a more restricted, yet often sufficient, rule whose preconditions are easier to evaluate [Shavlik87c, (also see Section 2.4.3)]. Evidence for this is found in the experiments involving the STD-EBL system. When building towers that contain on average about two blocks, rules that specify moving three blocks are preferentially chosen. This occurs because these three-block rules, while less efficient than rules for moving two blocks, cover a larger collection of the possible problems.

While this chapter's experiments indicate that learning can increase overall problem-solving performance, techniques for forgetting or reorganizing acquired rules are necessary [Markovitch88, Minton88b]. The experiments investigating rule access strategies (Section 4.3.6) demonstrate the value of dynamically organizing rules. The idea of organizing acquired rules so that rapidly evaluated special cases of more general rules are tried first is presented in Section 2.4.3 and [Shavlik87c]. An untested approach to forgetting is presented in [Fikes72], where it is suggested that statistics be kept on the frequencies acquired rules are learned, discarding those that fall below some threshold. This idea is successfully tested in [Minton85]. To prevent the accumulation of excessive number of rules, it is also important to wisely decide when to acquire a new rule. Some general heuristics have been proposed that estimate when it is a good idea to construct the generalization of a specific explanation. For example, [Minton85] proposes selectively generalizing those solutions that initially move away from the direction indicated by a hill-climbing measure. A similar idea appears in [Iba85]. Only solutions that achieve *thematic* goals [Schank77] are generalized in the GENESIS system [Mooney85]. Additional conditions for generalization are presented in [DeJong83b].

5 Conclusion

5.1 Contributions

Most research in explanation-based learning involves relaxing constraints on the entities in a situation, rather than generalizing the number of entities themselves. Nonetheless, many important concepts require generalizing number. This can be accomplished in an explanation-based fashion by generalizing the *structure* of the explanations. This book presents two theories of how this can be done; implementations of both theories have been successfully tested.

PHYSICS 101 is a mathematical reasoning system, offered as a psychologically plausible model, that performs explanation-based learning in mathematically oriented domains. Mathematically based domains are an area where the strengths of explanation-based learning are particularly appropriate, because explanation-based learning supports the construction of large concepts by analyzing how smaller concepts can be pieced together to solve a specific problem. Combining "small" concepts to form "larger" ones is the basis of progress in mathematical domains. PHYSICS 101's understanding and generalization processes are guided by the manner in which variables are canceled in a specific problem. Attention focuses on how *obstacles* are eliminated in the specific problem. Obstacles are variables that preclude the direct evaluation of the unknown. Canceling these variables allows the determination of the value of the unknown. One important feature of analyzing variable cancellations is that the generalization of number is motivated. The explanation of a specific calculation closely guides the construction of a general version of the calculation, from which PHYSICS 101 extracts a new general concept.

BAGGER is a domain-independent approach to the problem of generalizing the structure of explanations. It is based on the properties of the form of explanations, unlike PHYSICS 101, which is based on the semantics of obstacle cancellation. BAGGER's approach relies on a shift in representation which accommodates indefinite numbers of rule applications. This system analyzes explanation structures and detects repeated, inter-dependent applications of rules. Once the system finds a rule on which to focus attention, it determines how an *arbitrary* number of instantiations of this rule can be concatenated together. It then conceptually merges the indefinite-length collection of rules into the explanation, replacing the specific-length collection of rules, and an extension of a standard explanation-based algorithm produces a new rule from the augmented explanation. BAGGER2 is the result of extending BAGGER so that it can acquire recursive concepts.

The major contributions of this research are:

(1) *The claim that explanations that suffice to understand a specific example are not always sufficient to directly produce the complete underlying general concept.* Often the structure of the explanation must be generalized. This is the central theme

running throughout this book. Three implemented systems, tested on a number of problems from several domains and a large scale empirical investigation, substantiate this claim.

(2) *The idea that mathematical calculations can be understood and properly generalized by focusing on the idea of **obstacles** and their cancellation.* This hypothesis is successfully tested in the PHYSICS 101 system. It is claimed that reasoning about mathematical cancellations makes apparent constraints inherent in mathematically-based domains. The construct of a *cancellation graph* is offered as a data structure for representing obstacle cancellations and forms the backbone of PHYSICS 101's understanding and generalization algorithms.

(3) *An alternate notion of explanation-based generalization.* In PHYSICS 101 the explanation of a specific solution closely guides the *reconstruction* of the solution in the general case. Other generalization algorithms directly use the specific explanation. During PHYSICS 101's construction of the general calculation no problem-solving search is performed — construction follows deterministically from the specific calculation, leading to a relatively efficient process. The new calculation is often substantially more general, in terms of its structure as well as its variables, than the specific calculation. The number of entities and the identity of the operations performed may be generalized.

(4) *The notion of a **special case** as a way to address the operationality/generality problem.* By properly organizing acquired concepts, the advantages of both operational and general rules can be obtained, while minimizing the disadvantages of both.

(5) *A domain-independent approach to the problem of generalizing to* N. The BAGGER algorithm generalizes the structure of explanations so that an indefinite number of rule applications are supported. This algorithm is particularly applicable to domains expressed using situation calculus. The concept of *unwindable* rules supports the goal of expressing the preconditions of acquired rules only in terms of the initial state. The idea of a *rule instantiation sequence* (RIS) is presented as a data structure that accommodates an arbitrary number of applications of a specific rule. BAGGER reformulates specific explanations in terms of this rule instantiation sequence.

(6) *A graceful extension of a standard explanation-based generalization algorithm.* The BAGGER2 algorithm learns recursive and iterative concepts, integrates results from multiple examples, and extracts useful subconcepts during generalization. On problems where learning a recursive rule is not appropriate, the system produces the same result as Mooney's EGGS algorithm [Mooney86, Mooney89c].

(7) *An empirical demonstration of the value of generalizing number in particular, and of explanation-based learning in general.* Although some problems will be solved more slowly after learning, this negative effect is overwhelmed by the speedups afforded by learning on the majority of problems.

(8) *An empirical demonstration of the advantages of learning by observing the intelligent behavior of external agents.* The high cost a system must frequently pay if it solves all of its problems on its own can dissipate much of the gains it achieves from

148

learning. A substantial improvement can be achieved by initially observing an expert solve several sample problems. No special ordering of these training examples examples is necessary.

5.2 Relation to Other Work

Besides PHYSICS 101, BAGGER and BAGGER2, several other explanation-based approaches to generalizing the structure of explanations have been recently proposed; this section reviews these approaches and discusses related work in other paradigms. Additional related work is discussed in the following section, which presents several open research issues. Also, Section 2.1.3 reviews additional work on learning in mathematically-based domains.

5.2.1 Other Explanation-Based Approaches

Prieditis

Prieditis [Prieditis86] has developed a system which learns macro-operators representing sequences of repeated STRIPS-like operators. His approach analyzes the constraints imposed by the connections of the precondition, *ADD*, and *DELETE* lists of the operators determined to be of interest. This produces an iterative macro-operator that accommodates an indefinite number of repeated operator inter-connections.

While BAGGER is very much in the spirit of Prieditis' work, STRIPS-like operators impose unwarranted representational restrictions (see Section 3.1.2). For instance, BAGGER's use of predicate calculus allows generalization of repeated structure and repeated actions in a uniform manner. In addition, the BAGGER approach accommodates the use of additional inference rules to reason about what is true in a state. Everything need not appear explicitly in the focus rule. For example, in the stacking example, other rules are used to determine the height of a tower and that an object is clear when the only object it supports is transferred. Also, instantiations of the focus rule do not have to connect directly — intervening inference rules can be involved when determining that the results of one instantiation partially support the preconditions of another. There is nothing in Prieditis' approach that corresponds to BAGGER's unwinding operation, nor are disjunctive rules learned. Finally, unlike BAGGER2, Prieditis' system cannot learn recursive rules.

Cheng and Carbonell

In the FERMI system [Cheng86], cyclic patterns are recognized using empirical methods and the detected repeated pattern is generalized using explanation-based learning techniques. Unlike the other systems for number generalization, cyclic patterns are detected by analyzing changes in subgoals. The cost of this is explained in the next paragraph. Except for PHYSICS 101, which analyzes obstacle cancellations, the other number generalization systems focus directly on rule applications in order to decide where to generalize number. A major strength of the FERMI system is the incorporation of conditionals within the learned macro-operator, allowing this system to learn disjunctive rules. Shell and Carbonell [Shell89] present improvements that increase the efficiency of the macro-operators FERMI learns.

However, unlike the techniques implemented in BAGGER, BAGGER2, and PHYSICS 101, the rules acquired by FERMI are not fully based on an explanation-based analysis of an example, and so are not guaranteed to always work. For example, FERMI learns a strategy for solving a set of linear algebraic equations. None of the preconditions of the strategy check that the equations are linearly independent. The learned strategy will appear applicable to the problem of determining x and y from the equations $3x + y = 5$ and $6x + 2y = 10$. After a significant amount of work, the strategy will terminate unsuccessfully. This is one of the costs of focusing on changes at the subgoal level. Since several rules can cause the same subgoal change, the problem of analyzing the interactions between successive cycles is greatly complicated. A flexible agenda-based problem solver is used to circumvent this complication.

Cohen

Cohen's ADEPT system [Cohen88] generalizes number by constructing a finite-state control mechanism that deterministically directs the construction of proofs similar to the one used to justify the specific example. This is accomplished by first producing a linear *proof automaton*, a variant of a finite state automaton, that produces only one proof — that of the specific example. This proof automaton is then repeatedly reduced by merging states according to the constraints imposed by the inference rules used. Each reduction produces a loop in the automaton, while still keeping the automaton deterministic. Because the final automaton is deterministic, no search need be performed when applying it to future problems.

One significant property of Cohen's method is that it can generate proof procedures involving tree traversals and nested loops; it can also learn from multiple examples. However, in order to eliminate backtracking when applying the learned rule, his system assumes that operational terms can be matched by no more than one fact in the database. By disallowing backtracking, ADEPT improves efficiency at the cost of some expressiveness. This means that, unlike BAGGER2, it cannot learn how to build towers in a situation where Blocks A, C, and E are initially clear and then apply its learned strategy in a situation where Blocks B, D, and F are initially clear. Another difference from BAGGER2 is that, to learn from multiple examples, ADEPT requires the previous examples be present in their entirety. Cohen's method also differs from other explanation-based algorithms in that it does not eliminate "internal nodes" of the explanation during generalization. In other approaches, only the leaves of the operationalized explanation appear in the acquired rule's antecedents. In Cohen's approach, every inference rule used in the original explanation is explicitly incorporated into the final result. Each rule may again be applied when satisfying the acquired rule, thereby reducing efficiency. Finally, unlike BAGGER2, Cohen's system does not separately extract subconcepts from portions of an explanation.

Mooney

A related task is generalizing the *organization* of the nodes in the explanation, rather than generalizing their *number*. Mooney [Mooney88] presents an approach along these lines. His method, which is limited to domains expressed in the STRIPS formalism, determines the minimal set of constraints on the order of a plan's actions. Without this knowledge, the actions in the generalized plan must occur in the same order as in the training example. Strictly speaking, his approach does not alter the explanation structure. Rather, it produces the most general partial ordering of the plan's actions that maintains all connections between preconditions and effects in the original example. Though his technique cannot handle it, Mooney discusses an example where the generalization of operator order requires alteration of the explanation.

5.2.2 Related Work in Similarity-Based Learning

The problem of generalizing to N has also been addressed within the paradigms of similarity-based learning [Andreae84, Dietterich84, Dufay84, Holder89, Kodratoff86, Michalski83, Sammut86, Whitehall87, Wolff82]. A general specification of number generalization has been advanced in [Michalski83]. Michalski proposes a set of generalization rules including a *closing interval rule* and several *counting arguments rules* which can generate number-generalized structures. Kodratoff and Ganascia [Kodratoff86] propose a technique they call *structural matching* that generalizes the number of parts in an object when specifying this number is not necessary in order to distinguish the positive and negative training examples. Like BAGGER and BAGGER2, the MARVIN system of Sammut and Banerji [Sammut86] uses Horn clauses to represent concepts. The recursive concept *column*, which is a stack of objects, is one of the objects it learns to recognize. It learns by inductively generalizing training instances; these generalizations are corroborated by generating new examples and asking the user if they are a member of the concept being taught. The primary difference between MARVIN's and BAGGER's (and BAGGER2's) approaches is that the latter's explanation-based concepts are deductively supported by the domain theory; hence confirmation and revision are unnecessary.

5.2.3 Related Work in Automatic Programming

As previously discussed, BAGGER2 recurrences are essentially recursive programs. Unlike the simple template-matching rules EGGS learns, BAGGER's rules can produce solutions of various sizes. Some research in automatic programming shares many characteristics with this approach, namely that involving program synthesis from examples [Bauer79, Biermann78, Kodratoff79, Smith84, Summers77]. In these approaches, sequences of input/output pairs for recursive functions provide information on the control structure of the algorithm being specified. A major problem with input/output pairs is that for complex operations the amount of search needed to find the proper algorithm is prohibitive. Automatic programming systems that use examples must search for a consistent hypothesis because, unlike an explanation-based system, they do not have the information that specifies the dependencies between successive recursive calls. In this sense, they are similar to similarity-based learning algorithms; both must make unjustified generalizations, unlike those an explanation-based system makes.

There have been some recent efforts to apply explanation-based learning to automatic programming [Hill87, Steier87]. These systems, however, do not generalize explanation structures. Thus, they are incapable of extracting recursive or iterative programs from examples where the recursion or iteration is only implicitly represented. Arguments that explanation-based learning should be viewed in terms of partial evaluation, a technique of automatic programming, appear in [Prieditis88, Van Harmelen88]. Partial evaluation [Beckman76] transforms a program by performing as much of the computation in advance as possible, either fully independently of the input values or for various classes of possible input values. The result is a more efficient program. This is much like explanation-based learning speeding up a problem solver that uses a domain theory (see Chapter 4).

5.3 Some Open Research Issues

The PHYSICS 101, BAGGER, and BAGGER2 systems have taken important steps towards the solution to the problem of generalizing the structure of explanations. However, the research is still incomplete. From the vantage point of the current results, several avenues of future research are apparent. While there are many issues related to performing, understanding, and generalizing mathematical calculations, this section only addresses issues related to the problem of generalizing explanation structures. Most of the discussion relates to the approach taken in BAGGER and BAGGER2 in addressing the generalizing to N problem.

5.3.1 Deciding When to Learn

Detecting Fortuitous Circumstances

Possibly the major issue in generalizing the structure of explanations is that of deciding when there is enough information in the specific explanation to generalize its structure. Due to the finiteness of a specific problem, fortuitous circumstances in the specific situation may have allowed shortcuts in the solution. Complications in the general case may not have been faced. Hence the specific example provides no guidance as to how they should be addressed.

One aspect of this issue is recognizing the general problems inherent in the specific example. The notion of *obstacles* serves this role in PHYSICS 101. The specific solution must eliminate all of the specific counterparts of the general versions of the obstacles. If a general obstacle has no counterpart in the specific example, PHYSICS 101 does not save the generalization. This is the reason that a two-ball collision does not provide enough information from which to learn the concept of momentum conservation (see Appendix A.5).

In BAGGER, the requirement that for an application of a focus rule to be generalized, it be viewable as the arbitrary *ith* application also addresses the problem of recognizing fortuitous circumstances. If there is not enough information to view it as the *ith* application, it is likely that some important issue is not addressed in this focus rule application. However, more powerful techniques for detecting fortuitous circumstances need to be developed. One approach may be to abstract the notion of *obstacle* to cover more than mathematical cancellations.

An example in Appendix B.2.3 shows that BAGGER does not always acquire the fully general concept. From a particular example BAGGER only learns that a block is clear in the situation following the one in which the block on it is moved, rather than learning that a cleared block remains clear as long as nothing else is placed on it. From a more complicated example, BAGGER learns the more general concept. A second aspect of the issue of fortuitous circumstances is realizing that an acquired rule is overly-specific and should be refined or replaced. BAGGER also needs to be capable of adding disjuncts to existing rules, rather than storing multiple specializations of the same general rule. Determining which acquired rule "almost" solves a problem and, hence, is a candidate for refinement or replacement is a sizable problem. This is especially complicated when rules are insufficient because they are overly restrictive, rather than because they lead to incorrect results.

BAGGER2 partially addresses this issue in its ability to add a new disjunct to a recursive rule it previously acquired. However, learning too many disjuncts can lead to efficiency problems; this issue needs to be investigated further.

A learning system must insure that the rules it tries to apply to problems are likely to prove successful, otherwise the gains achieved by learning can be dissipated by the time spent attempting to apply rules that usually fail. This problem can be more severe when generalizing number because the specific explanation is generalized further than in standard explanation-based learning. There are three basic ways to address the problem of potentially being swamped by too many acquired rules [Fikes72]. One, care can be taken when deciding when to learn. Two, the collection of rules can be organized so that those most likely to be successful are tried first. Three, rules can be refined or replaced when they are found to be insufficient. The PHYSICS 101 and BAGGER system investigate the first two approaches; BAGGER2 addresses the third. All three merit additional research.

Choosing a Focus Rule

BAGGER's method of choosing a rule on which to focus attention should be improved. Currently the first detected instance of interconnected applications of a rule is used as the focus rule. (BAGGER2 does essentially the same thing when it chooses a predicate to head a recurrence.) However, there could be several occurrences that satisfy these requirements. Techniques for comparing alternative focus rules are needed. Inductive inference approaches to detecting repeated structures [Andreae84, Dietterich83, Dufay84, Holder89, Weld86, Whitehall87, Wolff82] may be applicable to the generation of candidate focus rules, upon which the explanation-based capabilities of BAGGER can build. It may also be necessary to rearrange the nodes in an explanation so that it is in a form where the BAGGER algorithm can apply.

BAGGER uses the heuristic of requiring multiple instantiations of a rule in order for it to be a focus rule. The same heuristic is used when deciding if an instantiation should be viewed as an unwindable rule (Section 3.2.1). It is possible to generalize number on the basis of one application of a rule [Cohen87 (Appendix B), Shavlik87d]. However, it is more intuitively pleasing that multiple instantiations are needed to trigger the extension, thereby increasing the chance that the acquired rule will prove frequently applicable in the future.

BAGGER2 uses a relatively simple technique for parsing explanations (see Figure 3.15). The class of recursive concepts this technique recognizes needs to be characterized, and BAGGER2 needs to be extended to cover a wider range of recursive rule applications. Techniques for detecting recursive patterns developed in automatic programming research may be applicable to this task [Smith84]. However, such approaches can introduce backtracking search into the generalization process, thereby leading to problems of intractability. Also, if there are multiple parses of an explanation, techniques for choosing the best parse may be required.

Deciding when to repeatedly apply a rule is more directly motivated in PHYSICS 101. The goal of canceling all of the general obstacles determines when a rule (such as Newton's Third Law) is to be repeatedly applied. While deciding when to learn is more directed in this system, the approach is specific to mathematical calculations.

5.3.2 Improving What is Learned

Representing Preconditions in Terms of Sets Rather than Sequences

Investigating the generalization of operator application orderings within learned rules is another opportunity for future research. Currently, in the rules learned by the BAGGER algorithm, the order interdependence among rule applications is specified in terms of sequences of vectors. However, this is unnecessarily constraining. When valid, these constraints should be specified in terms of *sets* or *bags*[1] of vectors. This could be accomplished by reasoning about the semantics of the system's predicate calculus functions and predicates. Properties such as symmetry, transitivity, and reflexivity may help determine constraints on order independence [Shavlik87d]. Mooney [Mooney89c] presents an algorithm for generalizing the order of a fixed number of actions in a plan expressed in the STRIPS formalism.

If a set satisfies a learned rule's antecedents, then *any* sequence derived from that set suffices. Conversely, if the vectors in a set fail to satisfy a rule's antecedents, there is no need to test each permutation of the elements. Unfortunately, testing all permutations occurs if the antecedents are unnecessarily expressed in terms of sequences. For example, assume the task at hand is to find enough heavy rocks in a storehouse to serve as ballast for a ship. A sequential rule may first add the weights in some order, find out that the sum weight of all the rocks in the room is insufficient, and then try another ordering for adding the weights. A rule specified in terms of sets would terminate after adding the weights once.

Efficiently Ordering Conjunctive Goals

An additional area of future research involves investigating the most efficient ordering of conjunctive goals. Consider an acquired sequential rule which builds towers of a desired height, subject to the constraint that no block can be placed upon a narrower block. The goal of building such towers is conjunctive: the correct height must be achieved and the width of the stacked blocks must be monotonically non-increasing. The optimal ordering is to select the blocks subject only to the height requirement and then sort them by size to determine their position in the tower. The reason this works is that a non-increasing ordering of widths on any set of blocks is guaranteed, so no additional block-selection constraints are imposed by this conjunct. The system should ultimately detect and exploit this kind of decomposability

---

[1] A bag (or multi-set) is an *unordered* collection of elements in which an element can appear more than once.

to improve the efficiency of the new rules. Work on ordering conjunctive goals appears in [Smith85, Treitel86].

Guaranteeing Termination

One important aspect of generalizing number is that the acquired rules may produce data structures whose size can grow without bound (for example, the rule instantiation sequence in BAGGER) or the algorithms that satisfy these rules may fall into infinite loops [Cohen87]. This means the issue of termination is significant. Although the *halting problem* is undecidable in general, in restricted circumstances termination can be proved [Manna74]. Techniques for proving termination need to be incorporated into systems that generalize number. BAGGER2 contains a partial solution to this problem. If a recurrence involves "unchanging" variables, before calling the recurrence the problem solver checks those terms which involve these variables and which also appear in all of the recurrence's terminating disjuncts. If it cannot satisfy these terms, the problem solver does not call the recurrence. These checks reduce the chance of unbounded recursive calls, but they do not guarantee termination. A less appealing, but safe, solution is to place resource bounds on the algorithms that apply number-generalized rules [Cohen87], potentially excluding successful applications.

5.3.3 Extending What can be Learned

Adding Extra Preconditions for Efficiency

Analyzing the properties of the predicates in the preconditions can lead to the insertion of additional preconditions that prevent unfruitful attempts to extend rule instantiation sequences. The example in Appendix B.4 demonstrates the value of adding extra terms to the preconditions of sequential rules. Adding extra preconditions can also support proofs of termination. For example, knowing that block heights are always positive can terminate the extension of the *RIS* when the size of the tower being constructed exceeds the upper bound on the goal height. Domain-independent ways of analyzing number-generalized rules and adding such additional preconditions need to be developed.

Satisfying Global Constraints

Satisfying global constraints poses an additional research problem. The recursive rules investigated in this book are all *incremental* in that successive operator applications converge toward the goal achievement. This is not necessarily the case for all number-generalized plans. Consider a plan for unstacking complex block structures subject to the global constraint that the partially dismantled structure always be stable. Removing one block can drastically alter the significance of another block with respect to the structure's stability. For some structures, only the subterfuge of adding a temporary support block or a counter-balance will allow unstacking to proceed. A block may be safe to remove at one point but be essential to the over-all structural stability at the next, even though the block actually removed was physically distant from it.

BAGGER's *RIS*, besides recording the focus rule's variable bindings, is used to store intermediate calculations, such as the height of the tower currently planned. Satisfying global constraints may require that the information in an *RIS* vector increase as the sequence lengthens. For example, assume that each block to be added to a tower can only support some block-dependent weight. The *RIS* may have to record the projected weight on each block while BAGGER plans the construction of a tower. Hence, as the sequence lengthens, each successive vector in the *RIS* will have to record information for one additional block. Figuratively speaking, the *RIS* will be getting longer and wider. The current BAGGER algorithm does not support this.

Acquiring Accessory Intersituational Rules

BAGGER, BAGGER2, and other such systems need to acquire accessory intersituational rules, such as frame axioms, to complement their composite rules. Currently, each of BAGGER's new sequential inference rules specifies how to achieve a goal involving some arbitrary aggregation of objects by applying some number of operators. These rules are useful in directly achieving goals that match the consequent, but do not effectively improve BAGGER's back-chaining problem-solving ability. This is because currently BAGGER does not construct new frame axioms for the rules it learns. (This problem is not specific to generalizing to *N*. Standard explanation-based learning algorithms must also face it when dealing with situation calculus.)

There are several methods of acquiring accessory rules. They can be constructed directly by combining the accessory rules of operators that make up the sequential rule. This may be intractable as the number of accessory rules for initial operators may be large and they may increase combinatorially in sequential rules. Another, potentially more attractive, approach is to treat the domain theory, augmented by sequential rules, as intractable. Since the accessory rules for learned rules are derivable from existing knowledge of initial operators, the approach in [Chien89] might be used to acquire the unstated but derivable accessory rules when they are needed. Chien's system makes simplifying assumptions during plan understanding in order to keep the task tractable. Failure in later applying a learned plan leads to in-depth investigation of the assumptions and then refinement of the plan.

Generalizing the Structure of Goals

A major weakness of current EBL algorithms that generalize explanation structures is that they do not generalize the structure of the *goal*. The examples studied do not require this type of generalization. For example, the goal of having a block at a given height should not be generalized to having *N* blocks at *M* heights. Instead, the number of blocks stacked should be generalized so that a given block can be placed at any height. However, if the specific plan involves finding the average of five numbers in an array, the general plan acquired should support the determination of the average of any size array. One approach to this issue is to develop methods for determining general versions of specific goals, then construct the explanation for the general goal, using the specific problem's explanation for guidance.

Solving Recurrences

Often a repeated process has a closed form solution. For example, summing the first *N* integers produces $\frac{N(N+1)}{2}$. There is no need to compute the intermediate partial summations.

156

A *recurrence relation* is a recursive method for computing a sequence of numbers [Liu68].

Many recurrences can be solved to produce efficient ways to determine the *n*th result in a sequence. It is this property that motivates the requirement that BAGGER and BAGGER2's preconditions be expressed solely in terms of the initial state. However, their acquired rules still hold intermediate results (e.g., in BAGGER's *RIS*). While often this information is needed (if, for instance, the resulting sequence of actions is to be executed in the external world), these systems would be more efficient if they could produce, whenever possible, number-generalized rules that did not require calculations of all the intermediate steps. If they observe the summation of, say, four numbers, they will not produce the efficient result mentioned above. Instead BAGGER will produce a rule that stores the intermediate summations in the *RIS*. One extension that could be attempted would be to create a library of templates for soluble recurrences, matching them against explanations [Shell89]. However, a more direct approach would be more appealing; Weld's [Weld86] technique of *aggregation* may be a fruitful approach. Aggregation is an abstraction technique that creates a description of a continuous process from a series of discrete events.

Extending BAGGER2

Often explanations are not trees, as BAGGER2 assumes, and some portions of the explanations will be shared. These shared portions can arise when one action satisfies preconditions for several subsequent actions (see Figure 3.14). The BAGGER2 algorithm can handle shared subexplanations by replicating them. Although this will lead to a more general concept, the efficiency of sharing is lost. The problem with shared nodes in a system that performs multiple generalizations to *N* involves synchronization. In one recurrence the shared node can be encountered on the *i*th cycle, while in another it may be the *j*th cycle. This complicates the identification of variables that should be equated. One solution involves having recurrences check for shared nodes during problem solving. If a node is marked, then there is no need to continue the recurrence. Instead, the current term can be unified with the term that did the marking.

5.3.4 Additional Issues

Empirically Analyzing EBL in a Domain-Independent Manner

The empirical analysis presented in Chapter 4 largely involves the blocks world domain. While providing a major test of standard EBL and BAGGER under a variety of conditions, it is not clear how much the results depend on the peculiarities of that domain. A domain-independent analysis is needed.

One approach would be to randomly generate rules, initial states, and goals. Since an underlying assumption of EBL is that past problems are indicative of future problems, and hence the generalizations of their solutions are worth saving, with excessive randomness it is unlikely that learning will prove beneficial. However, varying such things as the ratio of the number of different predicates to the number of domain rules may provide an indication of the domains in which standard explanation-based learning and BAGGER perform well. Other properties to vary include the average number of antecedents in a rule, the number of different consequents, the probability that a predicate in the antecedents also appears in the consequents, and the probability that a variable appears in more than one antecedent of a rule. To complement empirical analyses of EBL, theoretical analyses are needed, as has been done for similarity-based learning [Angluin83, Gold67, Kearns87, Valiant84]. Formal analysis of EBL include [Cohen89, Greiner89, Mahadevan88].

Handling Incomplete, Imperfect, and Intractable Domain Models

Finally, it is important to investigate the issue of generalizing the structure of explanations in the context of incomplete, imperfect, and intractable domain models [Mitchell86, Rajamoney87]. In any real-world domain, a computer system's model can only approximate reality. Needed inference rules may be missing, while many of those possessed will lead to incorrect results in some situations. Furthermore, the complexity of problem solving prohibits any semblance of completeness. BAGGER and BAGGER2 have relied on a correct domain model, and have not addressed correcting domain theories. Issues of intractability have not been addressed either, other than the use of an outside expert to provide sample solutions when the construction of solutions from first principles is intractable. In PHYSICS 101, reasoning about intractability and incompleteness could be incorporated by assuming obstacles are *negligible* and, hence, can be ignored (see Section 2.3.3).

Explanation-based approaches to handling the problem of intractability appear in [Bennett87, Braverman88a, Chien89, Doyle86, Gupta87, Hall88, Hammond87, Mostow87, Tadepalli89]. A popular approach is to make simplifying assumptions when initially learning, then attempt to correct these assumptions if they later lead to failure. Work addressing issues related to imperfect and incomplete domain theories is presented in [Carbonell87, Duval88, Falkenhainer87, Hall88, Mahadevan88, Rajamoney85, VanLehn87]. These issues can also be addressed by combining explanation-based techniques with other approaches to machine learning [Anderson87, Bergadano88, Danyluk87, Dietterich88, Lebowitz86, Mooney89c, Pazzani88, Porter86, Shavlik89a, Shavlik90c, Sims87, Tecuci89]. Reducing the dependence of explanation-based learning on the assumption of tractable, complete, and correct domain theories is currently one of the most active areas in EBL. The techniques proposed must be extendible to handle the important problem of generalizing the structure of explanations.

5.4   Final Summary

This book opens with the claim that current approaches to explanation-based learning have a fundamental shortcoming — they do not alter the structure of their explanations and, hence, do not generalize number. However, many concepts cannot be captured properly unless explanation-based learning systems possess this property. This research contributes to the theory and practice of explanation-based learning by developing and testing methods for extending the structure of explanations during generalization. As such, it brings machine learning closer to its goal of being able to acquire all of the knowledge inherent in the solution to a specific problem.

Appendix A   Additional PHYSICS 101 Examples

A.1   Overview

Several additional examples of the operation of PHYSICS 101 appear in this appendix. The first example, involving the concept of energy conservation, illustrates the effect that a problem-specific equation has on the generalization process. The next demonstrates how the system can use the result of one learning episode in a later learning episode. The final example shows how fortuitous circumstances in the specific example can influence the learning process. The cancellation graphs and the acquired rules for these examples are presented, as is a special-case law for energy conservation.

A.2   Learning about Energy Conservation

Figure A.1 contains a sample energy problem; a brick is falling under the influence of gravity. Information at two different states is presented; the mass of the brick, its initial velocity, and its height in the two states. Also, the system is told the net force on the brick is $M g X_y(t)$. The goal is to find the brick's velocity in the second state. PHYSICS 101's problem solver cannot solve this problem using its initial collection of physics formulae. The teacher's solution to this problem uses energy conservation and is shown in Table A.1. In this solution, the kinetic energy ($\frac{1}{2} mass \times velocity^2$) plus the potential energy ($mass \times g \times height$) in the two states is equated.

As in Chapter 2's momentum problem, in the provided solution a previously-unseen equation is evaluated at two different points and the two results equated. In order to justify the use of this equation, the system first attempts to produce an expression, where time is explicit, that describes the general form of one side of the initial equation in Table A.1. The system's problem solver cannot meet this goal, so another approach is taken. In the second

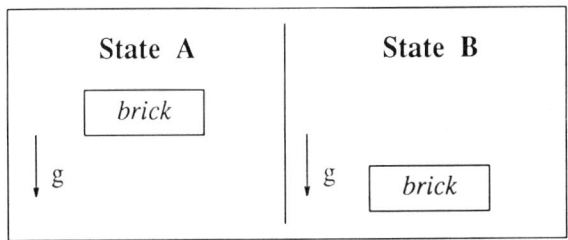

Figure A.1   A Falling Brick

Table A.1   The Teacher's Solution to the Energy Problem

$$\frac{1}{2} M_1 V^2_{1,y(A)} + M_1 g X_{1,y(A)} = \frac{1}{2} M_1 V^2_{1,y(B)} + M_1 g X_{1,y(B)}$$

$$\frac{1}{2} (2\,kg)(0\,\frac{m^2}{s^2}) + (2\,kg)(9.8\,\frac{m}{s^2})(5\,m) = \frac{1}{2} (2\,kg) V^2_{1,y(B)} + (2\,kg)(9.81\,\frac{m}{s^2})(0\,m)$$

$$0\,\frac{kg\,m^2}{s^2} + 98.1\,\frac{kg\,m^2}{s^2} = 1\,kg\,V^2_{1,y(B)} + 0\,\frac{kg\,m^2}{s^2}$$

$$98.1\,\frac{kg\,m^2}{s^2} = 1\,kg\,V^2_{1,y(B)}$$

$$V^2_{1,y(B)} = 98.1\,\frac{m^2}{s^2}$$

$$V_{1,y(B)} = 9.91\,\frac{m}{s}$$

approach, the system takes the temporal derivative of the underlying expression to see if it is zero. If so, it is valid to equate the expression at any two time points. The second approach succeeds, using the calculation steps shown in Table A.2.

The cancellation graph for the calculation of Table A.2 is presented in Figure A.2. There are two members in the obstacle set of the unknown velocity; one is the net force on the falling object, while the other is the velocity itself. This possibly confusing state of affairs, where the obstacle set contains the unknown *plus* another variable, arises because the calculus rule

$$\frac{d}{dt} ?x^{?n} = ?n\ ?x\ \frac{d}{dt} ?x^{?n-1}$$

is used in line 3 of Table A.2. This rule replaces the original instantiation of $V_{1,y}$ with two new, distinct instantiations. The two primary obstacles are partners in the cancellation of line 10. However, before this additive cancellation can take place, the multiplicative blockers of $F_{net,\,1,y}$ must be eliminated. There are two blockers; the mass term introduced in line 7, and the number 2 introduced in line 3. (Although not shown in Table A.2, the "2" is also a blocker of $V_{1,y}$.) Both of these blockers are cancelled by terms that are present in the left-hand side of the calculation, and their cancellation introduces no new obstacles.

The cancellers of the primary obstacles are produced by the remaining variables in the left-hand side of the calculation. Since M_1 is blocking the net force, the producer of its canceller must also appear in the left-hand side. Requiring the presence of the variables that produce the cancellers does not lead to any more obstacles. The role of each term in the

Table A.2   Verifying the Teacher's Solution to the Energy Problem

$$\frac{d}{dt}\left(\frac{1}{2}M_1 V^2{}_{1,\,y}(t) + M_1 g X_{1,\,y}(t)\right)$$

(1)	SeparateDerivatives	$= \frac{d}{dt}\left(\frac{1}{2}M_1 V^2{}_{1,\,y}(t)\right) + \frac{d}{dt}\left(M_1 g X_{1,\,y}(t)\right)$

(2)	ConstsOutOfDerivatives	$= \frac{1}{2}M_1 \frac{d}{dt}V^2{}_{1,\,y}(t) + M_1 g \frac{d}{dt}X_{1,\,y}(t)$

(3)	Differentiate	$= \frac{2}{2}M_1 V_{1,\,y}(t)\frac{d}{dt}V_{1,\,y}(t) + M_1 g \frac{d}{dt}X_{1,\,y}(t)$

(4)	MultiplyNumbers	$= 1\, M_1 V_{1,\,y}(t)\frac{d}{dt}V_{1,\,y}(t) + M_1 g \frac{d}{dt}X_{1,\,y}(t)$

(5)	RemoveIdentities	$= M_1 V_{1,\,y}(t)\frac{d}{dt}V_{1,\,y}(t) + M_1 g \frac{d}{dt}X_{1,\,y}(t)$

(6)	SubstCalculus	$= M_1 V_{1,\,y}(t) A_{1,\,y}(t) + M_1 g V_{1,\,y}(t)$

(7)	SubstToCancel	$= \dfrac{M_1 V_{1,\,y}(t) F_{net,\,1,\,y}(t)}{M_1} - \dfrac{M_1 F_{net,\,1,\,y}(t) V_{1,\,y}(t)}{M_1}$

(8)	SubstMultIdentities	$= 1\, V_{1,\,y}(t) F_{net,\,1,\,y}(t) - 1\, F_{net,\,1,\,y}(t) V_{1,\,y}(t)$

(9)	RemoveIdentities	$= V_{1,\,y}(t) F_{net,\,1,\,y}(t) - F_{net,\,1,\,y}(t) V_{1,\,y}(t)$

(10)	SubstAddIdentities	$= 0 \;\dfrac{kg\,m^2}{s^3}$

initial expression is understood.

The next several tables illustrate the construction of the general calculation. The first one, Table A.3, derives the primary obstacles from the generalized unknown.

Next, PHYSICS 101 must eliminate the blockers of the primary obstacles. Table A.4 shows how these unblockers are introduced into the calculation.

Finally, the system must introduce the cancellers of the primary obstacles into the calculation, as shown in Table A.4. Because the formula $F_{net} = MgX$ does not hold in all worlds, it is not used in the general calculation. Instead, the calculation is reconstructed without using this formula, which means that the net force needed to cancel the primary obstacles must appear in the left-hand side of the calculation. These new left-hand side variables produce no secondary obstacles, so reconstruction of the calculation is complete.

The general law PHYSICS 101's produces by analyzing the sample solution appears in Table A.6.

This general energy conservation law (Table A.6) applies whenever the total force on an object is known. Notice, though, that a potentially complicated integral needs to be computed if this general law is to be used. To use this formula, it is not sufficient to possess knowledge of the values of variables at two different times. A problem solver must also know how the

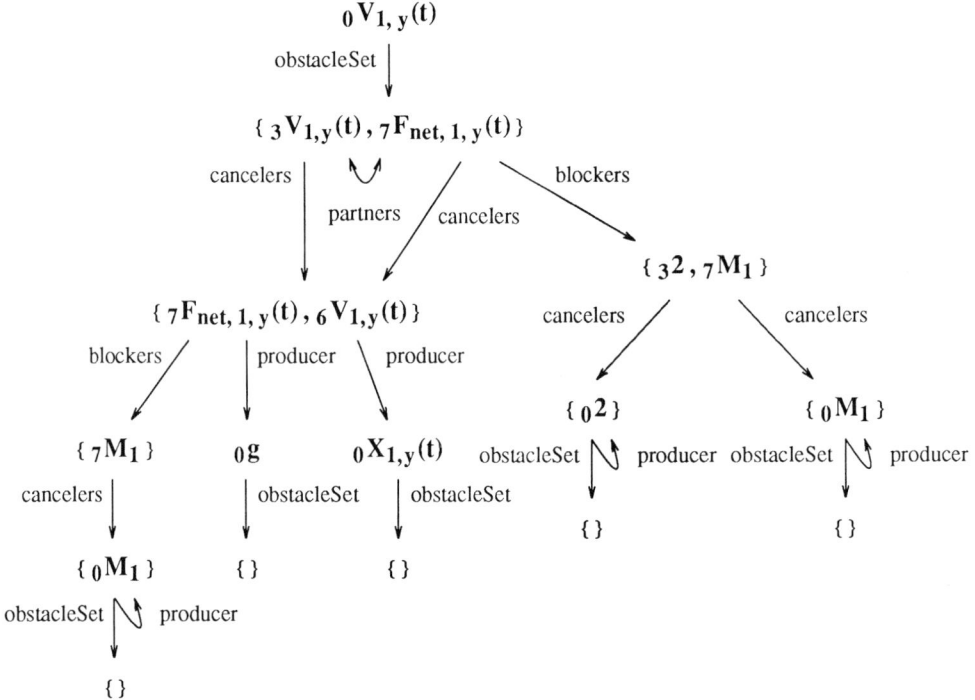

Figure A.2   The Cancellation Graph for the Energy Problem

Table A.3 Introducing the Primary Obstacles

$$\frac{d}{dt} V^2{}_{?s,\ ?c}(t)$$

(2) $$= 2\ V_{?s,\ ?c}(t)\ \frac{d}{dt} V_{?s,\ ?c}(t)$$

(5) $$= 2\ V_{?s,\ ?c}(t)\ A_{?s,\ ?c}(t)$$

(6) $$= 2\ V_{?s,\ ?c}(t)\ \frac{F_{?s,\ ?c}(t)}{M_{?s}}$$

Table A.4 Introducing Terms to Unblock the Primary Obstacles

$$\frac{d}{dt}\left(\frac{1}{2}\ M_{?c}\ V^2{}_{?s,\ ?c}(t)\right)$$

(1) $$= \frac{1}{2}\ M_{?c}\ \frac{d}{dt} V^2{}_{?s,\ ?c}(t)$$

(2) $$= \frac{2}{2}\ M_{?c}\ V_{?s,\ ?c}(t)\ \frac{d}{dt} V_{?s,\ ?c}(t)$$

(3) $$= 1\ M_{?c}\ V_{?s,\ ?c}(t)\ \frac{d}{dt} V_{?s,\ ?c}(t)$$

(4) $$= M_{?c}\ V_{?s,\ ?c}(t)\ \frac{d}{dt} V_{?s,\ ?c}(t)$$

(5) $$= M_{?c}\ V_{?s,\ ?c}(t)\ A_{?s,\ ?c}(t)$$

(6) $$= \frac{M_{?c}\ V_{?s,\ ?c}(t)\ F_{?s,\ ?c}(t)}{M_{?s}}$$

(7) $$= 1\ V_{?s,\ ?c}(t)\ F_{?s,\ ?c}$$

(8) $$= V_{?s,\ ?c}(t)\ F_{?s,\ ?c}$$

Table A.5 Introducing the Cancellers of the Primary Obstacles

$$\frac{d}{dt}\left(\frac{1}{2} M_{?c} V^2_{?s, ?c}(t) - \int F_{net, ?s, ?c}(t)\, dX_{?s, ?c}(t)\right)$$

$$(1) \quad = \frac{1}{2} M_{?c} \frac{d}{dt} V^2_{?s, ?c}(t) - \frac{d}{dt}\int F_{net, ?s, ?c}(t)\, dX_{?s, ?c}(t)$$

$$(2) \quad = \frac{2}{2} M_{?c} V_{?s, ?c}(t) \frac{d}{dt} V_{?s, ?c}(t) - F_{net, ?s, ?c}(t) \frac{d}{dt} X_{?s, ?c}(t)$$

$$(3) \quad = 1\, M_{?c} V_{?s, ?c}(t) \frac{d}{dt} V_{?s, ?c}(t) - F_{net, ?s, ?c}(t) \frac{d}{dt} X_{?s, ?c}(t)$$

$$(4) \quad = M_{?c} V_{?s, ?c}(t) \frac{d}{dt} V_{?s, ?c}(t) - F_{net, ?s, ?c}(t) \frac{d}{dt} X_{?s, ?c}(t)$$

$$(5) \quad = M_{?c} V_{?s, ?c}(t) A_{?s, ?c}(t) - F_{net, ?s, ?c}(t) V_{?s, ?c}(t)$$

$$(6) \quad = \frac{M_{?c} V_{?s, ?c}(t) F_{?s, ?c}(t)}{M_{?s}} - F_{net, ?s, ?c}(t) V_{?s, ?c}(t)$$

$$(7) \quad = 1\, V_{?s, ?c}(t) F_{?s, ?c} - F_{net, ?s, ?c}(t) V_{?s, ?c}(t)$$

$$(8) \quad = V_{?s, ?c}(t) F_{?s, ?c} - F_{net, ?s, ?c}(t) V_{?s, ?c}(t)$$

$$(9) \quad = 0 \frac{kg\, m^2}{s^3}$$

Table A.6 The Final Result of the Energy Problem

Equation

$$\frac{d}{dt}\left[\frac{1}{2} M_{?i} V^2_{?i, ?c}(t) - \int F_{net, ?i, ?c}(t)\, dX_{?i, ?c}\right] = 0 \frac{kg\, m^2}{s^3}$$

Preconditions

$$Object(?i) \wedge IsaComponent(?c) \wedge IndependentOf(M_{?i}, t) \wedge NOT(ZeroValued(M_{?i}))$$

net force depends on position for a continuum of times. In the specific problem there is a *constant* net force (gravity), and when this force is constant the problem is greatly simplified. Integrating a constant force leads to a potential energy determined by that constant force multiplied by the object's position. The position only needs to be known at the two distinct times, and not for *all* intervening times. The special case schema for energy conservation is contained in Table A.7. Again, since this is a conservation schema, the time at which each state occurs need not be known.

Table A.7 The Special-Case Energy Law

Equation

$$\frac{1}{2} M_{?i} V^2_{?i}(t) + M_{?i} \, g \, X_{?i, \, ?c}(t) \;\; = \;\; constant$$

Preconditions

Object(?i) ∧ IsaComponent(?c) ∧

IndependentOf($M_{?i}$, t) ∧ NOT(ZeroValued($M_{?i}$))

Special Case Conditions

$\overline{F}_{net, \, ?i}(t) = M_{?i} \, g \, ?c$

Problem Solving Schema Used

conserved-quantity-schema

A.3 Learning about the Sum of Internal Forces

In a third exercise, PHYSICS 101 is again given a problem describing the state of a collection of three balls at two different times. The internal forces of balls 2 and 3 are specified for both states, while ball 1's internal force is only known in the initial state. The goal is to determine the internal force on ball 1 in the second state. In the solution provided, the teacher evaluates the sum of the three internal forces in each state and equates the results. PHYSICS 101 must explain this new equation. As shown in Table A.8, the system is able to construct an expression describing how the sum of the internal forces depends on time. Since this sum is constant, it can be equated in any two states.

Figure A.3 contains the cancellation graph for the calculation in Table A.8. This problem is actually a subproblem of Chapter 2's momentum example, and the two problems' cancellation graphs are somewhat similar. The main difference is that in the internal force

Table A.8   Verifying the Teacher's Solution to the Internal Force Problem

$$F_{int,\,1,\,z}(t) + F_{int,\,2,\,z}(t) + F_{int,\,3,\,z}(t)$$

(1) SubstSameType $= F_{2,\,1,\,z}(t) + F_{3,\,1,\,z}(t) + F_{1,\,2,\,z}(t) + F_{3,\,2,\,z}(t) + F_{1,\,3,\,z}(t) + F_{2,\,3,\,z}(t)$

(2) SubstToCancel $= F_{2,\,1,\,z}(t) + F_{3,\,1,\,z}(t) - F_{2,\,1,\,z}(t) + F_{3,\,2,\,z}(t) - F_{3,\,1,\,z}(t) - F_{3,\,2,\,z}(t)$

(3) SubstAddIdentities $= 0\,\dfrac{kg\ m}{s^2} + 0\,\dfrac{kg\ m}{s^2} + 0\,\dfrac{kg\ m}{s^2}$

(4) AddNumbers $= 0\,\dfrac{kg\ m}{s^2}$

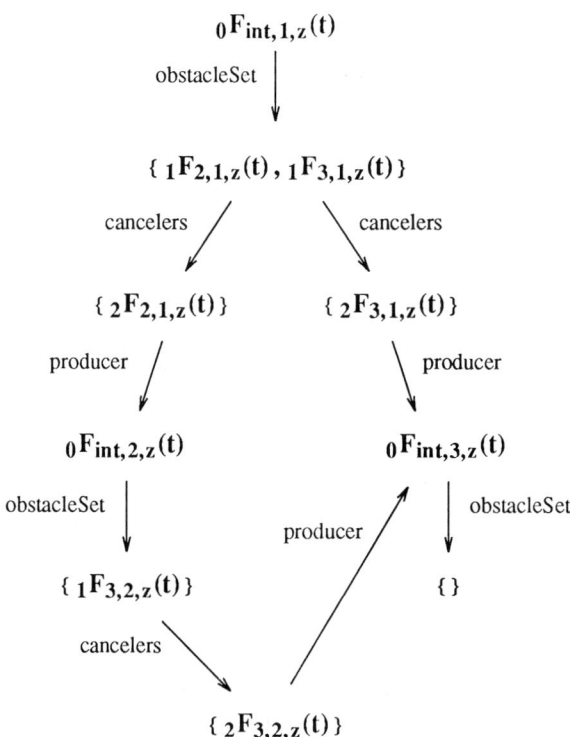

Figure A.3   The Cancellation Graph for the Internal Force Problem

problem there are no cancellation blockers. As in the momentum example, the primary obstacle set contains the two inter-object forces acting on ball 1. These unblocked obstacles are cancelled by forces descended from the internal forces of the other two balls. However, cancelling the primary obstacles produces a secondary obstacle — the force between balls 2 and 3. Cancelling this obstacle does not produce any additional obstacles.

The result of generalizing the internal force calculation is presented in Table A.9. Again, *all* the inter-object forces acting on an object must be cancelled. This results in the need for the presence of every object's internal force in the left-hand side of the equation. With this left-hand side, all the inter-object forces cancel, and PHYSICS 101 acquires the concept that the sum of the internal forces of any system is conserved.

Table A.9 The Final Result of the Internal Force Problem

Equation

$$\sum_{j \in ObjectsInWorld} F_{int,\ j,\ ?c}(?t) = 0 \ \frac{kg\ m}{s^2}$$

Preconditions

$$IsaTime(?t) \wedge IsaComponent(?c)$$

A.4 Using the New Force Law to Learn about Momentum

This example demonstrates the important property that PHYSICS 101 can use, in subsequent problem solving and learning episodes, an equation schema it acquires. The initial momentum problem (Figure 2.9) is rerun after the system acquires the concept illustrated in Table A.9. Table A.10 contains those lines in Table 2.7 that change. (Line 7 of Table 2.7 has no corresponding step in this calculation. That is, the system goes directly from line 6' to line 8'.) Now that PHYSICS 101 has an equation specifying a useful relationship among the internal forces, it can be used to eliminate the three internal forces from the calculation. There is no need to rewrite them in terms of the inter-object forces.

The cancellation graph for this calculation is in Figure A.4. This graph is substantially different from the one for the original solution to the momentum problem (Figure 2.13). In this problem the only primary obstacle is $F_{int,\,1,x}$, which is blocked by a mass term and cancelled by an internal force descended from the velocity of ball 3. Cancelling the primary obstacle introduces one secondary obstacle, namely $F_{int,\,2,\,x}$. In order to cancel this obstacle, $V_{2,\,x}$ must be present in the left-hand of the calculation. The presence of this variable, and the variable needed to cancel its blocker, does not introduce any additional obstacles. Even though their cancellation graphs differ, generalizing this calculation produces the same result as generalizing the calculation in Table 2.7.

Table A.10 Verifying the Momentum Problem after the Internal Force Problem

(6') SubstSameType $= \int (F_{ext,\,1,\,x}(t) + F_{int,\,1,\,x}(t))\,dt \; + \; \int (F_{ext,\,2,\,x}(t) + F_{int,\,2,\,x}(t))\,dt$

$+ \; \int (F_{ext,\,3,\,x}(t) + F_{int,\,3,\,x}(t))\,dt$

(8') SubstToCancel $= \int (F_{ext,\,1,\,x}(t) + F_{int,\,1,\,x}(t))\,dt \; + \; \int (F_{ext,\,2,\,x}(t) + F_{int,\,2,\,x}(t))\,dt$

$+ \; \int (F_{ext,\,3,\,x}(t) - F_{int,\,1,\,x}(t) - F_{int,\,2,\,x}(t))\,dt$

(9') CombineCalculus $= \int (F_{ext,\,1,\,x}(t) + F_{int,\,1,\,x}(t) + F_{ext,\,2,\,x}(t) + F_{int,\,2,\,x}(t)$

$+ F_{ext,\,3,\,x}(t) - F_{int,\,1,\,x}(t) - F_{int,\,2,\,x}(t))\,dt$

(10') SubAddIdentities $= \int (F_{ext,\,1,\,x}(t) + 0\,\frac{kg\,m}{s^2} + F_{ext,\,2,\,x}(t) + 0\,\frac{kg\,m}{s^2} + F_{ext,\,3,\,x}(t))\,dt$

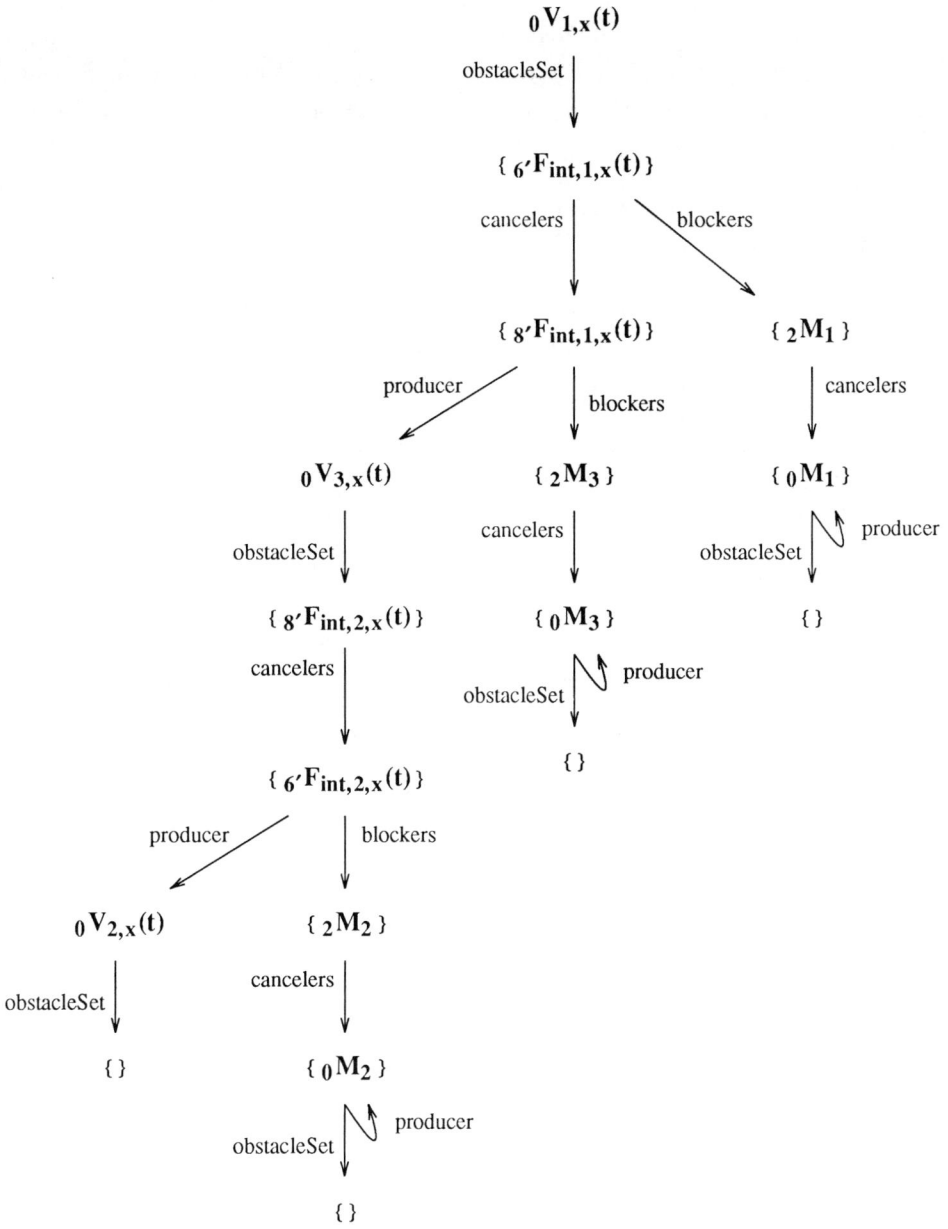

Figure A.4   The Cancellation Graph for the Second Solution of the Momentum Problem

A.5 Attempting to Learn from a Two-Ball Collision

It was stated in Chapter 2 that at least a three-ball collision problem is needed to properly acquire the concept of momentum conservation. This section describes the results of analyzing a two-ball collision.[1] Again, the teacher equates the momentum in the two states and the system needs to verify this new equation. Verification is nearly identical to the calculation in Table 2.7 and is not shown here. The main difference is that variables involving ball 3 are not present.

The cancellation graph for this simpler calculation appears in Figure A.5. It is virtually identical to the left half of Figure 2.13. The only significant difference is that the presence of $V_{2,x}$ produces no obstacles because canceling the obstacles of the unknown cancels all the potential obstacles of this variable. The fortuitous circumstances of the two-body example mean that the problem of what to do with the additional inter-object forces need not be faced in solving the specific example. This difference becomes important in the generalization phase, as described in Section 2.4.2. Since PHYSICS 101 does no problem solving during generalization, these inter-object forces remain, as shown in Table A.11.

One way to handle the case where there are no specific representatives of a variable in the general calculation would be to save the final result, marking it for possible later refinement. However, in PHYSICS 101 whenever there are variables without representatives in the specific calculation, no learning takes place.

This example illustrates an important issue in generalizing the structure of explanations. When generalizing an explanation to handle more entities, a learning system must be able to recognize any new issues that arise due to the presence of these additional entities. The sample problem's solution may not have had to address all of these issues, due to fortuitous circumstances in the example, and the learner must possess some facility to recognize and either surmount these extra issues or wait for a better training example.

---

[1] The two-ball problem is identical to the original three-ball problem of Figure 2.9, except that ball 3 is not included.

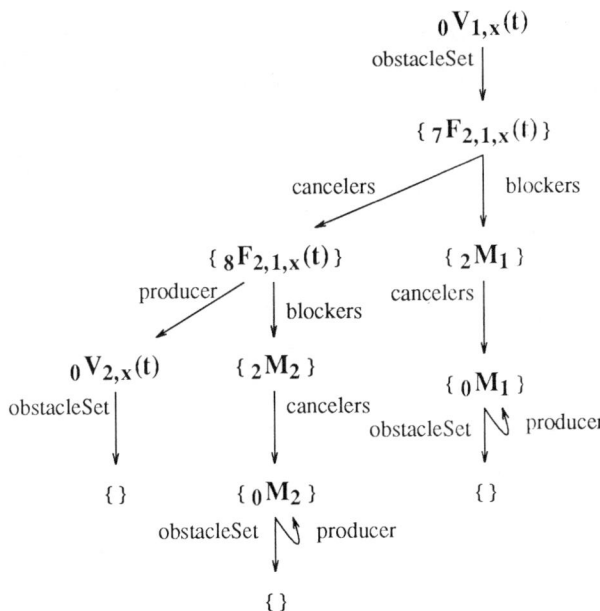

$$_0 V_{1,x}(t)$$

obstacleSet

$$\{\,_7 F_{2,1,x}(t)\,\}$$

cancelers   blockers

$$\{\,_8 F_{2,1,x}(t)\,\}$$ $$\{\,_2 M_1\,\}$$

producer   blockers   cancelers

$$_0 V_{2,x}(t)$$ $$\{\,_2 M_2\,\}$$ $$\{\,_0 M_1\,\}$$

obstacleSet   cancelers   obstacleSet producer

$$\{\,\}$$ $$\{\,_0 M_2\,\}$$ $$\{\,\}$$

obstacleSet producer

$$\{\,\}$$

Figure A.5   The Cancellation Graph for a Two-Ball Momentum Problem

---

Table A.11   The Potential Final Result of the Two-Ball Momentum Problem

Equation

$$\frac{d}{dt} \sum_{i \in ObjectsInWorld} M_i V_{i,\,?c}(t) \;=\; \sum_{i \in ObjectsInWorld} F_{ext,\,i,\,?c}(t) \;+\; \sum_{j \neq ?s} \sum_{k \neq j,\,?s} F_{k,\,j,\,?c}(t)$$

Preconditions

    IsaComponent($?c$) $\wedge$

    Member($?s$, $ObjectsInWorld$) $\wedge$

    $\forall\ i \varepsilon ObjectsInWorld$ NOT(ZeroValued(M_i)) $\wedge$

    $\forall\ i \varepsilon ObjectsInWorld$ IndependentOf(M_i ,t)

Eliminated Terms

    $\forall\ i \neq ?s\ \ F_{?s,\,i,\,?c}(t)$, $F_{i,\,?s,\,?c}(t)$

Appendix B Additional BAGGER Examples

B.1 Overview

This appendix presents the details of BAGGER's acquisition of several sequential rules.[1] Besides providing the details of the examples briefly mentioned previously in Section 3.1, plus a few others, it illustrates several interesting aspects of the BAGGER generalization algorithm. For instance, unlike in other works in explanation-based learning, a rule learned by BAGGER does not always subsume the problem solution from which it is derived. Other topics discussed include how extra terms can be added to a sequential rule in order to increase its efficiency, how the process of unwinding may limit the generality of an acquired sequential rule, and how the complexity of the sample solution can effect the generality of the rule learned.

As stated previously, after BAGGER initially produces a rule, it rearranges antecedents in order to speed-up the process of satisfying the rule. Thus, two adjacent antecedents in an explanation structure need not be near one another in an acquired rule.

B.2 More Tower Building Rules

The examples in this section consider some variants on the tower-building rule presented in Section 3.2.4. First, the results of applying standard explanation-based generalization to Figure 3.13's proof tree are presented. Next, using the same proof, BAGGER produces a more operational rule. Finally, using a slightly more complicated example, the acquisition of a more general rule is described.

B.2.1 The Result of Standard Explanation-Based Learning

The result of directly applying EGGS to the proof in Figure 3.13 appears in Table B.1. This rule specifies how to move from the initial state to the state that results from three transfers, where the moved blocks are stacked upon one another, creating the desired tower. Notice that this rule requires the first and second blocks to be moved be initially clear, while the third block to be moved must only support the second block to be moved. This rule cannot be used to construct a tower from a scene with three blocks all directly on a table, nor can it be used to move a three-block tower from one location to another.

Chapter 4 presents an empirical determination of the performance gains obtained by using the sequential rules learned by BAGGER rather than the rules learned by standard EBL.

---

[1] Remember that all variables contain a leading ''?'' and are universally quantified. The construct *{?h | ?t}* matches a list with head *?h* and tail *?t*.

Table B.1 The Standard EBL Version of the Tower Rule

Antecedents

(1) AchievableState(s0) ∧ Liftable(?x2, s0) ∧ FlatTop(?x2) ∧ Height(?x2, ?hx) ∧

(2) Block(?x) ∧ Height(?x,?hx2) ∧ ?x2 ≠ ?x ∧ FreeSpace(?y,s0) ∧ Xpos(?y,?xpos,s0) ∧

(3) Ypos(?y, ?pyy, s0) ∧ ?x ≠ ?y ∧ ?x2 ≠ ?y ∧ Supports(?x, {?x1}, s0) ∧

(4) NotMember(?x2, {?x1}) ∧ Supports(?x1, φ, s0) ∧ Block(?x1) ∧ FlatTop(?x1) ∧

(5) Height(?x1, ?hx1) ∧ ?x1 ≠ ?y ∧ ?x2 ≠ ?x1 ∧ ?x ≠ ?x1 ∧ ?xpos ≤ ?xmax ∧

(6) ?xpos ≥ ?xmin ∧ ?pyx = (?hx + ?pyy) ∧ ?pyx1 = (?hx1 + ?pyx) ∧

(7) ?pyx2 = (?hx2 + ?pyx1) ∧ ?pyx2 ≥ ?ymin

Consequents

(8) AchievableState(Do(Transfer(?x,?x1),Do(Transfer(?x1,?x2),Do(Transfer(?x2,?y),s0)))) ∧

(9) Xpos(?x,?xpos,Do(Transfer(?x,?x1),Do(Transfer(?x1,?x2),Do(Transfer(?x2,?y),s0)))) ∧

(10) ?xpos ≤ ?xmax ∧ ?xpos ≥ ?xmin ∧

(11) Ypos(?x,?pyx2,Do(Transfer(?x,?x1),Do(Transfer(?x1,?x2),Do(Transfer(?x2,?y),s0)))) ∧

(12) ?pyx2 ≥ ?ymin

B.2.2 A More Operational Tower Building Rule

An issue in explanation-based learning is deciding which portions of a specific problem's explanation can be considered easily reconstructable and, hence, disregarded when the explanation is generalized. Allowing such reconstruction during problem solving produces a more *general* rule since alternative reconstructions are possible, but the resulting rule is less *operational* because significant effort can be expended recalculating. As described in Chapter 3, BAGGER considers a term easily evaluatable if it is expressed in terms of the initial state only. A more restricted definition, one that incorporates all of the constraints in the explanation, is to consider a node acceptable only if it is a leaf node in the explanation. Being a leaf node means it is either an axiom or is a term used to specify the initial state. In latter case, it is reasonable to assume that these terms will also be specified in future problems and will require minimal effort to test.

BAGGER can be instructed to construct sequential rules that are more operational. This entails forming the initial antecedents by collecting the leaf nodes that support the first application of the focus rule[2] and altering the algorithm for constructing the remainder of the sequential rule to only accept a situation-independent rule if it is a leaf node. The results of using this more operational form of generalization with the previous tower-building proof (Figure 3.13) appears in Table B.2. Terms appearing in this rule, but not in the more general version (Table 3.5), are in all capitals and in a bold font.

Comparing the two versions, a clear table[3] is required for the location to place the first block moved, as opposed to a possibly hard to find arbitrary free space. Also, rather than specifying any liftable object, a clear box is specified as the first object to be moved. The new requirements on successive moved blocks are that each must be a box, which is a specialization of block. Finally, the previously moved object must be a box, as that insures it will have a flat top.

B.2.3   A More General Tower Building Rule

The rules learned by BAGGER depend on the complexity of the specific problem from which they are derived. If the specific problem's solution took advantage of some fortuitous circumstances, some issues inherent in the underlying general concept may not have been addressed. Because BAGGER performs no additional problem solving during generalization, the rule acquired may not fully reflect the possible generality. One way this can occur is if each application of the focus rule is satisfied in the same manner, even though alternatives are possible. In this case, BAGGER will not produce a disjunctive rule. This section further illustrates the issue of fortuitous circumstances using a slightly more complicated tower-building example; the result is a rule more general than that produced from the previous example.

Figure B.1 contains the initial and final states of the example, where four blocks are stacked to reach a goal height. The relevant portion of the resulting proof tree appears in Figure B.2. This subtree shows how BAGGER determines that Block D can be lifted. Some rules are numbered, using subscripts on their ampersands, for purposes of reference. The sequential rule that results is nearly identical to that in Table 3.5, with one major difference. The existential term in Table B.3 replaces the second disjunct in that rule (lines 9-11). This new term says that it is possible to plan to move a block in the ith step if it originally supports only one other block, which is to be moved in some *earlier* step, and no other block is to be placed on it in any intervening step. This is more general than the other plan, which said a block could be moved if the only block on top of it is moved in the *previous* step.

The proof tree in Figure B.2 contains two connected unwindable rules, which explains why BAGGER produces the existential term. The rule in that figure subscripted with a three is unwindable. When unwound, it says a block continues to support nothing as long as the block moved in each step is not placed upon it (producing line 4 in the table). This gets

---

[2] This could be easily extended to view *each* application of the focus rule as the first and using the disjunction of all the results to construct the initial antecedents.

[3] Although a known rule says that tables are always clear, that rule is not used in the explanation of the specific example.

Table B.2   The More Operational Version of the Tower Rule

Antecedents$_{initial}$

(1)   Sequence(?seq) $\wedge$ InitialVector(?v$_1$, ?seq) $\wedge$ State(s0) $\wedge$?v$_{1,1}$ = s0 $\wedge$

(2)   **TABLE**(?v$_{1,3}$) $\wedge$ **SUPPORTS**(?v$_{1,3}$,ϕ,s0) $\wedge$ **BOX**(?v$_{1,2}$) $\wedge$ **SUPPORTS**(?v$_{1,2}$,ϕ,s0) $\wedge$

(3)   Height(?v$_{1,2}$, ?v$_{1,4}$) $\wedge$ Xpos(?v$_{1,3}$, ?px, s0) $\wedge$ Ypos(?v$_{1,3}$, ?new, s0) $\wedge$

(4)   ?v$_{1,2}$ $\neq$?v$_{1,3}$ $\wedge$?v$_{1,5}$ = (?v$_{1,4}$ + ?new) $\wedge$?px $\geq$?xmin $\wedge$?px $\leq$?xmax

Antecedent$_{intermediate}$

(5)   [Member(?v$_i$, ?seq) $\wedge$?v$_i$ $\neq$?v$_1$ $\wedge$ Member(?v$_{i-1}$, ?seq) $\wedge$ Predecessor(?v$_{i-1}$, ?v$_i$, ?seq)

$\rightarrow$

(6)   ?v$_{i,3}$ = ?v$_{i-1,2}$ $\wedge$?v$_{i,1}$ = Do(Transfer(?v$_{i-1,2}$, ?v$_{i-1,3}$), ?v$_{i-1,1}$) $\wedge$ **BOX**(?v$_{i,3}$) $\wedge$

(7)   **BOX**(?v$_{i,2}$) $\wedge$ Height(?v$_{i,2}$, ?v$_{i,4}$) $\wedge$?v$_{i,2}$ $\neq$?v$_{i,3}$ $\wedge$?v$_{i,5}$ = (?v$_{i,4}$ + ?v$_{i-1,5}$)

(8)   [[[Member(?v$_j$,?seq) $\wedge$ Earlier(?v$_j$,?v$_i$,?seq) $\rightarrow$?v$_{i,2}$ $\neq$?v$_{j,3}$] $\wedge$ Supports(?v$_{i,2}$,ϕ,s0)]

(9) $\vee$ [[Member(?v$_j$,?seq) $\wedge$ Earlier(?v$_j$,?v$_{i-1}$,?seq) $\rightarrow$ NotMember(?v$_{j,2}$,{?v$_{i-1,2}$})] $\wedge$

(10)   [Member(?v$_j$, ?seq) $\wedge$ Earlier(?v$_j$, ?v$_{i-1}$, ?seq) $\rightarrow$?v$_{i,2}$ $\neq$?v$_{j,3}$] $\wedge$

(11)   Supports(?v$_{i,2}$, (?v$_{i-1,2}$), s0) $\wedge$?v$_{i,2}$ $\neq$?v$_{i-1,3}$]]]

Antecedents$_{final}$

(12)   FinalVector(?v$_n$, ?seq) $\wedge$?py = ?v$_{n,5}$ $\wedge$?state = Do(Transfer(?v$_{n,2}$, ?v$_{n,3}$), ?v$_{n,1}$) $\wedge$

(13)   ?object = ?v$_{n,2}$ $\wedge$?py $\geq$?ymin

Consequents

(14)   State(?state) $\wedge$ Xpos(?object, ?px, ?state) $\wedge$?px $\leq$?xmax $\wedge$?px $\geq$?xmin $\wedge$

(15)   Ypos(?object, ?py, ?state) $\wedge$?py $\geq$?ymin

This rule extends sequences 1 $\rightarrow$ N.

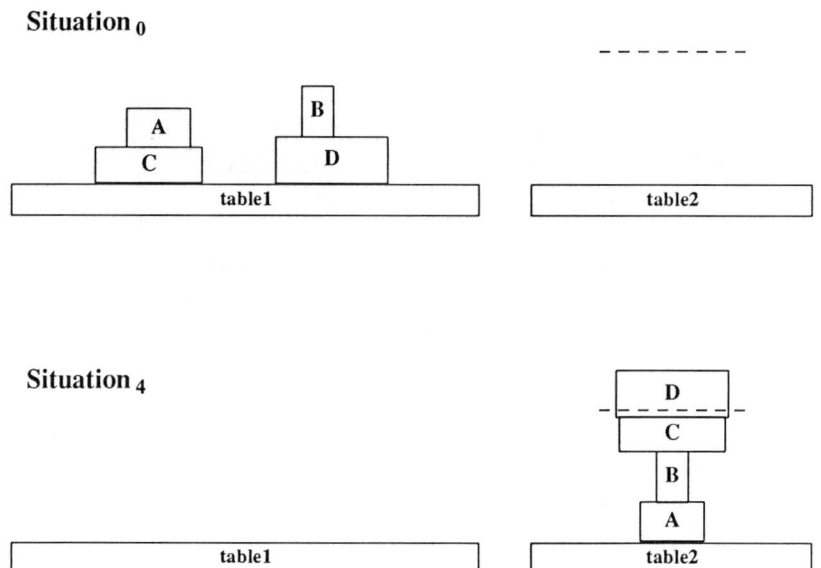

Situation $_0$

Situation $_4$

Figure B.1   Constructing a Four-Block Tower

unwound to Rule 2, which states that moving the only block on an object clears it. BAGGER unwinds the first unwound rule to an arbitrary step k, so this clearing occurs in step $k-1$. Next, BAGGER unwinds Rule 1. This rule instantiation says an object supporting only one other object stays that way as long as nothing else is set on it. Unwinding it to the initial state produces the third term in line 1, plus the terms in lines 2 and 3.

This example illustrates the need for recognizing when a newly-acquired rule subsumes a previously learned rule (BAGGER2 partially addresses this issue be adding new disjuncts to existing recurrences). If this can be done, BAGGER can remove the redundant rule from the database. A final point is that additional analysis of an explanation (e.g., considering the insertion of extra unwindable rules), may prove beneficial in acquiring the general concept underlying a sample solution.

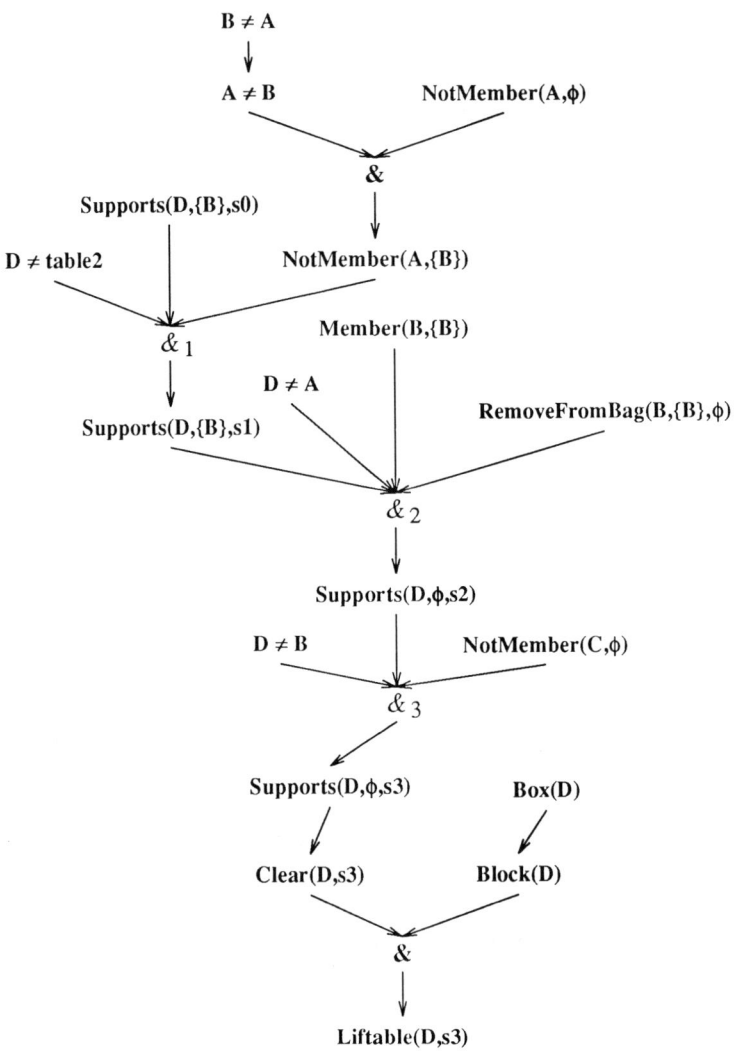

Figure B.2 **Partial Situation Calculus Plan for Stacking Four Blocks**

Abbreviation Key

s0 *the initial state*	s2 Do(Transfer(B,A),Do(Transfer(A,table2),s0))
s1 Do(Transfer(A,table2),s0)	s3 Do(Transfer(C,B),Do(Transfer(B,A),Do(Transfer(A,table2),s0)))

Table B.3 A More General Way to Find a Liftable Block

$\exists \; ?v_k \in ?seq$

   (1) NotEarlier($?v_i$, $?v_k$, $?seq$) $\wedge$ $?v_{i,2} \neq ?v_{k-1,3}$ $\wedge$ Supports($?v_{i,2}$, $\{?v_{k-1,2}\}$, s0) $\wedge$

   (2) [Member($?v_j$, $?seq$) $\wedge$ Earlier($?v_j$, $?v_{k-1}$, $?seq$) $\rightarrow ?v_{i,2} \neq ?v_{j,3}$] $\wedge$

   (3) [Member($?v_j$, $?seq$) $\wedge$ Earlier($?v_j$, $?v_{k-1}$, $?seq$) $\rightarrow$ NotMember($?v_{j,2}$, $\{?v_{k-1,2}\}$)] $\wedge$

   (4) [Member($?v_j$, $?seq$) $\wedge$ Earlier($?v_j$, $?v_i$, $?seq$) $\wedge$ NotEarlier($?v_j$, $?v_k$, $?seq$) $\rightarrow ?v_{i,2} \neq ?v_{j,3}$]

B.3 Clearing an Object

This section presents three examples dealing with the clearing of blocks. The first two produce orthogonal plans for clearing blocks, while the third demonstrates why BAGGER does not learn a plan combining the approaches in the first two.

B.3.1 Unstacking a Tower

The section presents the acquisition of the rule sketched earlier in Figure 3.3. The sequence of moves from which BAGGER learns a plan for unstacking towers appears in Figure B.3. Here three blocks are moved to clear Block *D*. The explanation of these transfers appears in Figure B.4, while the rule that results appears in Table B.4.

This rule's *RIS*, which only contains the variables in the focus rule, is satisfied from *N* to 1. The last term in line 6 and the first in line 10 require that the block to be moved in step *i-1* must be the only one directly upon the block to be moved in step *i*. In addition, the block to be moved in step *i* is placed upon the block to be moved in the previous step (last term of line 4). That is, clear a tower of blocks by inverting the tower at another location. Once a solver calculates a location to place the first block, it need not expend any more effort finding acceptable locations to place the other blocks.

There is one additional interesting point about this example. Unlike the results of most other learning algorithms, the learned rule does not apply to the sample problem which motivated it! The acquired rule clears an object by inverting, at another location, the stack of blocks upon it. However, this will not work if the block on top of the stack does not have a flat top, as is the case in the sample problem.

The BAGGER generalization algorithm analyzes each application of the focus rule. It only incorporates into the intermediate antecedents of the acquired rule the results of those applications that are suitably general. If an application performs some operation in an overly-specific way, the acquired rule will not reflect this nuance, and the rule's generality may be limited.

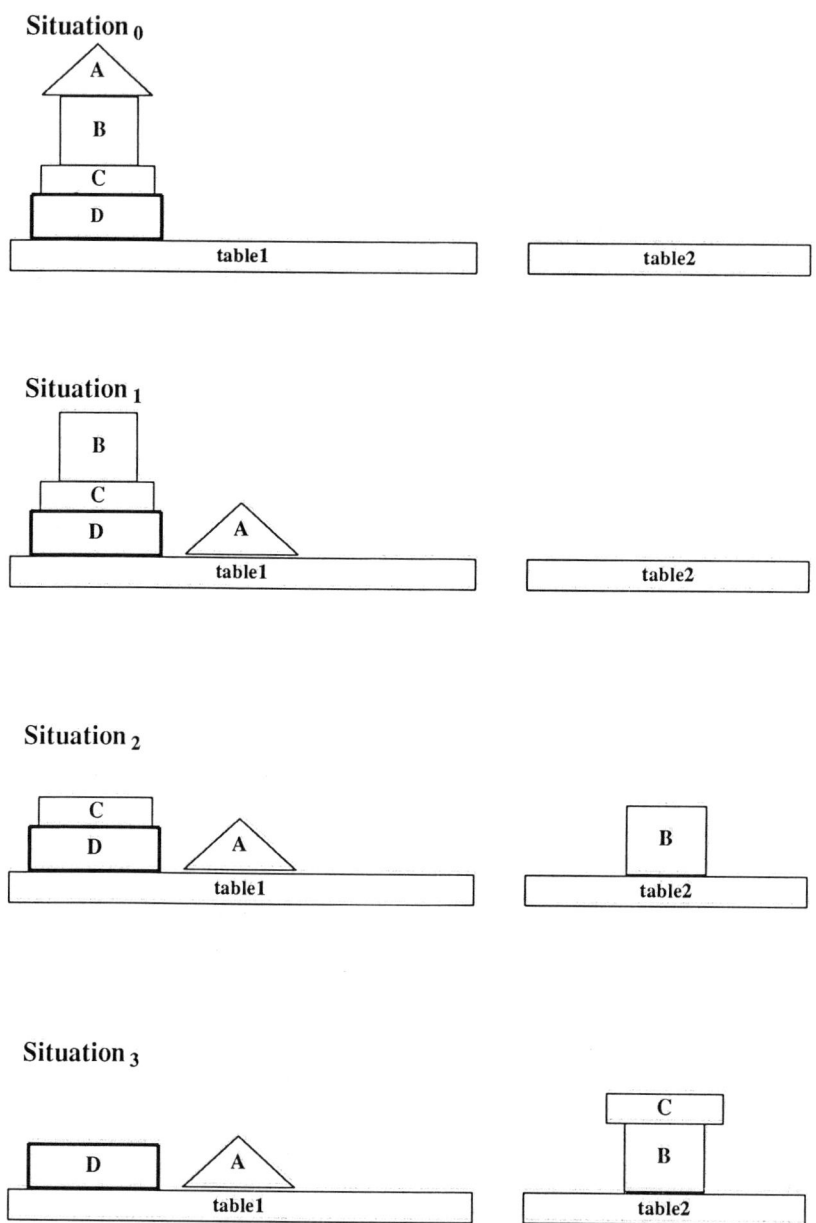

Figure B.3   Moving Three Blocks to Clear Another Block

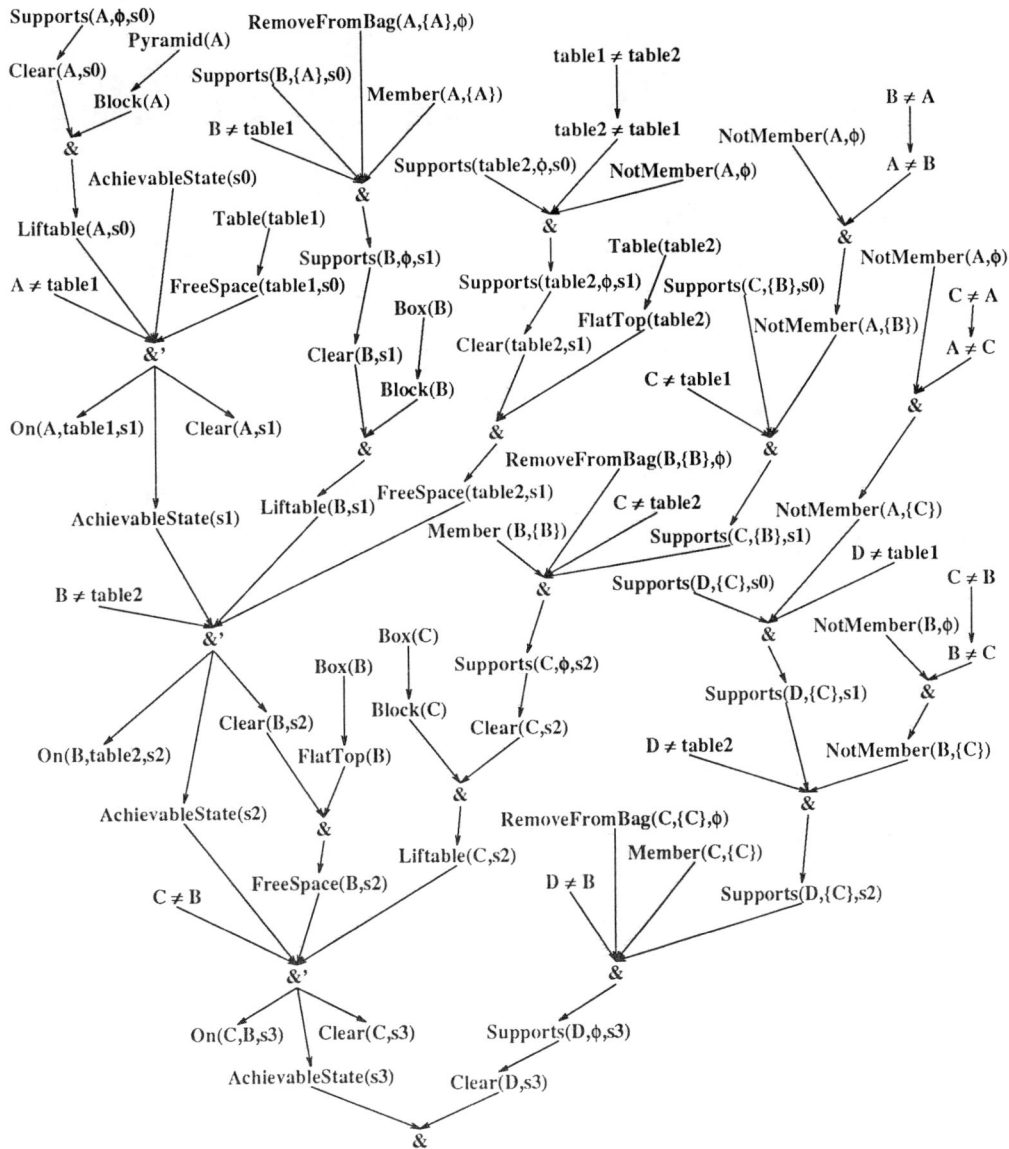

Figure B.4   Situation Calculus Plan for Clearing Block D

Abbreviation Key

s0 *the initial state*   s2 Do(Transfer(B,table2),Do(Transfer(A,table1),s0))

s1 Do(Transfer(A,table1),s0)   s3 Do(Transfer(C,B),Do(Transfer(B,table2),Do(Transfer(A,table1),s0)))

181

Table B.4 Unstacking a Tower

Antecedents$_{\text{initial}}$

(1) InitialVector($?v_1$, ?seq) $\wedge$ State(s0) $\wedge$ $?v_{1,1}$ = s0 $\wedge$ FreeSpace($?v_{1,3}$, s0) $\wedge$

(2) Liftable($?v_{1,2}$, s0) $\wedge$ $?v_{1,2} \neq ?v_{1,3}$

Antecedent$_{\text{intermediate}}$

(3) [Member($?v_i$, ?seq) $?v_i \neq ?v_1$ Member($?v_{i-1}$, ?seq)   Predecessor($?v_{i-1}$, $?v_i$, ?seq)
$\rightarrow$

(4) FlatTop($?v_{i,3}$) $\wedge$ Block($?v_{i,2}$) $\wedge$ $?v_{i,2} \neq ?v_{i,3}$ $\wedge$ $?v_{i,3} = ?v_{i-1,2}$ $\wedge$

(5) $?v_{i,1}$ = Do(Transfer($?v_{i-1,2}$, $?v_{i-1,3}$), $?v_{i-1,1}$) $\wedge$ Supports($?v_{i,2}$, $\{?v_{i-1,2}\}$, s0) $\wedge$

(6) $?v_{i,2} \neq ?v_{i-1,3}$ $\wedge$ [Member($?v_j$, ?seq) $\wedge$ Earlier($?v_j$, $?v_{i-1}$, ?seq) $\rightarrow$ $?v_{i,2} \neq ?v_{j,3}$] $\wedge$

(7) [Member($?v_j$,?seq) $\wedge$ Earlier($?v_j$,$?v_{i-1}$,?seq) $\rightarrow$ NotMember($?v_j$, 2,$\{?v_{i-1,2}\}$)] $\wedge$

(8) ?object $\neq ?v_{i-1,3}$ $\wedge$ NotMember($?v_{i-1,2}$, $\{?v_{n,2}\}$)]

Antecedents$_{\text{final}}$

(9) Sequence(?seq) $\wedge$ FinalVector($?v_n$,?seq) $\wedge$?state = Do(Transfer($?v_{n,2}$,$?v_{n,3}$),$?v_{n,1}$) $\wedge$

(10) Supports(?object, $\{?v_{n,2}\}$, s0) $\wedge$?object $\neq ?v_{n,3}$

Consequents

(11) State(?state) $\wedge$ Clear(?object, ?state)

This rule extends sequences N $\rightarrow$ 1.

If the sample problem is more complicated, BAGGER learns a disjunctive rule for clearing. For example, this will occur if a tower is moved and some of the intermediate blocks are placed on a table (which are known to always have free space) and others on some other blocks that are clear in the initial state. In these situations, the learned rule would subsume the example of Figure B.3.

B.3.2 Horizontally Clearing an Object

Unlike many other blocks-world formalizations, the rules used by BAGGER do not assume a block can support only one other block. Figure B.5 contains the results of a sequence of moves from which another plan (Figure 3.4) for clearing an object is acquired. Blocks A and B are moved in order to clear table 1. Here, the clearing is called "horizontal" because in general it involves clearing an object that is supporting any number of clear objects. This compares to the previous example of "vertical" clearing, where a stack of objects is moved.

Figure B.6 contains the explanation of these transfers, and Table B.5 contains the rule that results. In this new acquired rule, the initial antecedents determine which objects are being supported in the initial state by the object that is to be cleared. One of these is chosen as the first object to be moved. At each successive step, another object in the collection is chosen to be moved and is scheduled to be placed upon the block to be moved in the previous step. This continues until the collection is empty, at which time the goal will be achieved. The final term in line 8 insures that no block is moved on to the object to be cleared. The RIS's vectors contains one variable in addition to the three in the focus rule. This fourth variable records how many blocks will still be on the block being cleared after the ith step.

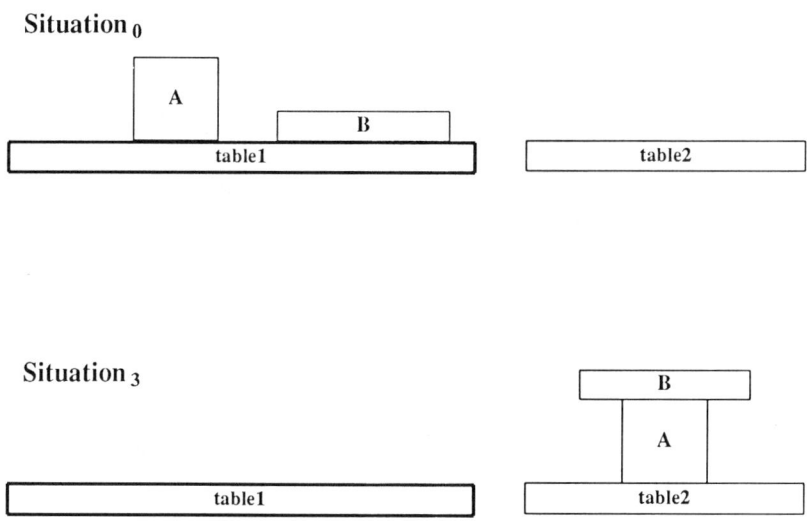

Figure B.5 · **Moving Two Blocks to Clear a Table**

Figure B.6   Situation Calculus Plan for Clearing Table 1

184

Table B.5 "Horizontally" Clearing an Object

Antecedents$_{initial}$

(1) Sequence(?seq) $\wedge$ InitialVector(?v_1, ?seq) $\wedge$ State(s0) $\wedge$?$v_{1,1}$ = s0 $\wedge$

(2) FreeSpace(?$v_{1,3}$, s0) $\wedge$ Liftable(?$v_{1,2}$, s0) $\wedge$?$v_{1,2}$ $\neq$?$v_{1,3}$ $\wedge$?object $\neq$?$v_{1,3}$ $\wedge$

(3) Member(?$v_{1,2}$,?new) $\wedge$ RemoveFromBag(?$v_{1,2}$,?new,?$v_{1,4}$) $\wedge$ Supports(?object,?new,s0)

Antecedent$_{intermediate}$

(4) [Member(?v_i, ?seq) $\wedge$?v_i $\neq$?v_1 $\wedge$ Member(?v_{i-1}, ?seq) $\wedge$ Predecessor(?v_{i-1}, ?v_i, ?seq)

$\rightarrow$

(5) ?$v_{i,3}$ = ?$v_{i-1,2}$ $\wedge$?$v_{i,1}$ = Do(Transfer(?$v_{i-1,2}$, ?$v_{i-1,3}$), ?$v_{i-1,1}$) $\wedge$

(6) Member(?$v_{i,2}$,?$v_{i-1,4}$) $\wedge$ RemoveFromBag(?$v_{i,2}$, ?$v_{i-1,4}$, ?$v_{i,4}$) $\wedge$ FlatTop(?$v_{i,3}$) $\wedge$

(7) Block(?$v_{i,2}$) $\wedge$ Supports(?$v_{i,2}$, ϕ, s0) $\wedge$?$v_{i,2}$ $\neq$?$v_{i,3}$ $\wedge$

(8) [Member(?v_j, ?seq) $\wedge$ Earlier(?v_j, ?v_i, ?seq) $\rightarrow$?$v_{i,2}$ $\neq$?$v_{j,3}$] $\wedge$?object $\neq$?$v_{i,3}$]

Antecedents$_{final}$

(9) FinalVector(?v_n, ?seq) $\wedge$?$v_{n,4}$ = ϕ $\wedge$?state = Do(Transfer(?$v_{n,2}$, ?$v_{n,3}$), ?$v_{n,1}$)

Consequents

(10) State(?state) $\wedge$ Clear(?object, ?state)

This rule extends sequences 1 $\rightarrow$ N.

B.4 Setting a Table

Occasionally BAGGER's problem solver will expend much effort trying to construct an *RIS* that satisfies the current goal before it determines all possible variable bindings lead to failure. This section presents an example in which additional analysis can lead to the system recognizing when it will be futile to try to instantiate a satisfactory *RIS*. From this example, BAGGER produces a plan for setting N places on a table. Additional analysis determines that it is futile to attempt to apply this rule unless the capacity of the table is at least N.

BAGGER produces the graph and rule presented in this section. However, the algorithm for constructing the extra terms is unappealingly narrow and is not discussed outside of this section. The technique is intended to only illustrate the kind of post-processing that is necessary to improve the efficiency of the rules BAGGER learns. In the system, this technique is implemented within a production system architecture. There are a collection of rules that can add new terms into a sequential rule. These rules continually add new terms until none of the rules have their preconditions satisfied.

The example from which BAGGER acquires the new rule is sketched in Figure B.7. Initially a table with a seating capacity of four is empty. First one, then another, set of utensils is placed on this table in satisfying the goal of finding a table with two locations set.

The proof that Figure B.7's action satisfy the goal appears in Figure B.8 (some long predicate names are abbreviated in this graph). A known rule states that to set a place on a table, there must be a clear spot on the table and there must be a set of utensils available. This rule also states that after setting the empty place, the place is no longer empty and the previously free utensils are now in use. A second rule counts the number of table locations that are set in a given situation.

The rule that BAGGER produces by generalizing the explanation in Figure B.8 appears in Table B.6; the meaning of each of the eight components in this rule's *RIS* appears in Table B.7. Basically, the rule records, in the initial situation, the open locations on some table and the number of available utensils sets. Then utensil sets are placed on open table locations until enough locations are set.

However, if there are not enough locations on the table or not enough utensil sets, a problem solver may perform substantial useless work. By analyzing the initially-produced sequential rule, BAGGER adds the last term in line 6, which requires that the size of the table chosen be sufficient to set the desired number of places.

It produces the term $?settings \leq ?size$ because of the presence of a termination condition (second term of line 12) that is a mathematical constraint. This constraint contains two variables that are not effected by the *RIS* and a third known to never be negative (because it is the second argument to the predicate *Size*). For an acceptable non-negative $?n$ to be possible, it must be the case that the number of settings requested never exceed the capacity of the table selected.

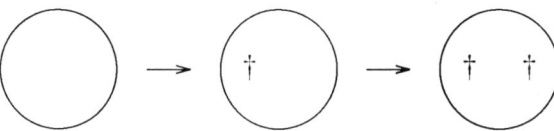

Figure B.7   Setting Two Places at a Table

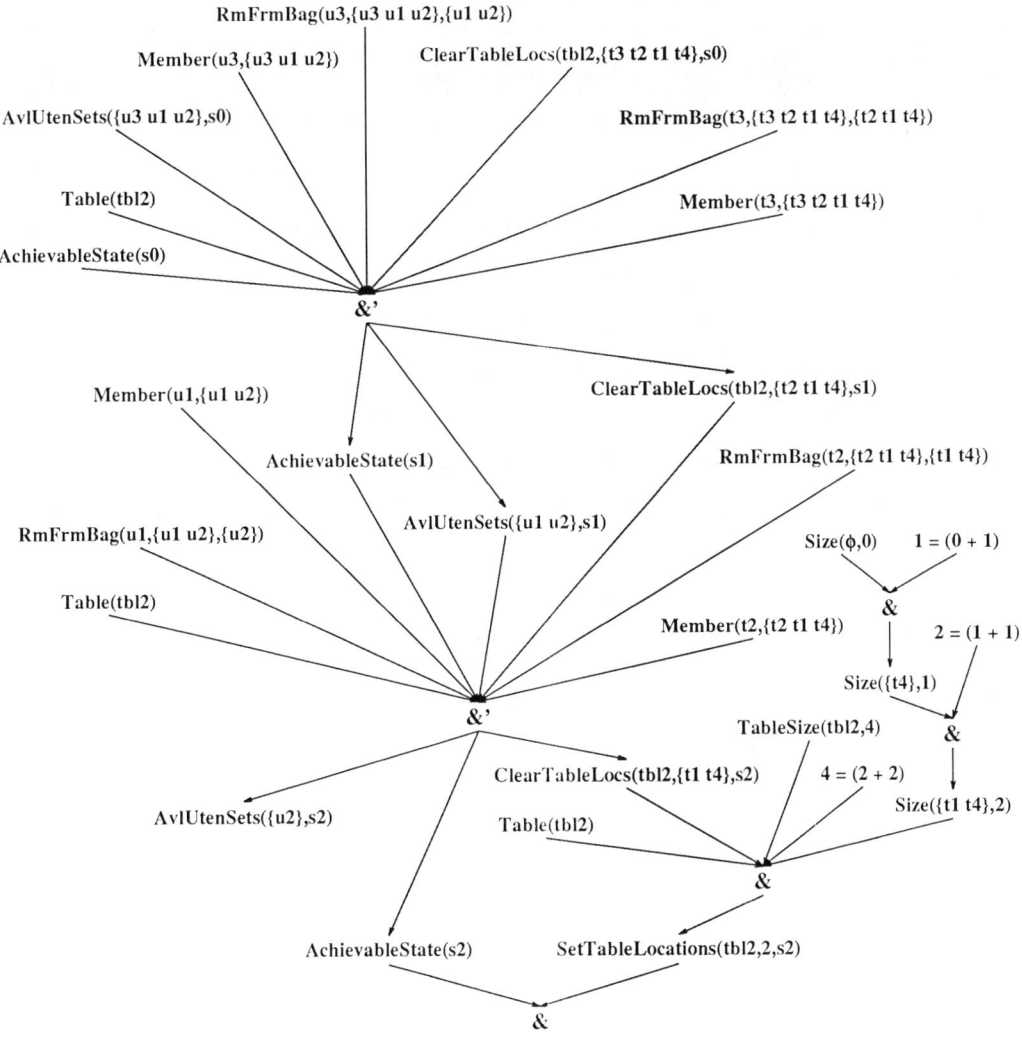

Figure B.8   Situation Calculus Plan for Setting Two Places at a Table

Abbreviation Key

s0   *the initial state*

s1   Do(SetTblLoc(tbl2,t3,u3),s0)

s2   Do(SetTblLoc(tbl2,t2,u1),Do(SetTblLoc(tbl2,t3,u3),s0))

Table B.6 A Rule for Setting Tables

Antecedents$_{\text{initial}}$

(1)   Sequence(?seq) $\wedge$ InitialVector(?v_1, ?seq) $\wedge$ AchievableState(s0) $\wedge$

(2)   AvailUtensilSets(?$v_{1,3}$, s0) $\wedge$?$v_{1,6}$ = {?$v_{1,7}$ | ?$v_{1,8}$} $\wedge$?$v_{1,3}$ = {?$v_{1,4}$ | ?$v_{1,5}$} $\wedge$

(3)   ?table = ?$v_{1,1}$ $\wedge$?$v_{1,2}$ = s0 $\wedge$ RemoveFromBag(?$v_{1,7}$, ?$v_{1,6}$, ?$v_{1,8}$) $\wedge$

(4)   Member(?$v_{1,7}$, ?$v_{1,6}$) $\wedge$ ClearTableLocs(?$v_{1,1}$, ?$v_{1,6}$, s0) $\wedge$

(5)   RemoveFromBag(?$v_{1,4}$, ?$v_{1,3}$, ?$v_{1,5}$) $\wedge$ Member(?$v_{1,4}$, ?$v_{1,3}$) $\wedge$ Table(?$v_{1,1}$) $\wedge$

(6)   TableSize(?$v_{1,1}$, ?size) $\wedge$?settings $\leq$?size

Antecedent$_{\text{intermediate}}$

(7)   [Member(?v_i, ?seq) $\wedge$?v_i $\neq$?v_1 $\wedge$ Member(?v_{i-1}, ?seq) $\wedge$ Predecessor(?v_{i-1}, ?v_i, ?seq)

$\rightarrow$

(8)   ?$v_{i,6}$ = ?$v_{i-1,8}$ $\wedge$?$v_{i,3}$ = ?$v_{i-1,5}$ $\wedge$

(9)   ?$v_{i,2}$ = Do(SetTblLoc(?$v_{1,1}$, ?$v_{i-1,7}$, ?$v_{i-1,4}$), ?$v_{i-1,2}$) $\wedge$

(10) ?$v_{i,6}$ = {?$v_{i,7}$ | ?$v_{i,8}$} $\wedge$?$v_{i,3}$ = {?$v_{i,4}$ | ?$v_{i,5}$}]

Antecedents$_{\text{final}}$

(11) FinalVector(?v_n, ?seq) $\wedge$?state = Do(SetTblLoc(?$v_{1,1}$, ?$v_{n,7}$, ?$v_{n,4}$), ?$v_{n,2}$) $\wedge$

(12) Size(?$v_{n,8}$, ?n) $\wedge$?size = (?settings + ?n)

Consequents

(13) AchievableState(?state) $\wedge$ SetTblLocs(?table, ?settings, ?state)

This rule extends sequences 1 $\rightarrow$ N.

Notice that the constraint that a sufficient number of utensils exist is not produced. This rule could waste much time attempting to set ten places on any of a hundred tables when only nine place settings exist. Improved reasoning about the implicit constraints in a sequential rule is an area for future research. This example is intended to motivate the need for doing so and illustrates a simple technique that demonstrates the feasibility of accomplishing this task.

A related theme is that the issue of generalizing to N involves more than merely going from a fixed number of rule applications to an arbitrary number. Rather, it also involves the acquisition of concepts where there is a constrained *range* of acceptable numbers of rule applications.

Table B.7 The Meaning of the Components in the RIS for Table Setting

Component	Meaning
1	the table
2	the current state
3	utensil sets available in the current state
4	the utensil set chosen at this step
5	the utensil sets left after this step
6	the clear locations on the table in the current state
7	the table location to set at this step
8	the table locations still clear after this step

Appendix C   BAGGER's Initial Inference Rules

C.1   Notation

The inference rules and axioms used in the BAGGER system appear in this appendix. In these rules, all variables contain a leading "?" and are universally quantified. The construct *{?a | ?b}* matches a list with head *?a* and tail *?b*. For example, if matched with *{x,y,z}*, variable *?a* is bound to *x* and *?b* to *{y,z}*.

C.2   Rules

Table C.1 contains those rules that describe properties of collections of objects. Included are rules for membership, rules for specifying how to add and remove elements, a rule about inequality, and rules about cardinality (size). These rules are used in the blocks world examples and in the example involving the setting of a table.

The second table contains *intra*situation rules for the blocks world examples. For example, in the blocks world, there are tables and blocks. There are two types of blocks: boxes, which have flat tops, and pyramids. Rules for inferring that free space is present, a block is liftable, and an object is clear are included.

The next two tables describe *inter*situation inferences for the blocks world. The first rule in Table C.3 is the definition of the transfer action used in the examples. The other accessory rules describe how the location of blocks change after a transfer. Table C.4 contains rules for reasoning about support relationships following a transfer.

As previously stated, BAGGER2 can only process tree-structured explanations. Table C.5 contains the formalization of transfer BAGGER2 uses. Notice that these rules, which replace the first rule in Table C.3, assume that a block can support at most one other block. That is, moving a block clears the block underneath it.

The last table, Table C.6, presents the two rules used in the Appendix B.4's example about setting up for dining.

Table C.1 Rules for Collections of Objects

Rule	Description
Member(?x,?bag) → Member(?x,{?y | ?bag})	If an object is a member of a collection of objects, it is also a member of a superset of that collection.
Member(?x,{?x | ?bag})	See if an object is in a collection of objects.
?x ≠ ?y ∧ NotMember(?x,?bag) → NotMember(?x,{?y | ?bag})	If two objects are distinct, and the first is not in a collection of objects, then the first is not a member of the collection that results from adding the second object to the original collection.
NotMember(?x,φ)	Nothing is a member of the empty set.
RemoveFromBag(?x,?bag1,?bag2) → RemoveFromBag(?x,{?y | ?bag1},{?y | ?bag2})	If two collections of objects are related by the removal of one object, then this same relation holds if a second object is added to each collection.
RemoveFromBag(?x,{?x | ?bag},?bag)	Remove this object from a collection of objects, producing a new collection of objects.
AddToBag(?x,?bag1,?bag2) → AddToBag(?x,{?y | ?bag1},{?y | ?bag2})	If two collections of objects are related by the addition of one object, then this same relation holds if a second object is added to each collection.
AddToBag(?x,?bag,{?x | ?bag})	Add this object to a collection of objects, producing a new collection of objects.
Size(?bag,?m) ∧ ?n = (?m + 1) → Size({?x | ?bag},?n)	The size of a collection of objects is increased by one if another object is added to the collection.
Size(φ,0)	The empty set has size zero.
?x ≠ ?y → ?y ≠ ?x	Inequality is reflexive.

Table C.2 Blocks World Intrasituation Rules

Rule	Description
Clear(?x,?s) ∧ FlatTop(?x) → FreeSpace(?x,?s)	If an object is clear and has a flat top, space is available.
Table(?x) → FreeSpace(?x,?s)	There always is room on a table.
Clear(?x,?s) ∧ Block(?x) → Liftable(?x,?s)	A block is liftable if it is clear.
Box(?x) → FlatTop(?x)	Boxes have flat tops.
Table(?x) → FlatTop(?x)	Tables have flat tops.
Box(?x) → Block(?x)	Boxes are a type of block.
Pyramid(?x) → Block(?x)	Pyramids are a type of block.
Supports(?x,φ,?s) → Clear(?x,?s)	An object is clear if it is supporting nothing.

Table C.3 Some Blocks World Intersituation Rules

Rule	Description
AchievableState(?s) ∧ Liftable(?x,?s) ∧ FreeSpace(?y,?s) ∧ ?x ≠ ?y → AchievableState(Do(Transfer(?x,?y),?s)) ∧ Clear(?x,Do(Transfer(?x,?y),?s)) ∧ On(?x,?y,Do(Transfer(?x,?y),?s))	If the top of an object is clear in some achievable state and there is free space on another object, then the first object can be moved from its present location to the new location. However, an object cannot be moved onto itself. Moving creates a new state in which the moved object is still clear but (possibly) at a new location.
AchievableState(S0)	The initial state is always achievable.
Xpos(?y,?xpos,?s) → Xpos(?x,?xpos,Do(Transfer(?x,?y),?s))	After a transfer, the object moved is centered (in the X-direction) on the object upon which it is placed.
?x ≠ ?y ∧ Height(?x,?hx) ∧ Ypos(?y,?ypos,?s) ∧ ?ypos2 = (?hx + ?ypos) → Ypos(?x,?ypos2,Do(Transfer(?x,?y),?s))	After a transfer, the Y-position of the object moved is determined by adding its height to the Y-position of the object upon which it is placed.
?a ≠ ?x ∧ Xpos(?a,?xpos,?s) → Xpos(?a,?xpos,Do(Transfer(?x,?y),?s))	All blocks, other than the one moved, remain in the same X-position after a transfer.
?a ≠ ?x ∧ Ypos(?a,?xpos,?s) → Ypos(?a,?xpos,Do(Transfer(?x,?y),?s))	All blocks, other than the one moved, remain in the same Y-position after a transfer.

Table C.4 Intersituation Rules about Block Support

Rule	Description
?a ≠ ?x ∧ On(?a,b,?s) → On(?a,?b,Do(Transfer(?x,?y),?s))	If an object is not moved, it remains on the same object.
?u ≠ ?y ∧ Supports(?u,?items,?s) ∧ NotMember(?x,?items) → Supports(?u,?items,Do(Transfer(?x,?y),?s))	If an object neither supports the moved object before the transfer, nor is the new supporter, then the collection of objects it supports remains unchanged.
?u ≠ ?y ∧ Supports(?u,?items,?s) ∧ Member(?x,?items) ∧ RemoveFromBag(?x,?items,?new) → Supports(?u,?new,Do(Transfer(?x,?y),?s))	If an object is not the new support of the moved object, but supported it before the transfer, then the moved object must be removed from the collection of objects being supported.
Supports(?y,?items,?s) ∧ NotMember(?x,?items) ∧ AddToBag(?x,?items,?new) → Supports(?y,?new,Do(Transfer(?x,?y),?s))	After the transfer, another item is supported if the new supporter did not previously support the moved object.
Supports(?y,?items,?s) ∧ Member(?x,?items) → Supports(?y,?items,Do(Transfer(?x,?y),?s))	If the moved object is transferred to the object that previously supported it, the new supporter still supports the same objects.

Table C.5   Formalizing Transfers for BAGGER2

Rule	Description
AchievableState(?s) ∧ Liftable(?x,?s) ∧ FreeSpace(?y,?s) ∧ ?x ≠ ?y → AchievableState(Do(Transfer(?x,?y),?s))	If the top of an object is clear in some achievable state and there is free space on another object, then the first object can be moved from its present location to the new location. However, an object cannot be moved onto itself.
AchievableState(Do(Transfer(?x,?y),?s)) → On(?x,?y,Do(Transfer(?x,?y),?s))	After an object is moved, it is on the destination object.
AchievableState(Do(Transfer(?x,?y),?s)) → Clear(?x,Do(Transfer(?x,?y),?s))	After an object is moved, it is clear.
On(?x,?z,?s) ∧ Block(?z) ∧ ?z ≠ ?y → Clear(?z,Do(Transfer(?x,?y),?s))	After an object is moved, the previously supporting object is clear, if it is a block and the moved object is not placed back on top of it.
Clear(?a,?s) ∧ ?a ≠ ?y → Clear(?a,Do(Transfer(?x,?y),?s))	If nothing is placed on it, an object stays clear.

Table C.6 Rules about Setting Tables

Rule	Description

Table(?tbl) ∧
AchievableState(?s) ∧
AvailUtensilSets(?utenSets,?s) ∧
Member(?utens,?utenSets) ∧
RemoveFromBag(?utens,?utenSets,?newUsets) ∧
ClearTableLocs(?tbl,?locs,?s) ∧
Member(?loc,?locs) ∧
RemoveFromBag(?loc,?locs,?newLocs)
   →
AchievableState(Do(SetTblLoc(?tbl,?loc,?utens))) ∧
ClearTableLocs(?tbl,?newLocs,
               Do(SetTblLoc(?tbl,?loc,?utens))) ∧
AvailUtensilSets(?newUsets,
               Do(SetTblLoc(?tbl,?loc,?utens)))
	To set a place on a table, there must be an available set of utensils and an open location on the table. Following the settings, the used resources are no longer available.

Table(?tbl) ∧ TableSize(?tbl,?size) ∧ ClearTableLocs(?tbl,?locs,?s) ∧ Size(?locs,?n) ∧ ?size = (?space + ?n) → SetTableLocations(?tbl,?spaces,?s)	The number of table locations that are set is determined by subtracting the number that are clear from the table capacity.

Appendix D   Statistics from Experiments

D.1   Description

The means and standard deviations for several experimental measurements are reported in this appendix, in order to provide an indication of the variability of the results. The standard deviation (σ) is defined as follows, where X contains the collection of results from the multiple experimental runs.

$$\sigma(X) = \sqrt{mean\,(X^2) - mean^2(X)}$$

The standard deviation is the positive square root of the difference between the mean of the square of each result and the square of the mean result.

D.2   Statistics

Table D.1 contains the statistics for Section 2.4.4's study of PHYSICS 101. Table D.2 presents the solution time data for a variety of Chapter 4's BAGGER experiments. Data in the autonomous mode is averaged over problems 26-50, while in the training mode the 20 problems in the training set are used. Data pertaining to the number of rules learned appears in Table D.3. Unless otherwise stated, the results in Tables D.2 and D.3 are for building towers. Table D.4 reports statistics from Section 4.3.8's study of BAGGER2.

Table D.1   Means and Standard Deviations for Figure 2.19

Number of Objects	Before Learning		After Learning	
	Mean	Std. Dev.	Mean	Std. Dev.
1	19.4 sec.	1.6	6.9	0.2
2	75.1	7.0	24.4	0.5
3	423.0	20.7	31.1	0.4
4	1530.0	87.1	48.1	0.7
5	na	na	61.5	1.5

na - not available (experiment not run)

199

Description	Operationality		Generality	
	Mean	Std. Dev.	Mean	Std. Dev.
Mean Solution Time				
autonomous mode				
NO-LEARN	64,500 sec.	36,500	79,300	26,900
STD-EBL	6,790	9,140	8,100	11,500
BAGGER	6,660	10,200	3,720	7,320
autonomous mode (external solutions after 10,000 sec)				
STD-EBL	318	239	1,290	498
BAGGER	197	251	133	171
autonomous mode (external solutions if all rules fail)				
STD-EBL	133	37.4	1,470	714
BAGGER	28.6	22.3	40.5	8.9
training mode				
NO-LEARN	91,000	36,900	68,400	38,600
STD-EBL	155	322	780	3,580
BAGGER	26.6	81.5	35.6	84.1
training mode (clearing)				
NO-LEARN	na	na	4,200,000	2,650,000
STD-EBL	na	na	57.9	132
BAGGER	na	na	15.4	20.5

Table D.2   Means and Standard Deviations for Various Experiments

na - not available (experiment not run)

Table D.3 Standard Deviations of Rules Learned for Various Experiments

Description	Operationality		Generality	
	Mean	Std. Dev.	Mean	Std. Dev.
Rules Learned				
autonomous mode				
STD-EBL	5.52	1.09	4.28	1.00
BAGGER	2.60	0.75	1.72	0.45
training mode				
STD-EBL	6.88	1.31	5.96	1.11
BAGGER	3.24	0.95	2.01	0.75
training mode (clearing)				
STD-EBL	na	na	3.96	0.68
BAGGER	na	na	1.36	0.53

Table D.4 Mean Solution Time and Standard Deviations for Figure 4.17

Circuit Size	NO-LEARN		STD-EBL		BAGGER2	
	Mean	Std. Dev.	Mean	Std. Dev.	Mean	Std. Dev.
5	0.3 sec.	0.01	0.1	0.00	0.2	0.01
6	0.4	0.02	0.2	0.01	0.3	0.01
7	0.5	0.01	0.4	0.02	0.3	0.01
8	0.6	0.03	1.0	0.03	0.4	0.02
9	0.7	0.02	2.0	0.09	0.5	0.03
10	0.8	0.03	na	na	0.6	0.02

na - not available (experiment not run)

References

[Ahn87]   W. Ahn, R. J. Mooney, W. F. Brewer and G. F. DeJong, "Schema Acquisition from One Example: Psychological Evidence for Explanation-Based Learning," *Proceedings of the Ninth Annual Conference of the Cognitive Science Society*, Seattle, WA, July 1987, pp. 50-57.

[Anderson86]   J. R. Anderson, "Knowledge Compilation: The General Learning Mechanism," in *Machine Learning: An Artificial Intelligence Approach, Vol. II*, R. S. Michalski, J. G. Carbonell and T. M. Mitchell (eds.), Morgan-Kaufmann, Los Altos, CA, 1986, pp. 289-309.

[Anderson87]   J. R. Anderson, "Causal Analysis and Inductive Learning," *Proceedings of the Fourth International Workshop on Machine Learning*, Irvine, CA, June 1987, pp. 288-299.

[Andreae84]   P. M. Andreae, "Justified Generalization: Acquiring Procedures from Examples," Ph.D. Thesis, Department of Electrical Engineering and Computer Science, MIT, Cambridge, MA, January 1984. (Also appears as Technical Report 834, MIT AI Laboratory.)

[Angluin83]   D. Angluin and C. H. Smith, "Inductive Inference: Theory and Methods," *Computing Surveys 15*, 3 (1983), pp. 237-269.

[Araya84]   A. Araya, "Learning Problem Classes by Means of Experimentation and Generalization," *Proceedings of the Fourth National Conference on Artificial Intelligence*, Austin, TX, August 1984, pp. 11-15.

[Bauer79]   M. A. Bauer, "Programming By Examples," *Artificial Intelligence 12*, 1 (1979), pp. 1-21.

[Beckman76]   L. Beckman, A. Haraldson, O. Oskassson and E. Sandewall, "A Partial Evaluator, and its Use as a Programming Tool," *Artificial Intelligence 7*, 4 (1976), pp. 319-357.

[Bennett87]   S. W. Bennett, "Approximation in Mathematical Domains," *Proceedings of the Tenth International Joint Conference on Artificial Intelligence*, Milan, Italy, August 1987, pp. 239-241.

[Bennett89]   S. W. Bennett, "Learning Approximate Plans for Use in the Real World," *Proceedings of the Sixth International Workshop on Machine Learning*, Ithaca, NY, June 1989, pp. 224-228.

[Bergadano88] F. Bergadano and A. Giordana, "A Knowledge Intensive Approach to Concept Induction," *Proceedings of the Fifth International Conference on Machine*

Learning, Ann Arbor, MI, June 1988, pp. 291-297.

[Biermann78]   A. W. Biermann, "The Inference of Regular LISP Programs from Examples," *IEEE Transactions on Systems, Man and Cybernetics 8*, 8 (1978), pp. 585-600.

[Bransford76]   J. D. Bransford and J. J. Franks, "Toward a Framework for Understanding Learning," in *The Psychology of Learning and Motivation, Volume 10*, G. H. Bower (ed.), Academic Press, New York, NY, 1976, pp. 93-127.

[Braverman88a]   M. S. Braverman and S. J. Russell, "IMEX: Overcoming Intractability in Explanation-Based Learning," *Proceedings of the Seventh National Conference on Artificial Intelligence*, St. Paul, MN, August 1988, pp. 575-579.

[Braverman88b]   M. S. Braverman and S. J. Russell, "Boundaries of Operationality," *Proceedings of the Fifth International Conference on Machine Learning*, Ann Arbor, MI, June 1988, pp. 221-234.

[Brown80]   J. S. Brown and K. VanLehn, "Repair Theory: A Generative Theory of Bugs in Procedural Skills," *Cognitive Science 4*, (1980), pp. 379-426.

[Bundy79]   A. Bundy, L. Byrd, G. Luger, C. Mellish and M. Palmer, "Solving Mechanics Problems using Meta-Level Inference," in *Expert Systems in the Micro-Electronic Age*, D. Michie (ed.), Edinburgh University Press, Edinburgh, Scotland, 1979, pp. 50-64.

[Bundy81]   A. Bundy and B. Welham, "Using Meta-Level Inference for Selective Application of Multiple Rewrite Rules in Algebraic Manipulation," *Artificial Intelligence 16*, 2 (1981), pp. 189-212.

[Bundy83]   A. Bundy, *The Computer Modelling of Mathematical Reasoning*, Academic Press, New York, NY, 1983.

[Bundy85]   A. Bundy, B. Silver and D. Plummer, "An Analytical Comparison of Some Rule Learning Programs," *Artificial Intelligence 27*, 2 (1985), pp. 137-181.

[Business Week88]   Business Week, "The Software Trap: Automate - Or Else," *Business Week*, May 9, 1988, pp. 142-151.

[Carbonell87]   J. G. Carbonell and Y. Gil, "Learning by Experimentation," *Proceedings of the Fourth International Workshop on Machine Learning*, Irvine, CA, June 1987, pp. 256-266.

[Chafe75]   W. Chafe, "Some Thoughts on Schemata," *Theoretical Issues in Natural Language Processing 1*, Cambridge, MA, 1975, pp. 89-91.

[Charniak76]   E. Charniak, "A Framed Painting: The Representation of a Common Sense Knowledge Fragment," *Cognitive Science 4*, (1976), pp. 355-394.

[Charniak80]   E. Charniak, C. Riesbeck and D. McDermott, *Artificial Intelligence Programming*, Lawrence Erlbaum and Associates, Hillsdale, NJ, 1980.

[Cheng86]   P. Cheng and J. G. Carbonell, "The FERMI System: Inducing Iterative Macro-operators from Experience," *Proceedings of the Fifth National Conference on Artificial Intelligence*, Philadelphia, PA, August 1986, pp. 490-495.

[Chi81]   M. T. Chi, P. J. Feltovich and R. Glaser, "Categorization and Representation of Physics Problems by Experts and Novices," *Cognitive Science 5*, 2 (1981), pp. 121-152.

[Chi82]   M. Chi, R. Glaser and E. Rees, "Expertise in Problem Solving," in *Advances in the Psychology of Human Intelligence, Volume 1*, R. Sternberg (ed.), Lawrence Erlbaum and Associates, Hillsdale, NJ, 1982, pp. 7-75.

[Chien89]   S. A. Chien, "Using and Refining Simplifications: Explanation-Based Learning of Plans in Intractable Domains," *Proceedings of the Eleventh International Joint Conference on Artificial Intelligence*, Detroit, MI, August 1989, pp. 590-595.

[Clocksin84]   W. F. Clocksin and C. S. Mellish, *Programming in PROLOG*, Springer Verlag, Berlin, 1984.

[Cohen87]   W. W. Cohen, "A Technique for Generalizing Number in Explanation-Based Learning," Technical Report ML-TR-19, Department of Computer Science, Rutgers University, New Brunswick, NJ, September 1987.

[Cohen88]   W. W. Cohen, "Generalizing Number and Learning from Multiple Examples in Explanation-Based Learning," *Proceedings of the Fifth International Conference on Machine Learning*, Ann Arbor, MI, June 1988, pp. 256-269.

[Cohen89]   W. W. Cohen, "Solution Path Caching Mechanisms which Provably Improve Performance," Technical Report DCS-TR-254, Department of Computer Science, Rutgers, New Brunswick, July 1989.

[Cullingford78] R. E. Cullingford, "Script Application: Computer Understanding of Newspaper Stories," Technical Report 116, Department of Computer Science, Yale University, New Haven, CT, January 1978.

[Danyluk87]   A. P. Danyluk, "The Use of Explanations for Similarity-Based Learning," *Proceedings of the Tenth International Joint Conference on Artificial Intelligence*, Milan, Italy, August 1987, pp. 274-276.

[Davis82]   R. Davis, "Teiresias: Applications of Meta-Level Knowledge," in *Knowledge-Based Systems in Artificial Intelligence*, R. Davis and D. B. Lenat (eds.), McGraw-Hill, New York, NY, 1982. (Based on a 1976 Stanford Ph.D. Thesis.)

[DeJong81]   G. F. DeJong, "Generalizations Based on Explanations," *Proceedings of the Seventh International Joint Conference on Artificial Intelligence*, Vancouver, B.C., Canada, August 1981, pp. 67-70.

[DeJong83a]   G. F. DeJong, "An Approach to Learning from Observation," *Proceedings of the Second International Workshop on Machine Learning*, Urbana, IL, June 1983.

[DeJong83b]   G. F. DeJong, "Acquiring Schemata through Understanding and Generalizing Plans," *Proceedings of the Eighth International Joint Conference on Artificial Intelligence*, Karlsruhe, West Germany, August 1983, pp. 462-464.

[DeJong86a]   G. F. DeJong, "Explanation Based Learning," in *Machine Learning: An Artificial Intelligence Approach, Vol. II*, R. S. Michalski, J. G. Carbonell and T. M.

Mitchell (eds.), Morgan-Kaufmann, Los Altos, CA, 1986.

[DeJong86b] G. F. DeJong and R. J. Mooney, "Explanation-Based Learning: An Alternative View," *Machine Learning 1*, 2 (1986), pp. 145-176.

[DeJong88] G. F. DeJong, "An Introduction to Explanation-Based Learning," in *Exploring Artificial Intelligence*, H. E. Shrobe (ed.), Morgan-Kaufmann, Los Altos, CA, 1988, pp. 45-81.

[Dietterich82] T. G. Dietterich, B. London, K. Clarkson and G. Dromney, "Learning and Inductive Inference," in *The Handbook of Artificial Intelligence, Vol. III*, P. R. Cohen and E. A. Feigenbaum (eds.), William Kaufman, Inc., Los Altos, CA, 1982.

[Dietterich83] T. G. Dietterich and R. S. Michalski, "A Comparative Review of Selected Methods for Learning from Examples," in *Machine Learning: An Artificial Intelligence Approach*, R. S. Michalski, J. G. Carbonell and T. M. Mitchell (eds.), Tioga Publishing Company, Palo Alto, CA, 1983, pp. 41-81.

[Dietterich84] T. G. Dietterich and R. S. Michalski, "Discovering Patterns in Sequences of Objects," *Artificial Intelligence 25*, (1984), pp. 257-294.

[Dietterich86] T. G. Dietterich, "Learning at the Knowledge Level," *Machine Learning 1*, 3 (1986), pp. 287-316.

[Dietterich88] T. G. Dietterich and N. Flann, "An Inductive Approach to Solving the Imperfect Theory Problem," *Proceedings of the AAAI Explanation-Based Learning Symposium*, March 1988, pp. 42-46.

[Dijkstra76] E. W. Dijkstra, *A Discipline of Programming*, Prentice-Hall, Englewood Cliffs, NJ, 1976.

[Doyle86] R. J. Doyle, "Constructing and Refining Causal Explanations from an Inconsistent Domain Theory," *Proceedings of the Fifth National Conference on Artificial Intelligence*, Philadelphia, PA, August 1986, pp. 538-544.

[Dufay84] B. Dufay and J. Latombe, "An Approach to Automatic Robot Programming Based on Inductive Learning," in *Robotics Research: The First International Symposium*, , MIT Press, Cambridge, MA, 1984, pp. 97-115.

[Duval88] B. Duval and Y. Kodratoff, "Learning Concepts by Asking Questions," in *Machine Learning, Meta-Reasoning, and Logics*, P. Brazdil (ed.), 1988.

[Egan74] D. E. Egan and J. G. Greeno, "Theory of Rule Induction: Knowledge Acquisition in Concept Learning, Serial Pattern Learning and Problem Solving," in *Knowledge and Cognition*, L. W. Gregg (ed.), Lawrence Erlbaum and Associates, Hillsdale, NJ, 1974.

[Ellman85] T. Ellman, "Generalizing Logic Circuit Designs by Analyzing Proofs of Correctness," *Proceedings of the Ninth International Joint Conference on Artificial Intelligence*, Los Angeles, CA, August 1985, pp. 643-646.

[Ellman89]   T. Ellman, "Explanation-Based Learning: A Survey of Programs and Perspectives," *Computing Surveys 21*, 2 (1989), pp. 163-221.

[Fahlman74]   S. Fahlman, "A Planning System for Robot Construction Tasks," *Artificial Intelligence 5*, 1 (1974), pp. 1-49.

[Falkenhainer86] B. C. Falkenhainer and R. S. Michalski, "Integrating Quantitative and Qualitative Discovery: The ABACUS System," *Machine Learning 1*, 4 (1986), pp. 367-401.

[Falkenhainer87] B. C. Falkenhainer, "Scientific Theory Formation Through Analogical Inference," *Proceedings of the Fourth International Workshop on Machine Learning*, Irvine, CA, June 1987, pp. 218-229.

[Fateman85]   R. J. Fateman, "Eleven Proofs of $Sin^2x+Cos^2x = 1$," *SIGSAM Bulletin 19*, 2 (1985), pp. 25-28.

[Fikes71]   R. E. Fikes and N. J. Nilsson, "STRIPS: A New Approach to the Application of Theorem Proving to Problem Solving," *Artificial Intelligence 2*, 3/4 (1971), pp. 189-208.

[Fikes72]   R. E. Fikes, P. E. Hart and N. J. Nilsson, "Learning and Executing Generalized Robot Plans," *Artificial Intelligence 3*, 4 (1972), pp. 251-288.

[Fikes75]   R. E. Fikes, "Deductive Retrieval Mechanisms for State Description Models," *Proceedings of the Fourth International Joint Conference on Artificial Intelligence*, Tiblisi, Georgia, U.S.S.R., August 1975, pp. 99-106.

[Floyd67]   R. W. Floyd, "Assigning Meanings to Programs," in *Mathematical Aspects of Computer Science*, J. T. Schwartz (ed.), American Mathematical Society, Providence, RI, 1967, pp. 19-32.

[Forbus86]   K. D. Forbus and D. Gentner, "Learning Physical Domains: Toward a Theoretical Framework," in *Machine Learning: An Artificial Intelligence Approach, Vol. II*, R. S. Michalski, J. G. Carbonell and T. M. Mitchell (eds.), Morgan-Kaufmann, Los Altos, CA, 1986, pp. 311-348.

[Forgy82]   C. L. Forgy, "RETE: A Fast Algorithm for the Many Pattern/Many Object Pattern Match Problem," *Artificial Intelligence 19*, (1982), pp. 17-37.

[Geddes82]   K. Geddes, G. Gonnet and B. Char, "MAPLE User's Manual, Second Edition," Technical Report CS-82-40, University of Waterloo, Ontario, Canada, December 1982.

[Gick83]   M. L. Gick and K. L. Holyoak, "Schema Induction and Analogical Transfer," *Cognitive Psychology 15*, (1983), pp. 1-38.

[Gold67]   E. M. Gold, "Language Identification in the Limit," *Information and Control 10*, (1967), pp. 447-474.

[Green69]   C. C. Green, "Application of Theorem Proving to Problem Solving," *Proceedings of the First International Joint Conference on Artificial Intelligence*, Washington, D.C., August 1969, pp. 219-239.

[Greiner88]   R. Greiner, "Learning by Understanding Analogies," *Artificial Intelligence 35*, 1 (1988), pp. 81-126.

[Greiner89]   R. Greiner and J. Likuski, "Incorporating Redundant Learned Rules: A Preliminary Formal Analysis of EBL," *Proceedings of the Eleventh International Joint Conference on Artificial Intelligence*, Detroit, MI, August 1989, pp. 744-749.

[Gupta87]   A. Gupta, "Explanation-Based Failure Recovery," *Proceedings of the Sixth National Conference on Artificial Intelligence*, Seattle, WA, July 1987, pp. 606-610.

[Hall88]   R. Hall, "Learning by Failing to Explain: Using Partial Explanations to Learn Incomplete or Intractable Domains," *Machine Learning 3*, 1 (1988), pp. 45-78.

[Hammond87]   K. J. Hammond, "Learning and Reusing Explanations," *Proceedings of the Fourth International Workshop on Machine Learning*, Irvine, CA, June 1987, pp. 141-147.

[Hearn84]   A. Hearn, "REDUCE User's Manual, Version 3.1," Technical Report CP-78, The RAND Corporation, Santa Monica, CA, April 1984.

[Hill87]   W. L. Hill, "Machine Learning for Software Reuse," *Proceedings of the Tenth International Joint Conference on Artificial Intelligence*, Milan, Italy, August 1987, pp. 338-344.

[Hinsley77]   D. A. Hinsley, J. R. Hayes and H. A. Simon, "From Words to Equations: Meaning and Representation on Algebra Word Problems," in *Cognitive Processes in Comprehension*, P. A. Carpenter and M. A. Just (eds.), Lawrence Erlbaum and Associates, Hillsdale, NJ, 1977, pp. 89-105.

[Hinton86]   G. E. Hinton and T. J. Sejnowski, "Learning and Relearning in Boltzmann Machines," in *Parallel Distributed Processing, Vol. I*, D. E. Rumelhart and J. L. McClelland (eds.), MIT Press, Cambridge, MA, 1986, pp. 282-317.

[Hinton89]   G. E. Hinton, "Connectionist Learning Procedures," *Artificial Intelligence 40*, 1 (1989), pp. 185-234.

[Hirsh87]   H. Hirsh, "Explanation-Based Generalization in a Logic-Programming Environment," *Proceedings of the Tenth International Joint Conference on Artificial Intelligence*, Milan, Italy, August 1987, pp. 221-227.

[Hirsh88]   H. Hirsh, "Reasoning about Operationality for Explanation-Based Learning," *Proceedings of the Fifth International Conference on Machine Learning*, Ann Arbor, MI, June 1988, pp. 214-220.

[Holder89]   L. B. Holder, "Empirical Substructure Discovery," *Proceedings of the Sixth International Workshop on Machine Learning*, Ithaca, NY, June 1989, pp. 133-136.

[Hunt66]   E. B. Hunt, J. Marin and P. J. Stone, *Experiments in Induction*, Academic Press, New York, NY, 1966.

[Iba85]   G. A. Iba, "Learning by Discovering Macros in Puzzle Solving," *Proceedings of the Ninth International Joint Conference on Artificial Intelligence*, Los Angeles, CA, August 1985, pp. 640-642.

[Jacobson51]   N. Jacobson, *Lectures in Abstract Algebra, Vol. 1*, Von Nostrand, Princeton, NJ, 1951.

[Kearns87]   M. Kearns, M. Li, L. Pitt and L. G. Valiant, "Recent Results on Boolean Concept Learning," *Proceedings of the Fourth International Workshop on Machine Learning*, Irvine, CA, June 1987, pp. 337-352.

[Kedar-Cabelli85] S. T. Kedar-Cabelli, "Purpose-Directed Analogy: A Summary of Current Research," *Proceedings of the Third International Workshop on Machine Learning*, Skytop, PA, June 1985, pp. 80-83.

[Kedar-Cabelli87] S. T. Kedar-Cabelli and L. T. McCarty, "Explanation-Based Generalization as Resolution Theorem Proving," *Proceedings of the Fourth International Workshop on Machine Learning*, Irvine, CA, June 1987, pp. 383-389.

[Keller87a]   R. M. Keller, "The Role of Explicit Contextual Knowledge in Learning Concepts to Improve Performance," Ph.D. Thesis, Department of Computer Science, Rutgers University, New Brunswick, NJ, January 1987. (Also appears as Technical Report ML-TR-7.)

[Keller87b]   R. M. Keller, "Concept Learning in Context," *Proceedings of the Fourth International Workshop on Machine Learning*, Irvine, CA, June 1987, pp. 91-102.

[Keller88a]   R. M. Keller, "Defining Operationality for Explanation-Based Learning," *Artificial Intelligence 35*, 2 (1988), pp. 227-241.

[Keller88b]   R. M. Keller, "Operationality and Generality in Explanation-Based Learning: Separate Dimensions or Opposite Endpoints?," *Proceedings of the AAAI Explanation-Based Learning Symposium*, Stanford, CA, March 1988, pp. 153-157.

[Kirkpatrick83]   S. Kirkpatrick, C. D. Gelatt and M. P. Vecchi, "Optimization by Simulated Annealing," *Science 220*, (1983), pp. 671-680.

[Kodratoff79]   Y. Kodratoff, "A Class of Functions Synthesized from a Finite Number of Examples and a LISP Program Scheme," *International Journal of Computer and Information Sciences 8*, 6 (1979), pp. 489-521.

[Kodratoff86]   Y. Kodratoff and J. Ganascia, "Improving the Generalization Step in Learning," in *Machine Learning: An Artificial Intelligence Approach, Vol. II*, R. S. Michalski, J. G. Carbonell and T. M. Mitchell (eds.), Morgan-Kaufmann, Los Altos, CA, 1986, pp. 215-244.

[Kokar86]   M. M. Kokar, "Determining Arguments of Invariant Functional Descriptions," *Machine Learning 1*, 4 (1986), pp. 403-422.

[Korf85]   R. E. Korf, "Depth-First Iterative-Deepening: An Optimal Admissible Tree Search," *Artificial Intelligence 27*, 1 (1985), pp. 97-109.

209

[Laird86]   J. Laird, P. Rosenbloom and A. Newell, "Chunking in SOAR: The Anatomy of a General Learning Mechanism," *Machine Learning 1*, 1 (1986), pp. 11-46.

[Langley81]   P. Langley, "Data-Driven Discovery of Physical Laws," *Cognitive Science 5*, 1 (1981), pp. 31-54.

[Langley87]   P. Langley, H. A. Simon, G. L. Bradshaw and J. M. Zytkow, *Scientific Discovery: Computational Explorations of the Creative Processes*, MIT Press, Cambridge, MA, 1987.

[Larkin80]   J. H. Larkin, J. McDermott, D. P. Simon and H. A. Simon, "Models of Competence in Solving Physics Problems," *Cognitive Science 4*, 4 (1980), pp. 317-345.

[Lebowitz86]   M. Lebowitz, "Integrated Learning: Controlling Explanation," *Cognitive Science 10*, 2 (1986), pp. 219-240.

[Lenat76]   D. B. Lenat, "AM: An Artificial Intelligence Approach to Discovery in Mathematics as Heuristic Search," Ph.D. Thesis, Department of Computer Science, Stanford University, Stanford, CA, 1976. (A version also appears in *Knowledge-Based Systems in Artificial Intelligence*, R. Davis and D. Lenat, McGraw-Hill, New York, NY, 1982.)

[Lewis78]   C. H. Lewis, "Production Systems Models of Practice Effects," Ph.D. Thesis, Department of Psychology, University of Michigan, Ann Arbor, MI, 1978.

[Liu68]   C. L. Liu, *Introduction to Combinatorial Mathematics*, McGraw-Hill, New York, NY, 1968.

[Maclin89]   R. Maclin and J. W. Shavlik, "Using Explanation-Based Learning to Acquire Programs by Analyzing Examples," Technical Report 858, Department of Computer Science, University of Wisconsin, Madison, WI, 1989.

[Mahadevan85]   S. Mahadevan, "Verification-Based Learning: A Generalization Strategy for Inferring Problem-Reduction Methods," *Proceedings of the Ninth International Joint Conference on Artificial Intelligence*, Los Angeles, CA, August 1985, pp. 616-623.

[Mahadevan88]   S. Mahadevan and P. Tadepalli, "On the Tractability of Learning from Incomplete Theories," *Proceedings of the Fifth International Conference on Machine Learning*, Ann Arbor, MI, June 1988, pp. 235-241.

[Manna70]   Z. Manna, "Termination of Programs Represented as Interpreted Graphs," *Proceedings of the Spring Joint Computer Conference*, 1970, pp. 83-89.

[Manna74]   Z. Manna, *Mathematical Theory of Computation*, McGraw-Hill, New York, NY, 1974.

[Markovitch88]   S. Markovitch and P. D. Scott, "The Role of Forgetting in Learning," *Proceedings of the Fifth International Conference on Machine Learning*, Ann Arbor, MI, June 1988, pp. 459-465.

[Markovitch89]   S. Markovitch and P. D. Scott, "Utilization Filtering: A Method for Reducing the Inherent Harmfulness of Deductively Learned Knowledge," *Proceedings of the Eleventh International Joint Conference on Artificial Intelligence*, Detroit, MI, August 1989, pp. 738-743.

[Mathlab83]   Mathlab, "MACSYMA Reference Manual, Version Ten," Laboratory for Computer Science, MIT, Cambridge, MA, December 1983.

[McCarthy63]   J. McCarthy, "Situations, Actions, and Causal Laws," memorandum, Stanford University, Stanford, CA, 1963. (Reprinted in *Semantic Information Processing*, M. Minsky (ed.), MIT Press, Cambridge, MA, 1968, pp. 410-417.)

[Michalski80a]   R. S. Michalski and R. L. Chilausky, "Learning by Being Told and Learning from Examples: An Experimental Comparison of the Two Methods of Knowledge Acquisition in the Context of Developing an Expert System for Soybean Disease Diagnosis," *Policy Analysis and Information Systems 4*, 2 (1980), pp. 125-160.

[Michalski80b]   R. S. Michalski, "Pattern Recognition as Rule-Guided Inductive Inference," *IEEE Transactions on Pattern Analysis and Machine Intelligence 2*, 4 (1980), pp. 349-361.

[Michalski83]   R. S. Michalski, "A Theory and Methodology of Inductive Learning," *Artificial Intelligence 20*, 2 (1983), pp. 111-161.

[Minsky75]   M. L. Minsky, "A Framework for Representing Knowledge," in *The Psychology of Computer Vision*, P. H. Winston (ed.), McGraw-Hill, New York, NY, 1975, pp. 211-277.

[Minton84]   S. N. Minton, "Constraint-Based Generalization: Learning Game-Playing Plans from Single Examples," *Proceedings of the Fourth National Conference on Artificial Intelligence*, Austin, TX, August 1984, pp. 251-254.

[Minton85]   S. N. Minton, "Selectively Generalizing Plans for Problem Solving," *Proceedings of the Ninth International Joint Conference on Artificial Intelligence*, Los Angeles, CA, August 1985, pp. 596-599.

[Minton87]   S. N. Minton, J. G. Carbonell, O. Etzioni, C. A. Knoblock and D. R. Kuokka, "Acquiring Effective Search Control Rules: Explanation-Based Learning in the PRODIGY System," *Proceedings of the Fourth International Workshop on Machine Learning*, Irvine, CA, June 1987, pp. 122-133.

[Minton88a]   S. N. Minton, *Learning Search Control Knowledge: An Explanation-Based Approach*, Kluwer Academic Publishers, Hingham, MA, 1988.

[Minton88b]   S. N. Minton, "Quantitative Results Concerning the Utility of Explanation-Based Learning," *Proceedings of the Seventh National Conference on Artificial Intelligence*, St. Paul, MN, August 1988, pp. 564-569.

[Mitchell78]   T. M. Mitchell, "Version Spaces: An Approach to Concept Learning," Ph.D. Thesis, Stanford University, Palo Alto, CA, 1978. (Also appears as Technical Report STAN-CS-78-711.)

[Mitchell82]	T. M. Mitchell, "Generalization as Search," *Artificial Intelligence 18*, 2 (1982), pp. 203-226.

[Mitchell83a]	T. M. Mitchell, "Learning and Problem Solving," *Proceedings of the Eighth International Joint Conference on Artificial Intelligence*, Karlsruhe, West Germany, August 1983, pp. 1139-1151.

[Mitchell83b]	T. M. Mitchell, P. E. Utgoff and R. Banerji, "Learning by Experimentation: Acquiring and Refining Problem-Solving Heuristics," in *Machine Learning: An Artificial Intelligence Approach*, R. S. Michalski, J. G. Carbonell and T. M. Mitchell (eds.), Tioga Publishing Company, Palo Alto, CA, 1983, pp. 163-190.

[Mitchell85]	T. M. Mitchell, S. Mahadevan and L. I. Steinberg, "LEAP: A Learning Apprentice for VLSI Design," *Proceedings of the Ninth International Joint Conference on Artificial Intelligence*, Los Angeles, CA, August 1985, pp. 573-580.

[Mitchell86]	T. M. Mitchell, R. M. Keller and S. Kedar-Cabelli, "Explanation-Based Generalization: A Unifying View," *Machine Learning 1*, 1 (1986), pp. 47-80.

[Mooney85]	R. J. Mooney and G. F. DeJong, "Learning Schemata for Natural Language Processing," *Proceedings of the Ninth International Joint Conference on Artificial Intelligence*, Los Angeles, CA, August 1985, pp. 681-687.

[Mooney86]	R. J. Mooney and S. W. Bennett, "A Domain Independent Explanation-Based Generalizer," *Proceedings of the Fifth National Conference on Artificial Intelligence*, Philadelphia, PA, August 1986, pp. 551-555.

[Mooney88]	R. J. Mooney, "Generalizing the Order of Operators in Macro-Operators," *Proceedings of the Fifth International Conference on Machine Learning*, Ann Arbor, MI, June 1988, pp. 270-283.

[Mooney89a]	R. J. Mooney, "The Effect of Rule Use on the Utility of Explanation-Based Learning," *Proceedings of the Eleventh International Joint Conference on Artificial Intelligence*, Detroit, MI, August 1989, pp. 725-730.

[Mooney89b]	R. J. Mooney, *A General Explanation-Based Learning Mechanism and its Application to Narrative Understanding*, Pitman, London, in press.

[Mooney89c]	R. J. Mooney and D. Ourston, "Induction Over the Unexplained: Integrated Learning of Concepts with Both Explainable and Conventional Aspects," *Proceedings of the Sixth International Workshop on Machine Learning*, Ithaca, NY, June 1989, pp. 5-7.

[Mostow83]	J. Mostow, "Machine Transformation of Advice into a Heuristic Search Procedure," in *Machine Learning: An Artificial Intelligence Approach*, R. S. Michalski, J. G. Carbonell and T. M. Mitchell (eds.), Tioga Publishing Company, Palo Alto, CA, 1983, pp. 367-404.

[Mostow87]	J. Mostow and N. Bhatnagar, "FAILSAFE -- A Floor Planner that uses EBG to Learn from its Failures," *Proceedings of the Tenth International Joint Conference on Artificial Intelligence*, Milan, Italy, August 1987, pp. 249-255.

212

[Neves81]	D. M. Neves and J. R. Anderson, "Knowledge Compilation: Mechanisms for the Automatization of Cognitive Skills," in *Cognitive Skills and Their Acquisition*, J. R. Anderson (ed.), Lawrence Erlbaum and Associates, Hillsdale, NJ, 1981.
[Neves85]	D. M. Neves, "Learning Procedures from Examples and by Doing," *Proceedings of the Ninth International Joint Conference on Artificial Intelligence*, Los Angeles, CA, August 1985, pp. 624-630.
[Nilsson80]	N. J. Nilsson, *Principles of Artificial Intelligence*, Tioga Publishing Company, Palo Alto, CA, 1980.
[Novak76]	G. S. Novak, "Computer Understanding of Physics Problems Stated in Natural Language," Technical Report NL-30, Ph.D. Thesis, Department of Computer Science, University of Texas at Austin, March 1976.
[O'Rorke84]	P. V. O'Rorke, "Generalization for Explanation-Based Schema Acquisition," *Proceedings of the Fourth National Conference on Artificial Intelligence*, Austin, TX, August 1984, pp. 260-263.
[O'Rorke87a]	P. V. O'Rorke, "LT Revisited: Experimental Results of Applying Explanation-Based Learning to the Logic of Principia Mathematica," *Proceedings of the Fourth International Workshop on Machine Learning*, Irvine, CA, June 1987, pp. 148-159.
[O'Rorke87b]	P. V. O'Rorke, "Explanation-Based Learning Via Constraint Posting and Propagation," Ph.D. Thesis, Department of Computer Science, University of Illinois, Urbana, IL, January 1987. (Also appears as CSL Technical Report UILU-ENG-87-2239.)
[Palmer83]	M. S. Palmer, "Inference-Driven Semantic Analysis," *Proceedings of the Eighth International Joint Conference on Artificial Intelligence*, Karlsruhe, West Germany, August 1983, pp. 310-313.
[Pazzani85]	M. J. Pazzani, "Explanation and Generalization Based Memory," *Proceedings of the Seventh Annual Conference of the Cognitive Science Society*, Irvine, CA, August 1985, pp. 323-328.
[Pazzani88]	M. J. Pazzani, "Integrated Learning with Incorrect and Incomplete Theories," *Proceedings of the Fifth International Conference on Machine Learning*, Ann Arbor, MI, June 1988, pp. 291-297.
[Porter85]	B. W. Porter and D. F. Kibler, "A Comparison of Analytic and Experimental Goal Regression for Machine Learning," *Proceedings of the Ninth International Joint Conference on Artificial Intelligence*, Los Angeles, CA, August 1985, pp. 555-559.
[Porter86]	B. W. Porter and D. F. Kibler, "Experimental Goal Regression: A Method for Learning Problem Solving," *Machine Learning 1*, 3 (1986), pp. 249-286.
[Press86]	W. H. Press, B. P. Flannery, S. A. Teukolsky and W. T. Vetterling, *Numerical Recipes: The Art of Scientific Computing*, Cambridge University Press, Cambridge, England, 1986.

[Prieditis86]   A. E. Prieditis, "Discovery of Algorithms from Weak Methods," *Proceedings of the International Meeting on Advances in Learning*, Les Arcs, Switzerland, 1986, pp. 37-52.

[Prieditis87]   A. E. Prieditis and J. Mostow, "PROLEARN: Towards a PROLOG Interpreter that Learns," *Proceedings of the Sixth National Conference on Artificial Intelligence*, Seattle, WA, July 1987, pp. 494-498.

[Prieditis88]   A. E. Prieditis, "Environment-Guided Program Transformation," *Proceedings of the AAAI Explanation-Based Learning Symposium*, Stanford, CA, March 1988, pp. 201-209.

[Quinlan79]   J. R. Quinlan, "Discovering Rules from Large Collections of Examples: A Case Study," in *Expert Systems in the Micro Electronic Age*, D. Michie (ed.), Edinburgh University Press, Edinburgh, Scotland, 1979.

[Rajamoney85]   S. Rajamoney, G. F. DeJong and B. Faltings, "Towards a Model of Conceptual Knowledge Acquisition through Directed Experimentation," *Proceedings of the Ninth International Joint Conference on Artificial Intelligence*, Los Angeles, CA, August 1985.

[Rajamoney87]   S. Rajamoney and G. F. DeJong, "The Classification, Detection and Handling of Imperfect Theory Problems," *Proceedings of the Tenth International Joint Conference on Artificial Intelligence*, Milan, Italy, August 1987, pp. 205-207.

[Reiter78]   R. Reiter, "On Closed World Data Bases," in *Logic and Data Bases*, H. Gallaire and J. Minker (ed.), Plenum Press, NY, 1978.

[Rendell83]   L. Rendell, "A New Basis for State-Space Learning Systems and a Successful Implementation," *Artificial Intelligence 20*, 4 (1983), pp. 203-226.

[Rendell85]   L. Rendell, "Substantial Constructive Induction using Layered Information Compression: Tractable Feature Formation in Search," *Proceedings of the Ninth International Joint Conference on Artificial Intelligence*, Los Angeles, CA, August 1985, pp. 650-658.

[Rosenblatt58]   F. Rosenblatt, "The Perceptron: A Probabilistic Model for Information Storage and Organization," *Psychological Review 65*, (1958), pp. 386-407.

[Rosenbloom86]   P. Rosenbloom and J. Laird, "Mapping Explanation-Based Generalization into SOAR," *Proceedings of the Fifth National Conference on Artificial Intelligence*, Philadelphia, PA, August 1986, pp. 561-567.

[Rumelhart86]   D. E. Rumelhart, G. E. Hinton and J. L. McClelland, "A General Framework for Parallel Distributed Processing," in *Parallel Distributed Processing: Explorations in the Micro-Structure of Cognition*, D. E. Rumelhart and J. L. McClelland (eds.), MIT Press, Cambridge, MA, 1986, pp. 46-73.

[Sammut86]   C. Sammut and R. B. Banerji, "Learning Concepts by Asking Questions," in *Machine Learning: An Artificial Intelligence Approach, Vol. II*, R. S. Michalski, J. G. Carbonell and T. M. Mitchell (eds.), Morgan-Kaufmann, Los Altos, CA, 1986, pp. 167-192.

[Samuel59]   A. L. Samuel, "Some Studies in Machine Learning using the Game of Checkers," *IBM Journal of Research and Development 3*, (1959), pp. 211-229.

[Schank77]   R. C. Schank and R. P. Abelson, *Scripts, Plans, Goals and Understanding: An Inquiry into Human Knowledge Structures*, Lawrence Erlbaum and Associates, Hillsdale, NJ, 1977.

[Schank82]   R. C. Schank, *Dynamic Memory*, Cambridge University Press, Cambridge, England, 1982.

[Schank86]   R. C. Schank, G. C. Collins and L. E. Hunter, "Transcending Inductive Category Formation in Learning," *Behavioral and Brain Sciences 9*, 2 (1986), pp. 639-686.

[Schoenfeld82] A. H. Schoenfeld and D. Herrmann, "Problem Perception and Knowledge Structure in Expert and Novice Mathematical Problem Solvers," *Journal of Experimental Psychology: Learning, Memory, and Cognition 8*, 5 (1982), pp. 484-494.

[Segre85]   A. M. Segre and G. F. DeJong, "Explanation Based Manipulator Learning: Acquisition of Planning Ability Through Observation," *Proceedings of the IEEE International Conference on Robotics and Automation*, St. Louis, MO, March 1985, pp. 555-560.

[Segre87]   A. M. Segre, "On the Operationality/Generality Trade-off in Explanation-Based Learning," *Proceedings of the Tenth International Joint Conference on Artificial Intelligence*, Milan, Italy, August 1987, pp. 242-248.

[Segre88a]   A. M. Segre, "Operationality and Real-World Plans," *Proceedings of the AAAI Explanation-Based Learning Symposium*, Stanford, CA, March 1988, pp. 153-157.

[Segre88b]   A. M. Segre, *Machine Learning of Robot Assembly Plans*, Kluwer Academic Publishers, Hingham, MA, 1988.

[Sejnowski87]   T. J. Sejnowski and C. R. Rosenberg, "Parallel Networks that Learn to Pronounce English Text," *Complex Systems 1*, (1987), pp. 145-168.

[Selfridge59]   O. G. Selfridge, "Pandemonium: A Paradigm for Learning," *Proceedings of the Symposium on Mechanization of Thought Processes*, London, 1959, pp. 511-529.

[Shavlik85a]   J. W. Shavlik and G. F. DeJong, "Building a Computer Model of Learning Classical Mechanics," *Proceedings of the Seventh Annual Conference of the Cognitive Science Society*, Irvine, CA, August 1985, pp. 351-355.

[Shavlik85b]   J. W. Shavlik, "Learning about Momentum Conservation," *Proceedings of the Ninth International Joint Conference on Artificial Intelligence*, Los Angeles, CA, August 1985, pp. 667-669.

[Shavlik86a]   J. W. Shavlik and G. F. DeJong, "Computer Understanding and Generalization of Symbolic Mathematical Calculations: A Case Study in Physics Problem Solving," *Proceedings of the 1986 Symposium on Symbolic and Algebraic*

Computation, Waterloo, Ontario, Canada, July 1986, pp. 148-153.

[Shavlik86b] J. W. Shavlik and G. F. DeJong, "A Model of Attention Focussing During Problem Solving," *Proceedings of the Eighth Annual Conference of the Cognitive Science Society*, Amherst, MA, August 1986, pp. 817-822.

[Shavlik87a] J. W. Shavlik and G. F. DeJong, "Analyzing Variable Cancellations to Generalize Symbolic Mathematical Calculations," *Proceedings of the Third IEEE Conference on Artificial Intelligence Applications*, Orlando, FL, February 1987.

[Shavlik87b] J. W. Shavlik and G. F. DeJong, "BAGGER: An EBL System that Extends and Generalizes Explanations," *Proceedings of the Sixth National Conference on Artificial Intelligence*, Seattle, WA, July 1987, pp. 516-520.

[Shavlik87c] J. W. Shavlik and G. F. DeJong, "An Explanation-Based Approach to Generalizing Number," *Proceedings of the Tenth International Joint Conference on Artificial Intelligence*, Milan, Italy, August 1987, pp. 236-238.

[Shavlik87d] J. W. Shavlik and G. F. DeJong, "Modelling the Use of Examples to Teach General Concepts in Mathematically-Based Domains," *Third International Conference of Artificial Intelligence and Education*, Pittsburgh, PA, May 1987.

[Shavlik87e] J. W. Shavlik, G. F. DeJong and B. H. Ross, "Acquiring Special Case Schemata in Explanation-Based Learning," *Proceedings of the Ninth Annual Conference of the Cognitive Science Society*, Seattle, WA, July 1987, pp. 851-860.

[Shavlik88] J. W. Shavlik and R. Maclin, "An Approach to Acquiring Algorithms by Observing Expert Behavior," *Proceedings of the AAAI-88 Workshop on Automating Software Design*, St. Paul, MN, August 1988.

[Shavlik89a] J. W. Shavlik and G. Towell, "Combining Explanation-Based Learning and Artificial Neural Networks," *Proceedings of the Sixth International Workshop on Machine Learning*, Ithaca, NY, June 1989, pp. 90-92.

[Shavlik89b] J. W. Shavlik, "An Empirical Analysis of EBL Approaches for Learning Plan Schemata," *Proceedings of the Sixth International Workshop on Machine Learning*, Ithaca, NY, June 1989, pp. 183-187.

[Shavlik90a] J. W. Shavlik, "Acquiring Recursive and Iterative Concepts with Explanation-Based Learning," *Machine Learning*, in press.

[Shavlik90b] J. W. Shavlik and G. F. DeJong, "Learning in Mathematically-Based Domains: Understanding and Generalizing Obstacle Cancellations," *Artificial Intelligence*, in press.

[Shavlik90c] J. W. Shavlik and G. G. Towell, "An Approach to Combining Explanation-Based and Neural Learning Algorithms," *Connection Science: The Journal of Neural Computing, Artificial Intelligence and Cognitive Research*, in press.

[Shell89] P. Shell and J. Carbonell, "Towards a General Framework for Composing Disjunctive and Iterative Macro-operators," *Proceedings of the Eleventh International Joint Conference on Artificial Intelligence*, Detroit, MI, August

216

1989, pp. 596-602.

[Silver83]   B. Silver, "Learning Equation Solving Methods from Examples," *Proceedings of the Third National Conference on Artificial Intelligence*, Washington, D.C., August 1983, pp. 429-431.

[Silver86]   B. Silver, *Meta-Level Inference*, North-Holland, New York, NY, 1986.

[Sims87]   M. H. Sims, "Empirical and Analytic Discovery in IL," *Proceedings of the Fourth International Workshop on Machine Learning*, Irvine, CA, June 1987, pp. 274-280.

[Sleeman82]   D. H. Sleeman and J. S. Brown (eds.), *Intelligent Tutoring Systems*, Academic Press, New York, NY, 1982.

[Smith84]   D. Smith, "The Synthesis of LISP Programs from Examples: A Survey," in *Automatic Program Construction Techniques*, A. Biermann (ed.), MacMillan, 1984, pp. 307-324.

[Smith85]   D. E. Smith and M. R. Genesereth, "Ordering Conjunctive Queries," *Artificial Intelligence 26*, 2 (1985), pp. 171-215.

[Soloway78]   E. Soloway, "Learning = Interpretation + Generalization: A Case Study in Knowledge-Directed Learning," Ph.D. Thesis, University of Massachusetts, Amherst, MA, 1978. (Also appears as COINS Technical Report 78-13.)

[Steier87]   D. Steier, "CYPRESS-SOAR: A Case Study in Search and Learning in Algorithm Design," *Proceedings of the Tenth International Joint Conference on Artificial Intelligence*, Milan, Italy, August 1987, pp. 327-330.

[Summers77]   P. D. Summers, "A Methodology for LISP Program Construction from Examples," *Journal of the Association for Computing Machinery 24*, (1977), pp. 161-175.

[Sussman75]   G. J. Sussman, *A Computational Model of Skill Acquisition*, American Elsevier, New York, 1975.

[Sweller85]   J. Sweller and G. A. Cooper, "The Use of Worked Examples as a Substitute for Problem Solving in Learning Algebra," *Cognition and Instruction 2*, 1 (1985), pp. 59-89.

[Tadepalli89] P. Tadepalli, "Lazy Explanation-Based Learning: A Solution to the Intractable Theory Problem," *Proceedings of the Eleventh International Joint Conference on Artificial Intelligence*, Detroit, MI, August 1989, pp. 694-700.

[Tambe88]   M. Tambe and A. Newell, "Some Chunks are Expensive," *Proceedings of the Fifth International Conference on Machine Learning*, Ann Arbor, MI, June 1988, pp. 451-458.

[Tecuci89]   G. Tecuci and Y. Kodratoff, "Multi-Strategy Learning in Nonhomogeneous Domain Theories," *Proceedings of the Sixth International Workshop on Machine Learning*, Ithaca, NY, June 1989, pp. 14-16.

[Treitel86]   R. Treitel, "Re-arranging Rules," *Proceedings of the Workshop on Knowledge Compilation*, Otter Crest, OR, September 1986.

[Utgoff86]   P. E. Utgoff, *Machine Learning of Inductive Bias*, Kluwer Academic Publishers, Hingham, MA, 1986.

[Valiant84]   L. G. Valiant, "A Theory of the Learnable," *Communications of the Association for Computing Machinery 27*, 11 (1984), pp. 1134-1142.

[VanLehn87]   K. VanLehn, "Learning One Subprocedure per Lesson," *Artificial Intelligence 31*, 1 (1987), pp. 1-40.

[Van Harmelen88] F. Van Harmelen and A. Bundy, "Explanation-Based Generalization = Partial Evaulation (Research Note)," *Artificial Intelligence 36*, (1988), pp. 401-412.

[Van de Velde89] W. Van de Velde, "(Re)Presentation Issues in Second Generation Expert Systems," in *Knowledge Representation and Organization in Machine Learning*, K. Morik (ed.), Springer Verlag, 1989, pp. 17-49.

[Vere78]   S. A. Vere, "Inductive Learning of Relational Productions," in *Pattern Directed Inference Systems*, D. A. Waterman and F. Hayes-Roth (eds.), Academic Press, New York, 1978.

[Waldinger77]   R. Waldinger, "Achieving Several Goals Simultaneously," in *Machine Intelligenge 8*, E. Elcock and D. Michie (eds.), Ellis Horwood Limited, London, 1977.

[Watanabe87]   L. Watanabe and R. Elio, "Guiding Constructive Induction for Incremental Learning from Examples," *Proceedings of the Tenth International Joint Conference on Artificial Intelligence*, Milan, Italy, August 1987, pp. 293-296.

[Waterman70]   D. Waterman, "Generalization Learning Techniques for Automating the Learning of Heuristics," *Artificial Intelligence 1*, (1970), pp. 121-170.

[Weld86]   D. S. Weld, "The Use of Aggregation in Casual Simulation," *Artificial Intelligence 30*, 1 (1986), pp. 1-34.

[Wenger87]   E. Wenger, *Artificial Intelligence and Tutoring Systems: Computational and Cognitive Approaches to the Communication of Knowledge*, Morgan-Kaufmann, Los Altos, CA, 1987.

[Whitehall87]   B. L. Whitehall, "Substructure Discovery in Executed Action Sequences," M.S. Thesis, Department of Computer Science, University of Illinois, Urbana, IL, 1987. (Also appears as CSL Technical Report UILU-ENG-87-2256.)

[Wilkins88]   D. C. Wilkins, "Knowledge Base Refinement Using Apprenticeship Learning Techniques," *Proceedings of the Seventh National Conference on Artificial Intelligence*, St. Paul, MN, August 1988, pp. 646-651.

[Winston75]   P. H. Winston, "Learning Structural Descriptions from Examples," in *The Psychology of Computer Vision*, P. H. Winston (ed.), McGraw-Hill, New York, NY, 1975, pp. 157-210.

[Winston82]   P. H. Winston, "Learning New Principles From Precedents and Exercises," *Artificial Intelligence 19*, (1982), pp. 321-350.

[Winston83]   P. H. Winston, T. O. Binford, B. Katz and M. Lowry, "Learning Physical Descriptions from Functional Definitions, Examples, and Precedents," *Proceedings of the Third National Conference on Artificial Intelligence*, Washington, D.C., August 1983, pp. 433-439.

[Wolff82]   J. G. Wolff, "Language Acquisition, Data Compression and Generalization," *Language and Communication 2*, 1 (1982), pp. 57-89.

[Wolfram83]   S. Wolfram, "SMP Reference Manual," Computer Mathematics Group, Inference Corporation, Los Angeles, CA, 1983.